America's Lone Star Constitution

America's Lone Star Constitution

How Supreme Court Cases from Texas Shape the Nation

Lucas A. Powe, Jr.

UNIVERSITY OF CALIFORNIA PRESS

University of California Press, one of the most
distinguished university presses in the United States,
enriches lives around the world by advancing scholarship
in the humanities, social sciences, and natural sciences. Its
activities are supported by the UC Press Foundation and
by philanthropic contributions from individuals and
institutions. For more information, visit www.ucpress.edu.

University of California Press
Oakland, California

Library of Congress Cataloging-in-Publication Data

Names: Powe, L. A. Scot, author.
Title: America's Lone Star constitution : how Supreme
    Court cases from Texas shape the nation / Lucas
    A. Powe, Jr..
Description: Oakland, California : University of
    California Press, [2018] | Includes bibliographical
    references and index. |
Identifiers: LCCN 2017046014 (print) | LCCN 2017059012
    (ebook) | ISBN 9780520970014 (e-edition) | ISBN
    9780520297807 (cloth) | ISBN 9780520297814 (pbk.)
Subjects: LCSH: Law—Texas—History. | Law—Political
    aspects—Texas—Cases. | Law—Political aspects—
    United States—Cases.
Classification: LCC KFT1278 (ebook) | LCC KFT1278 .P68 2018
    (print) | DDC 342.73—dc23
LC record available at https://lccn.loc.gov/2017046014

27 26 25 24 23 22 21 20 19 18
10 9 8 7 6 5 4 3 2 1

To the youngest Texans in the family: Jack, Reid, Nathan, Preston, and Sean

CONTENTS

ACKNOWLEDGMENTS

I started this book midway through 2013 and stopped it by the end of that summer, believing that I was unsure of what I was doing. In the spring of 2016 Dean Ward Farnsworth encouraged me to restart the project and promised all the help that he could provide. That turned out to be flying five of my friends and former Constitutional Law colleagues—Jack Balkin, Justin Driver, Doug Laycock, Mark Graber, and Ernie Young—to Austin where we talked about the project for a day, highlighted by barbeque lunch from Louie Mueller's. Without the Dean's support and the wise counsel of my friends I would not have completed the book.

Once completed, my colleagues Sandy Levinson and H.W. Perry plus my former colleague Mark Gergen read the entire manuscript. Tom Krattenmaker and Jordan Steiker read parts. All offered helpful suggestions and the final product is much better for the many suggestions I received and acted upon.

Throughout the process, Jane O'Connell, Associate Director of the Tarlton Law Library at the University of Texas, tracked down every source that I asked for, even if it took her many phone calls and occasional insisting. Without her ability to find what I needed, the book could not have been written.

My heartfelt thanks to all.

Introduction

> The Constitution, in all its provisions, looks to an
> indestructible Union composed of indestructible states.
> —*Texas v. White* (1869)

Texas is many things to many people: a Southern state, a Western state, a culturally conservative state, a racially diverse state, a physically diverse state, a rich state with too many poor people, a former nation— all of which, perhaps most importantly, converges to become a state of mind. Texans happily assert everything is bigger in Texas; that includes effects on constitutional law (whether or not Texans know this). More important United States Supreme Court cases have originated in Texas than in any other state, so many, in fact, that entire basic courses in Constitutional Law in both law schools and political science departments could be taught using nothing but Texas cases.

The various factors mentioned in the prior paragraph offer explanations as to why it is that Texas (rather than, say, California or Ohio) creates such an impact. Texas is a big state with a large population—especially since the second half of the twentieth century. Texas's Southern heritage guaranteed that race would be an issue in litigation, and it may have been that litigating racial issues outside of the Deep South was safer for those challenging the status quo. Texas was the only Southern state with a sizeable Hispanic population, and Anglo Texans believed that Hispanics should be second-class citizens (in violation of the Constitution). Texans are uncommonly proud of their heritage as a people who fought and won independence and established a Republic—which is emphasized from public schooling onward. Any drive through Texas offers countless opportunities to view the Lone Star flag. That heritage has translated into a belief in independence, and their version of independence means that government—especially the one in Washington, D.C.—should not be telling Texans what they can and cannot do. This has become decidedly marked in this century where Texas attorneys general have seen fighting the federal government as a means of fostering their own ambitions. And many Texans, and probably the overwhelming number of Republicans, hold culturally conservative values that are antithetical to modern liberalism. There are undoubtedly other reasons, but these help explain why it is Texas and not California that provides breadth and depth to constitutional adjudication.

The men and women—litigants, lawyers, politicians, and judges—add a rich texture to the underlying interplay of law and politics at the local, state, and national levels. The litigants include Heman Sweatt, Demetrio Rodriguez, Norma McCorvey (as Jane Roe), John Lawrence, and Billie Sol Estes; lawyers include Fletcher "Big Fish" Fischer, Sarah Weddington, Charles Alan Wright, and Ted Cruz. The state politicians range from Sam Houston to Alan Shivers to Rick Perry and Greg Abbott while the national ones include John Quincy Adams, Harry Truman, Dwight Eisenhower, and Barack Obama. Edith Jones, Jerry Smith, and Patrick Higginbotham on the Fifth Circuit Court of Appeals, and Sharon Keller and Barbara Hervey of the Texas Court of Criminal Appeals, are all Texas judges. At the United States Supreme Court Tom Clark was the sole Texan, but Texas cases brought out the jurisprudence of important justices from William O. Douglas on the left to William H. Rehnquist and Antonin Scalia on the right.

In all its facets, Texas offers a window to all constitutional law and the Supreme Court as well—hence my title *America's Lone Star Constitution: How Supreme Court Cases from Texas Shape Constitutional Law*. And Texas's impact literally started at the beginning by precipitating a debate over national powers and then a war with Mexico. No other state can make such a claim.

I

There was no greater American foe of the Texas War for Independence than Congressman John Quincy Adams. The ex-president had tried to purchase Texas while in office, but as an antislavery congressman he saw Texas independence as but a step toward statehood and ultimately civil war: "Are you ready for all these wars? A Mexican war? A war with Britain, if not with France? A general Indian war? A servile war? And, as an inevitable consequence of them all, a civil war? ... I avow it as my solemn belief that the annexation of an independent foreign power [Texas] would be *ipso facto* a dissolution of this Union."[1]

Americans, overwhelmingly from the South, had been moving to Texas since Stephen F. Austin convinced Mexico to allow immigration. In 1829 Mexico, over the objections of the Texans, banned slavery. But its control over its northern territory was slight at best and the ban was ignored. "Anglo Texans made bad Mexicans," accenting the many causes for the revolution: chaos in Mexico, the Texans' desires to be treated like the Americans they were, and maintaining slavery.[2] With Santa Anna's defeat at the Battle of San Jacinto and independence secured, Texans held the Republic's first election, adopting a constitution, electing Sam Houston as president, and by a vote of 3,277–91 authorizing annexation by the United States. The new Texas government showed Adams's fears were real because Houston—the most celebrated Texas politician of the century: first and third president of the Republic, first U.S. senator, and finally governor who opposed secession—petitioned President Andrew Jackson for annexation, describing Texans and those in the United States as "one people ... united by all the sacred ties that can bind one people to another."[3]

Jackson saw the situation similarly. In a message to Congress on Texas he stated that "a large portion of its civilized inhabitants are emigrants from the United States, speak the same language with ourselves, cherish the same principles, political and religious, and are bound to many of our citizens by ties of friendship and kindred blood; and, more than all, it is known that the people of that country have instituted the same form of government with our own."[4] But Jackson did not push for annexation (although he did recognize the Republic). There was too much opposition in the North, where free states would become a minority in the Senate, and Texas was claiming far more territory than Mexico accepted. His chosen successor, Martin Van Buren, didn't either, both for the same political reasons and because the economy tanked during his first year in office.

Yet petitions, pro and con, were arriving in Congress, and the House debated annexation with Adams speaking in opposition every day from June 16 to July 7, 1838. When Congress adjourned without taking action, President Sam Houston withdrew the request for annexation, and the Texas Congress ratified his action. Houston was followed by the anti-American Mirabeau B. Lamar; annexation remained off the table.

The 1840 election produced a Whig victory. The Whigs were an anti-expansionist party whose views were nicely summarized by its de facto leader Senator Henry Clay: "it is more important that we should unite, harmonize, and improve what we have than attempt to acquire more."[5] But in 1841 John Tyler became the first vice president to succeed a dying president—William Henry Harrison—to the office. "His Accidency," a not too popular Virginian, broke with the Whigs and hoped to gain the Democratic nomination in 1844. To do so he needed an issue, and annexation was just that. Tyler could note the danger of Texas making an alliance with Great Britain, something talked about but unlikely.

After the anti-annexation Daniel Webster resigned as secretary of state, Tyler replaced him with Virginian Abel P. Upshur, who engaged in secret negotiations with Texas over a treaty of annexation. When Upshur was killed in an accident, the new secretary, John C. Calhoun, swiftly completed negotiations. The treaty went to the Senate in April

1844. For ratification, it would need 35 of the 52 senators in a body that was evenly divided between slave and free states.

This offered one of those unique moments when the political parties reverse their constitutional position on a single issue by consciously (or unconsciously)—but never out loud—allowing policy to trump the Constitution. The Jacksonian Democrats were the party of limited federal government while the Whigs maintained an expansive view of federal powers. Yet the Democrats were enthusiastic territorial expansionists while the Whigs—especially Adams and the retired Supreme Court justice Joseph Story—believed annexation of a foreign country unconstitutional absent a constitutional amendment. (This had been Thomas Jefferson's position on Louisiana until he concluded that necessity must be able to trump law.) This made it difficult for Whigs to explain the additions of West Florida and East Florida. Webster tried, saying those were driven by national necessity, but "no such necessity existed with Texas."[6]

Opponents of acquiring Texas received a gift from Calhoun. He wrote to the British ambassador and framed annexation as the protection of Southern states "in order to preserve a domestic institution."[7] New York Democrat Silas Wright could thus comment, "the Texas treaty is made upon a record which is sure to destroy any man from a free state who will go for it."[8] The treaty was defeated by a better than two-thirds margin, 16–35. The Whigs followed Clay's lead and all but one voted no, while the Democrats split. Not accepting defeat, Tyler then proceeded to recommend annexing Texas by joint resolution that could be done by majority vote in each House, but would require ten or eleven senators to switch their votes. Tyler justified his end run around the Treaty Clause by claiming the "power of Congress is ... fully competent in some other form of proceeding to accomplish everything that a formal ratification of the treaty would have accomplished."[9]

The expected 1844 matchup between Clay and Van Buren would have left Texas on the sidelines because Clay opposed annexation and Van Buren was lukewarm, wishing it put off for another day. But at the

Democratic Convention Van Buren could not get the two-thirds delegates necessary for the nomination, which instead went to "Young Hickory," James K. Polk, a Tennessee slaveholder. He was an ardent expansionist who fully approved the party plank calling for "the annexation of Texas and the reoccupation of Oregon" (right up to the southern tip of Alaska, "54 / 40 or fight") at "the earliest practicable moment."[10]

Tyler interpreted Polk's victory over Clay as a referendum on annexation, which it wasn't. Nevertheless, he claimed that "a controlling majority of the people and a large majority of the States have declared in favor of immediate annexation," and proposed admitting Texas as a state by a joint resolution.[11] Whigs and antislavery Democrats were aghast and some Whigs went so far as to claim that the resolution would be null and void even if it passed. The Whigs were now on pretty strong constitutional ground, even if it wasn't the ground they normally inhabited in support of federal power—or the ground they had just adventitiously occupied (claiming a treaty could not acquire a foreign state). In *American Insurance v. Cantor* Chief Justice John Marshall held that the Constitution "confers absolutely on the government of the Union ... the power of acquiring territory, either by conquest or treaty."[12] A joint resolution was neither.

The resolution did pass, however, overwhelmingly in the House and by 27–25 in the Senate where three Southern Whigs joined the Democrats. The joint resolution offered Texas better terms than the treaty had, allowing the Republic at some future time to divide itself into five states. Texas would also retain title to all its public lands. The resolution extended the Missouri Compromise line to cover the northernmost claims of Texas, which the Republic abandoned.

In Texas President Anson Jones called a constitutional convention that proceeded to accept statehood with but a single dissenting vote. But the convention turned the issue over to the people for ratification of their decision. By approximately 4,000 to 200 the voters approved statehood and a new constitution (and protection against Indians and Mexico from the United States Army). Congress then approved, and Polk announced Texas as a state at the end of December 1845. Seven weeks later President Jones pronounced the Republic at an end.

Mexico had already informed the United States that annexation would be tantamount to a declaration of war. So, in preparation, Polk sent American troops, not to the Nueces River that had been Texas's southern border under Mexico, but to the Rio Grande, which was part of Texas's rather extravagant claims as to its borders. After Mexican troops attacked a party of dragoons, Polk sent Congress a message declaring that as "Mexico has passed the boundary of the United States, has invaded our territory and shed American blood on American soil . . . war exists . . . by an act of Mexico herself."[13]

Adams had lived to see his prophesized war with Mexico a reality, and like some Northern Whigs such as Abraham Lincoln, he believed the war unconstitutional (because Polk had started it). But Congress voted the necessary authorization. Then, three months later, a freshman Democratic congressman, David Wilmot of Pennsylvania, introduced an amendment to ban slavery in any territory acquired from Mexico; the House passed it with no support from Southern Democrats and that of all but two Southern Whigs. In an era heretofore of fairly strict party discipline, the Wilmot Proviso shattered it. The parties were created to argue economic issues, not slavery.

The Wilmot Proviso, which never became law, was the opening shot in the sectional struggle. Over the next decade there would be the Kansas-Nebraska Act, Bleeding Kansas, *Dred Scott v. Sandford*,[14] John Brown's raid on Harper's Ferry, and as a culminating event, the election of a sectional president, Abraham Lincoln, with exclusively free state support. The South saw itself under siege. The North saw an aggressive slavocracy.

II

Before 1860 was out, South Carolina had seceded and was soon followed by the Gulf South. Governor Sam Houston, an opponent of secession, was pressured to reluctantly call a secession convention, and in early February 1861, over only eight dissents, the convention voted to leave the Union. Having joined the Union with a vote of the people, Texas left with a similarly lopsided vote of 46,129 to 14,697, with the ten central Texas German counties and some North Texas votes accounting for the negatives. A month before Fort Sumter, Texas, which had successfully seceded from Mexico, seceded from the Union. (Only Virginia and Tennessee joined Texas in putting to a vote the decision to secede.)

Four years later, a defeated Confederacy faced the prospect of losing its slaves and perhaps some of its claims to be part of the national government. Radical Republicans like Thaddeus Stevens and Charles Sumner had no intention of readmitting the Southern states into the national fold until they had been reconstructed. They were conquered provinces, states who had committed suicide, to be governed by the victors.

With Ulysses Grant as president, the Supreme Court spoke to the status of the former states in *Texas v. White.*[15] Chief Justice Salmon P. Chase, once an antislavery Republican who hoped to get the nomination from Lincoln in 1864, but now a Democrat hoping for the 1872 nomination, kept the opinion for himself because the case played perfectly into his philosophy and needs. The principal issue was whether, having left the Union, Texas had the right to sue in federal court. Chase first made clear that secession was unlawful: the "Constitution, in all its provisions, looks to an indestructible Union composed of indestructible states."[16] Because of its own actions Texas's rights as a member of the Union had been suspended, but not destroyed, during the rebellion. It thus fell to Congress under Article IV to guarantee to each state a republican form of government. Congress had the discretion to choose the appropriate means to repair the suspended relationship between the states. Chase did not endorse the Republicans' Reconstruction plan: "We do not inquire here into the constitutionality of this legislation so far as it relates to military authority, or to the paramount authority of Congress."[17] What was important was that the Reconstruction program recognized the ongoing existence of the states: "It suffices to say, that the terms of the acts necessarily imply recognition of the actually existing governments."[18] (On the merits the Court ruled that Texas could prevail in a suit to recover bonds sold by the wartime state government because that government had been unlawful and its actions supporting the rebellion were null and void.)

As Michael Les Benedict, the leading constitutional historian of the era, observes, the "opinion was virtually a platform for a Democratic new departure [with Chase as the leading New Departure Democrat]. It confirmed that secession was unconstitutional which nearly all northern Democrats believed, and which southerners had to swallow in order to work with northern Democrats to regain power. It accepted the results of Reconstruction, without endorsing the program or even confirming the constitutionality of the specific means Republicans used."[19] Because the opinion could be a Democratic platform and would be widely published, Chase "wrote with real care and eloquence, aiming the opinion at a public audience as well as a legal one. It was as much constitutional politics as constitutional law."[20]

III

Fast forward fourteen decades. Heading for a reelection battle, in 2009 Texas governor Rick Perry suggested that at some future date Texas might have to consider secession once again because of a newly activist federal government. "If Washington continues to thumb their nose at the American people, you know, who knows what might come out of that. But Texas is a very unique place, and we're a pretty independent lot to boot."[21] Embracing that vision and independence, Texans overwhelmingly reelected him a year later.

Perry's successor, Greg Abbott, who as attorney general boasted that every day he went to the office and sued the federal government, proposed calling a constitutional convention of the states to consider amending the United States Constitution to, among others, allow two-thirds of the states to overrule a federal law or a Supreme Court decision and requiring a supermajority of seven justices to declare any law unconstitutional. It apparently is not enough that the fraught relationship between Texas, the nation, the Constitution, and the Supreme Court in the century and a half since *Texas v. White* has produced more constitutional law than any other state.

Most of these cases could have occurred elsewhere—but did not. In the current century Texas has taken an adversarial relationship to the federal government. There is an international treaty requiring consular notification if a foreign national is arrested. Although President George W. Bush asked states to comply with the treaty, Texas refused and executed a Mexican national who had not been given consular access before his confession to rape and murder. Just to the north, Oklahoma took the opposite position of assisting the United States in foreign affairs. The execution of Jose Ernesto Medellin was distinctly Texan.

"Don't Mess With Texas" is the state's antilitter highway slogan. But everyone knows it means so much more. Texas was a nation and still often acts as if it is a nation. That is why the constitutional law originating in Texas is so rich and pervasive.

PART I

Texas the Southern State

Like the rest of the Confederacy, Texas, once "redeemed," rejected everything about the national Republicans and endorsed the "Lost Cause" ideology of the past while it implemented Jim Crow to keep its African American population in their place as second-class citizens. Texas, like the rest of the South, has spent decades dealing with slavery, Jim Crow, and their legacies. Racial issues have been with Texas from the beginning and they continue to the present. With the exception of two cases claiming the Voting Rights Act unjustly punishes the South, all cases focus on the issue of discrimination—whether aimed at African Americans, Hispanics, or, more recently, Anglos—in the context of construing the Equal Protection Clause of the Fourteenth Amendment.

ONE

The All-White Primary

Their fido pack went bear hunting and treed a skunk.
—Richard Evans on a major loss at the Supreme Court

It was June 19, 1865, when, arriving in Galveston, General Gordon Granger of the victorious Union army issued General Order No. 3. That order announced that by Executive Proclamation the slaves were now forever free.[1] The Thirteenth Amendment codifying (and extending) the Emancipation Proclamation would not become part of the Constitution for another six months. But with General Order No. 3, approximately one-fourth of the population of Texas had been added to the lists of the free.

I

Once granted the vote, the adult freedmen, virtually all living in East Texas, became the base of the Texas Republican Party.[2] They were joined by the formerly apolitical Germans in Central Texas and other Anglos who had remained loyal to the Union—scalawags as they were soon labeled. The ex-Confederates held to the Democratic Party.

With Military Reconstruction replacing Presidential Reconstruction, Republicans came to power first with Unionist former governor Elisha Pease and then with scalawag lawyer Edmund J. Davis, who had raised the First Texas Cavalry for the Union. Davis's 1869 victory had been close, winning by fewer than a thousand votes out of 79,000 cast.[3] Looking to the future, Republicans had to hold the black vote while adding to their Anglo vote. That proved a fine line that the party found itself unable to walk.

As in other Southern states, success at the polls for Republicans did not translate into freedmen holding anywhere near their share of offices. Republicans accepted their votes but not their status as equals. Thus, like four other states, none were elected statewide and only 14 of 100 in the first Republican legislature were freedmen.[4]

In 1873 Davis was defeated by Democrat Richard Coke. There was continuing massive immigration to Texas by whites from ex-Confederate states. Thus the population jumped from 604,000 in 1860 to over three million at the turn of the century, and the black percentage of the population dropped to 18 percent.[5] This decisively shifted the balance to Democrats so that Coke prevailed—100,415 to 52,141.[6] Claiming a rigged election, Davis initially refused to give up the governorship, hoping President Ulysses S. Grant would use the army to sustain him in office.[7] But with such a resounding electoral defeat, that hope was in vain as President Grant believed the will of all the voters, not just Republicans, should prevail.[8] Texas was "redeemed," and Republicans, while competing in some counties for several decades, ceased being a factor in statewide politics well into the second half of the twentieth century. Nevertheless, as the nineteenth century ended, blacks still freely voted because Texas did not follow the ex-Confederate states in adopting literacy tests, good character requirements, or requirements that prospective voters be given a clause in the state constitution to interpret. (African Americans in those states were invariably given obscure and poorly written clauses to decipher and then informed they had failed the test.)

Democratic dominance was challenged, however, by the Populist revolt fueled in large part by the decline in the standard of living of the state's farmers both black and white. As one white Populist noted, "[t]hey are in the ditch just like we are."[9] While most blacks remained true to the Republicans, a not insignificant number bolted to the Populists who won some local races, but, like Republicans, could not win statewide. Everything came to a head in 1896 when the Republicans created a fusion ticket with the Populists and Texas Democrats adopted some of the proposed Populist reforms. And, of course, nationally the Democrats co-opted the Populist votes by nominating William Jennings Bryan. Texas Populists split their votes, nationally for the Democrats, locally for the Populists—and lost both ways, dooming the party.[10] Furthermore, Texas Democrats played the race card in urging whites to vote with the party of whites, once again the only party that could win statewide elections.

Democratic victories papered over a division between reformers and conservatives within the party. Reformers believed that electoral fraud was rampant. Actually, so did Populists. The remedy, reformers concluded, was a shrunken electorate. Conservatives were opposed because they controlled the Mexican American voting bloc in South Texas. When former Populists joined the reformers, a poll tax finally was adopted in 1902 after two decades of attempts.[11] Everyone understood that it would not only depress the black vote but also affect whites. And it did. In 1900, 80 percent of whites voted; in the 1906, 1908, and 1910 elections the white vote never exceeded 30 percent. In 1906 only 20 percent, some 5,000 blacks, voted.[12]

In the shrinking Texas electorate the influence of swing voters increased, and in the early twentieth century those included blacks who could pay the poll tax. In Houston there were black entrepreneurs and professionals who were economically independent of whites. In circumstances of a close race in the Democratic primaries—required by a 1903 law—Texas blacks "did not need a numerical majority to enjoy a political majority. Rather, if the total number of eligible Negro voters was greater than the difference in the number of votes cast for each [candidate] the Negroes had a 'majority.'"[13]

Democrats did not like the situation and in some counties it was "solved" by the county party chairman deciding that blacks could not vote in the primaries. But in other counties when the primary would be close, candidates wanted the black vote, however undesirable they found the situation. The number of counties allowing the black vote became fewer and fewer, but in the racially polarizing days of World War I and its aftermath any black voting was too much for whites.[14] Yet because some Democrats could not restrain themselves from seeking black votes, an external restraint was deemed necessary. In 1923, following the lead of other former Confederate states that had acted years earlier (between 1896 and 1915), the Texas legislature adopted the all-white primary, leaving blacks who paid the poll tax free to cast a meaningless vote in the general election (as well as to participate fully in the nonpartisan municipal elections). The legislation declared that "in no event shall a negro be eligible to participate in a Democratic Party primary election."[15] Texas differentiated itself from the other Southern states with all-white primaries because it acted legislatively while the others acted by internal decision of the Democratic Party. This was an important distinction because the Supreme Court since 1883 had drawn a clear distinction between state action and private action that discriminates.[16] The former was prohibited by the Fourteenth (and presumably the Fifteenth) Amendment, while the latter was a private wrong (if that) subject only to state law (if any).

II

Because Texas acted by legislation, Texas was a more appealing target for challenging the all-white primary than any other state. Texas lacked literacy and understanding tests that disenfranchised most Southern blacks. Texas had middle-class blacks who were registered to vote and did vote in general elections and municipal elections (except Houston). And best of all for a constitutional challenge, the Texas law was not, unlike the poll tax, race neutral. Texas specifically disadvantaged blacks.

In the two decades after the enactment of the all-white primary the determination of Texas Democrats to exclude blacks from any electoral influence (and the equal determination of challengers to enjoy rights guaranteed by the Reconstruction Amendments to the Constitution) would result in four Supreme Court decisions, the first in 1927, the last in 1944. It took three victories for the black challengers finally to prevail. And for Fort Bend County blacks it took a fifth trip and an additional nine years to win the right to vote in the Democratic Party primary.

In fact, there was one Supreme Court decision involving Texas preceding the ones just mentioned. In January 1921 the Democratic Party in Houston declared that blacks could not vote in their February 9 primary for local officials. C. N. Love, a Houston newsman, filed suit in state court for an injunction on February 5, charging the move violated both the Fourteenth and Fifteenth Amendments. The judge denied the injunction and a Texas appellate court agreed on the ground that the election was now in the past. The Democrats were so confident of victory that they neither briefed nor argued the case before the Supreme Court, and their confidence was not misplaced. Two weeks after argument a unanimous Court through Justice Oliver Wendell Holmes agreed that the Texas courts did not have "to extend the remedy beyond what was prayed."[17] Hinting at the merits, however, the Court stated that the underlying question of constitutional law was "grave."[18] That was quite a change from two decades earlier when a younger Holmes showed callous indifference to the disenfranchisement of Alabama blacks by refusing to order them registered because "the great mass of the white population intends to keep blacks from voting."[19]

The first challenge to the state's all-white primary was initiated by El Paso physician Lawrence A. Nixon at the behest of the local National Association for the Advancement of Colored People (NAACP) and with the help of the national NAACP. Nixon was a friend of the local election judge C. C. Herndon and was turned away with a polite "you know we can't let you vote."[20] Nixon's suit not only sought an injunction, but to get around any problems of mootness, also sought $5,000 in money damages. Herndon helpfully signed a statement that the only reason for turning Nixon away was Nixon's race. Nevertheless, a federal district court dismissed Nixon's case without the dignity of an opinion.

Once again the Texas Democrats did not even bother to argue before the Supreme Court, but this time, after oral argument, the Texas attorney general's office successfully moved to file an amicus brief defending the state law, claiming the primary was not an election within the meaning of the Fifteenth Amendment and therefore Nixon's claim was political, not legal.[21] If political it would not be within judicial cognizance. In *Nixon v. Herndon* a unanimous Court, again through Holmes, found it unnecessary to reach the Fifteenth Amendment because "it is too clear for extended argument that color cannot be made the basis for a statutory classification affecting the right set up in this case."[22] Holmes's two-page opinion was a bit too facile; historically the reason the Fifteenth Amendment was necessary was that the Fourteenth was thought not to reach political rights such as voting or office-holding. Still, although this was an era where dissents were rarely registered, unanimity was interesting because of the composition of the Court. Justice James McReynolds, an appointee of President Woodrow Wilson, was an out-and-out racist (among far too many undesirable traits). Holmes, like many other Progressives, ranged from skeptical to hostile to claims of racial discrimination. His fellow Progressive, Louis D. Brandeis, was simply unconcerned with the issue. But they all agreed Texas had crossed a constitutional line.

Governor Dan Moody responded to *Nixon v. Herndon*, adding to the call of a special legislative session a proposal to reinstate the all-white primary by legalistic legerdemain. The legislature responded by deregulating qualifications for primary elections, passing new legislation that left Texas, like the other Southern states, with the parties' executive committees determining the qualifications for adult voting in the primaries. The executive committee of the Texas Democrats in turn then limited voting in primaries to whites only. It took two weeks for Moody's proposal to become Texas law. Anglo Texans were nothing if not efficient in implementing their desire that blacks have no say in Texas state government.

In a replay, Dr. Nixon, again with the backing of the NAACP, sued a local Democratic election judge, seeking both an injunction and money damages. The new legislation, after all, had left him in exactly the same position that he had been before—excluded from voting the Democratic primary solely because of his race. But this time it was different, the attorney general's office argued, because the decision to exclude blacks was made by a private association, the Texas Democrats. Texas prevailed at both the trial and court of appeals level.

The Supreme Court, however, held for Dr. Nixon, this time in a 5–4 split that offered a precursor of the votes on economic issues that would prevail through 1937.[23] The conservatives, accepting the argument that had prevailed below, dissented in an opinion by McReynolds. The majority opinion, by Justice Benjamin Cardozo, who had just replaced the aged Holmes, found that the Democrats' decision was still tainted by the actions of the state legislature. The state had "lodged the power in a committee, which excluded the petitioner and others of his race, not by virtue of any authority delegated by the party, but by virtue of an authority originating or supposed to originate in the mandate of the law."[24] Whether the conclusion would be different if the state said nothing and the Democrats acted on their own "must be postponed until decision becomes necessary."[25]

It took Texas Democrats just twenty-two days to respond to Cardozo's opinion. With no state law operative, the state Democratic convention unanimously resolved: "All white citizens of the State who are qualified to vote under the Constitution and laws of Texas shall be eligible for membership in the party and as such be eligible for participation in the primaries."[26]

The national NAACP lawyers—who were white—had produced two victories at the Supreme Court but not a single black voter in the Democratic primaries. Local black lawyers, who had also filed a brief at the Court, thought they could do better and ultimately with Houston activist and barber Richard Randolph Grovey they sued election judge Allen Townsend, not for $5,000 as Dr. Nixon had claimed, but for a mere $10 and in a justice-of-the-peace court—where they lost.

Texas law did not allow an appeal in any case where the amount in controversy was less than $20 and so, with a decision by the highest court in the state wherein a decision could be had, Grovey's lawyers appealed directly to the Supreme Court, which agreed to hear the case. The lawyers then got an added break as neither the attorney general nor the state's Democrats bothered to brief or argue the case for excluding blacks from the primaries. They assumed they would win so why bother? One ought to be able to win a case when the other side is not represented. That was one of the powerful messages of fairness the Court sent in *Gideon v. Wainwright*[27] on the rights of indigent criminal defendants to be provided with counsel. But like William Marbury—of the famous *Marbury v. Madison*[28]—arguing unopposed can still lead to defeat. *Grovey v. Townsend*[29] not only upheld the right of the Texas Democrats in convention to exclude blacks from their primaries, it did so unanimously! Instead of gaining unsatisfying victories as the national NAACP had done in 1927 and then 1932, the local lawyers suffered a complete defeat in 1935. Richard Evans, an African American, Yale-educated Waco attorney, had begged the lawyers not to bring the case. With the defeat he groused, "Their fido pack went bear hunting and treed a skunk."[30] The formerly unanswered question was now answered; what Southern Democrats had done for decades complied with the Fourteenth and Fifteenth Amendments.

Justice Owen Roberts—otherwise the swing justice from 1934 through 1937 and famously "the switch in time that saved nine"[31] for his changed votes that helped scuttle President Franklin D. Roosevelt's Court-packing plan in 1937—wrote the Court's opinion finding a lack of state action. Like many a subsequent state action opinion, *Grovey* was hardly satisfying.[32] Texas required primaries, ordered that general election standards apply, mandated absentee voting. But Texas did not finance the primaries, nor did state officials count the ballots. So the state had some but not total involvement with the Democratic primary. Excluding blacks could have been called state action, but by a 9–0 vote it wasn't.

III

The national NAACP, which unlike the Texas lawyers had its eyes on the long term, did not see *Grovey* as a final defeat.[33] The NAACP hired Charles Hamilton Houston, the first African American to be invited to join the *Harvard Law Review*, to head up its lawyering. Houston then made the best legal hire ever with Thurgood Marshall, his former student at Howard Law School, to be his assistant and successor and eventually the most important lawyer of the century. (Houston retired in 1940 for health reasons.) Houston also determined that the national organization needed better relations with local branches to coordinate litigation. But what the NAACP could not anticipate was that in the six years after *Grovey*, President Roosevelt would have the good luck to replace seven justices on the Court. For the New Deal justices, the Old Constitutional Order was a complete misunderstanding of the Constitution.[34]

Marshall and the Texas NAACP agreed in the spring of 1940 that Marshall would file another challenge to the all-white primary. Marshall had two Houston NAACP members as choices for plaintiff: Dr. Lonnie Smith, a dentist, and Sidney Hasgett, a construction worker. Both tried to vote in the July Democratic primary as well as the August runoff, and naturally both had been denied on the basis of their race. Marshall settled on Hasgett, filed suit, lost at trial, and filed the appeal. But before briefing or argument the Supreme Court decided *United States v. Classic*,[35] which had the possibility of being a game changer.

Briefly, *Classic* involved a criminal indictment (dismissed by the district judge) charging voter fraud in a Louisiana primary. (Reform opponents of the Huey Long machine changed ballots to ensure the nomination of

Hale Boggs, a future Democratic majority leader, to the House of Representatives. The irony: The Justice Department discovered the fraud in an investigation targeting the Long machine.) Chief Justice Harlan Fiske Stone's opinion held that the indictment to deny anyone any "right or privilege ... secured by the Constitution" could stand because as a matter of established fact as well as Louisiana law, the primary election was "an integral part of the procedure of the popular choice of Congressman."[36] Besides its factual irony, an interesting sidelight to *Classic* is that the dissenters, Hugo Black, William O. Douglas, and Frank Murphy, increasingly represented the liberal wing of the Court.[37]

Classic was not a case of racial discrimination and did not mention *Grovey* or the all-white primaries. Nor did it encompass state offices. Furthermore, Louisiana paid for the primaries and required a primary if a party's candidate was to appear on the general election ballot; Texas did neither. Yet the language about primaries being integral to the general election process had implications. Throughout the South and in most of Texas, the winner of the Democratic primary was the foregone winner of the general election.

Hasgett's case had been litigated to protest his rejection for voting for state office. To be perfectly safe, Marshall decided to jettison Hasgett's appeal and begin anew with Dr. Smith as plaintiff, focusing on the July primary where all the federal offices had been settled. Marshall's decision was not universally popular. Thus he jokingly noted in a November 1941 letter that if he lost the new case he would have to move to Germany and live with "Adolph Hitler or some other peace loving individual who would be less difficult than the Negroes in Texas who had put up money for the case."[38]

The district judge and the Fifth Circuit Court of Appeals did not believe *Classic* had eroded *Grovey*. Maybe as significantly, neither did Herbert Wechsler, the successful government attorney in *Classic*. Marshall hoped the Justice Department would join the NAACP in asking the Court to reconsider *Grovey*. Wechsler (who eventually would win *New York Times v. Sullivan*[39] and became executive director of the prestigious

American Law Institute) was against it, and everyone who touched the issue raised the red flag of the need to retain Southern support for FDR and the Democrats. The political calculation prevailed and the NAACP was alone (eventually to be supported by an amicus brief by the American Civil Liberties Union and the National Lawyers Guild).

The NAACP may have been alone, but once again they were unopposed; neither S. E. Allwright, a Houston election judge, nor Texas nor Texas Democrats filed a brief nor bothered to show up for the November, 1943 argument. Marshall spoke the entire time as no justice bothered asking him a question. After argument, Texas and the Texas Democrats were allowed to file amicus briefs and the Court ordered reargument, and this time Marshall was opposed by an assistant state attorney general. It wasn't the mismatch of arguing unopposed, but it was a mismatch. The NAACP's claim that *Classic* undermined *Grovey* and that Texas functionally had disenfranchised over 11 percent of its adult population prevailed in *Smith v. Allwright*[40] by an 8–1 vote in an opinion written by Kentuckian Stanley Reed (who got the assignment after Felix Frankfurter declined, suggesting the opinion should not be written by a northeastern Jew). Reed tracked Marshall's argument, and after noting that the vote could not be denied on the basis of race, Reed observed that "this grant to the people of the opportunity of choice is not to be nullified by a State through casting its electoral process in a form that permits a private organization to practice racial discrimination in the election. Constitutional rights would be of little value if they could be thus indirectly denied."[41] Unmentioned but just below the surface was World War II, where whites and African Americans were fighting two totalitarian racist powers.

Roberts, the author of *Grovey*, was the lone dissenter and he let loose his anger at being isolated on a Court of New Deal appointees. He thought the New Dealers' penchant for overruling "indicates an intolerance for what those who have composed this court in the past have conscientiously and deliberately concluded, and involves an assumption that knowledge and wisdom reside in us which was denied to our predecessors."[42] The overrulings—and there were many as the New Dealers brushed aside the Old Constitutional Order—"tend[] to bring adjudications of this tribunal into the same class as a restricted railroad ticket, good for this day and train only."[43] He retired a year later (after only fifteen years on the Court), and his colleagues were so divided and bitter about his legacy that they could not agree on the traditional letter acknowledging his service on the Court.

After twenty years of litigation and four trips to the Court, the Texas all-white primary was dead. Reaction by white politicians across the Deep South was hostile, and the Texas State Bar Association let loose its unhappiness by passing a resolution that claimed that the "Supreme Court of the United States is losing, if it has not already lost, the high esteem in which it has been held by the people."[44]

Despite hostility, *Smith v. Allwright* was successful in allowing African Americans (who could otherwise qualify to vote) access to the Democratic primaries. Michael Klarman's magisterial *From Jim Crow to Civil Rights* details a number of reasons why: African Americans were united and intensely committed to the need for ballot access, while whites were far less united on denial of that access than they were on the other facets of Jim Crow (like segregated schools). Moreover, *Smith* could be easily enforced by the Justice Department.[45] In 1940 only 3 percent of Southern African Americans were registered to vote; by 1952 the number was 20 percent.[46] In Texas about 30,000 African Americans were registered to vote in 1940; by 1947 the number reached around 100,000 and then jumped to 214,000 for the 1956 elections.[47] In 1978 Justice Thurgood Marshall looked back: "The Texas primary case was the greatest ... it changed the whole complexion in the South."[48]

With *Smith* and the end of World War II, "Blacks participated in large numbers" in the 1946 Texas Democratic primary.[49] But in Fort Bend County, in the coastal plains to the west and south of Houston, their ability to participate was irrelevant because the white Democrats always decided the winner by a pre-primary vote of the Jaybird Democratic Association, a private group formed in 1889 as the Jaybird Club and, in the twentieth century, open to every white voter. If the Jaybirds could successfully exclude African Americans, then there would be a roadmap around *Smith*—create private organizations to determine the candidate who would ultimately prevail. Indeed, the Jaybird winner invariably won both the state primary and the general election, often being unopposed on the official ballots. (The justices had raised this at Conference.)

In another lawyer mismatch, the NAACP argued against local counsel and convinced eight justices that the Jaybird primary violated the Fifteenth Amendment, but it took the justices a while to get there as the initial vote was 5–4 to reject the constitutional claim. Then Frankfurter made it 4–4 by passing. Then he changed his mind again and made it 5–4 to strike down the Jaybird primary.[50] With the result thus sealed, three more justices switched to find the requisite state action, although the eight could not agree as to why. One opinion found the Jaybird primary an "integral" part of the election process (perhaps without regard to any state action). Another found state action in the participation of local officials without showing what that was, while a third simply assumed there was state action. The opinions are terrible, but the justices would not allow a retreat on the all-white primary. The dissenter, Sherman Minton, aptly observed: "When the Jaybird opinion comes down, there may be some questions about which election returns the Court follows! It will be damn clear they aren't following any law."[51]

The all-white primary was truly dead for those African Americans who could successfully register to vote. But that still wasn't easy because restrictions—such as the poll tax and literacy or understanding tests—set up to deny them the vote would last until the mid-1960s.[52] They were ended by the Voting Rights Act of 1965, pushed by President Lyndon Baines Johnson, a Texan who cared passionately about his legacy and justice in race relations—and who predicted he was handing the South to the Republicans for a generation. It may have taken more than a generation, but the numbers of Southern Democrats steadily declined as the century progressed and the handover to the Republicans has been solidly in place for over a generation.

TWO

After the Voting Rights Act

Throwing out preclearance when it has worked and is
continuing to work to stop discriminatory [election] changes
is like throwing away your umbrella in a rainstorm because
you are not getting wet.

    —Justice Ruth Bader Ginsburg dissenting
    in *Shelby County v. Holder* (2013)

In 1970 with the Vietnam War raging, Congress extended the franchise
to eighteen-year-olds. Texas, along with three other states, contested
the law. Four justices held that Congress properly exercised its power
under Section 5 of the Fourteenth Amendment to enforce the requirement of equal protection found in Section 1. Four justices held that
extending the franchise was beyond congressional authority.

I was clerking during this Term, and as oral argument approached,
Chief Justice Warren E. Burger circulated a memorandum to the effect
that the Constitution could not allow the federal government to set
qualifications in federal elections but simultaneously prohibit it from
regulating qualifications in state elections. As I recall, the law clerks
were incredulous. Why argue against an obviously absurd point? The
answer turned out to be eighty-four-year-old Hugo Black, Franklin D.
Roosevelt's first nominee to the Court. He held Congress had authority
to extend the franchise for federal elections because of Article 1, Section 4: "The Times, Places and Manner of holding elections for Senators and Representatives, shall be prescribed by each State by the Leg-

islature thereof; but the Congress may at any time by Law make or alter such regulations." Then he held Congress lacked the power to extend the franchise in state elections because of what he felt were the implications of Article 1, Section 2: "The House of Representative shall be composed of Members chosen every second year by the People of the several States and the Electors in each State shall have the Qualifications requisite for the Electors of the most numerous Branch of the State Legislature." He saw that as "a clear indication that the Framers intended the States to determine the qualifications of their own voters for state offices."[1]

Black's idiosyncratic opinion controlled the result but created an intolerable situation for state election officials. Three months later both the House and the Senate passed, by the needed two-thirds vote, a proposed constitutional amendment to give eighteen-year-olds the vote in all elections. In just 107 days the requisite three-quarters of the states ratified the Twenty-Sixth Amendment. Only one subsequent amendment has been ratified—in 1992—and it was one of the original twelve sent to the states in 1789 (of which ten were ratified by 1791).

I

In 1992 Edward Blum ran for the House seat once held by Barbara Jordan. Given that the district was configured to elect another African American, he lost. He then sued the state (with four others), claiming 24 of the state's 30 congressional districts were illegally drawn. To say that the legislature had created bizarrely shaped districts does not do justice to the creativity of the legislature. They had a minority "core area and many very narrow tentacles, (some only a block wide) at points extending outward to capture pockets of minority population in parts of the counties that were not necessarily contiguous with the core of the district."[2] In *Bush v. Vera*[3] the Court found this an unconstitutional racial gerrymander in three minority districts including the one where Blum lost. The lines were easily redrawn by the district court and the statewide gerrymander, perhaps the "best" of the 1990s, was otherwise left in place with Democrats controlling the congressional delegation even as Texas had turned Republican. This was Blum's introduction to the Supreme Court and over the next twenty years he would be there again and again, although never as a named litigant. He needed no introduction to Texas as he was a University of Texas alumnus (but not a lawyer).

In the 1980s, Austin began its explosive population growth especially to the northwest and southwest. In the Canyon Creek area, headwaters to Bull Creek (once owned by Congressman J.J. "Jake" Pickle), a developer created a municipal utility district (MUD) to issue bonds and service them to build infrastructure for an upscale residential community. Canyon Creek went from twelve residents in 1990 to 3,500 a decade later. In 2000 it was 93 percent Anglo with a mean family income of $103,000. While it was inside both Travis County and Austin, the MUD was not under the control of either.

The MUD was governed by five directors elected in biannual elections, only one of which has been contested. From its inception until 2006 the MUD made eight submissions for preclearance (prior permission to change voting procedures) to the United States attorney general under section 5 of the Voting Rights Act because it was making changes in how it conducted its (basically uncontested) elections. The annualized cost of the submissions was $223. These submissions dealt with changes in polling places, which prior to 2004 were in private residences. Then, for convenience, they were consolidated in a neighborhood school and placed on the countywide ballot for Travis.

The attorney general never objected to any changes. There has never been an election-related lawsuit against the MUD. Indeed, no one has ever complained about any election procedure of the MUD. Nor have any outside groups been able to identify any problems.

The Voting Rights Act, with its preclearance requirements for the South (areas listed in section 4), was adopted in 1965[4] and reauthorized in 1970[5] (for five years), 1975[6] (for seven years), 1982 (for twenty-five years), and 2006 for an additional twenty-five years by a 98–0 vote in the Senate and 390–33 in the House. President George W. Bush signed the bill, stating, "By reauthorizing this Act Congress has reaffirmed its belief that all men are created equal."[7]

A few days after the 2006 reauthorization, the MUD sued the attorney general, claiming that it should be allowed the advantage of the "bailout" (from preclearance) provisions of the Act. To obtain a bailout a jurisdiction must have had a pristine record on any possible voting rights issue for the previous ten years. The MUD argued that if it were not allowed to bail out, then the preclearance provision was unconstitutional. Given that preclearance had never been a burden regarding either time or money for the MUD, the lawsuit looks odd. That is, until one realizes that Ed Blum was the man behind it. In 2005 he created the Project on Fair Representation, funded by undisclosed donors with Blum as its sole employee. He described his approach as follows: "I find the plaintiff, I find the lawyer, and I put them together, and then I worry about it for four years."[8] Northwest Austin Municipal Utility District Number One was Blum's first plaintiff and its challenge to section 5 of the Voting Rights Act was the first of several cases Blum convinced the Court to hear. Blum noted that "[b]y getting cases to the Supreme Court it makes donors more generous. I can tell them I am going to take a case to the Supreme Court and now they believe me."[9] The case was handled by Greg Coleman, a UT law grad, former law clerk for Clarence Thomas, who had been the first solicitor general of Texas. Coleman made sure the Court knew that the MUD had clean hands from its inception.

At the Court the MUD got its bailout from preclearance with an opinion by Chief Justice John Roberts, the most qualified Supreme Court appointee since Thurgood Marshall. Roberts graduated from Harvard and Harvard Law School, clerked initially for the distinguished (and tough) Henry Friendly and then William Rehnquist. He went to the solicitor general's office and then private practice, where he was a leading member of the Supreme Court bar before taking a seat on the District of Columbia Circuit Court of Appeals.

To get the MUD its bailout, Roberts had to torture the statutory language in order to find that special purpose districts like the MUD were eligible for the bailout. As such, *Northwest Austin Municipal Utility District Number One v. Holder*[10] is of minimal importance. But what Roberts said in the opinion foreshadowed a future case of supreme importance.

Roberts praised the Voting Rights Act and the progress of the South under its regime—perhaps praised it to its death. In some states blacks register and vote at higher rates than whites. Blacks hold office and conditions have "unquestionably improved."[11] But asking the federal government for permission to change laws or procedures "imposes substantial 'federalism costs.'"[12] The "Act imposes current burdens and must be justified by current needs . . . and there is considerable evidence that it fails to account for current political conditions."[13] Thus the preclearance "requirements and its coverage formula raise serious constitutional questions."[14] Those questions could be delayed and avoided because of the construction that the Court put on the bailout provision. The opinion was channeling Blum, who had stated: "It simply isn't 1965 anymore in the Deep South. But it may take the Supreme Court to tell that to Congress."[15]

Every justice but Clarence Thomas joined the opinion. He went all the way to find section 5 unconstitutional.

II

What Roberts did was offer another Southern jurisdiction an open invitation to challenge section 5 as not being justified by current conditions. It fell to Ed Blum to find that plaintiff and of course he did—Shelby County, Alabama. If the Northwest Austin MUD had a clean record on race, Shelby County and Alabama most certainly did not. Located south and east of Birmingham, and ineligible for bailout, the county had submitted voting changes for preclearance that had been rejected by the attorney general. Furthermore Alabama was subject to more successful voter discrimination lawsuits between 1982 and 2006 than any other state—except Mississippi. State motto: "We're number two."

To argue Shelby County's case Blum turned to the very able Bert W. Rein, co-founder of the major D.C. law firm Wiley Rein. Rein was a Harvard law graduate who went on to clerk for Justice John Marshall Harlan. He had already argued a Texas affirmative action case for the Project for Fair Representation earlier in the Term. The oral argument was hard on Solicitor General Donald Verrilli. Roberts asked him which state had the worst ratio of white to black voter turnout. He didn't know so Roberts helped him: "Massachusetts. Do you know what has the best, where African American turnout actually exceeds white turnout? Mississippi."[16] There was no doubt where Roberts was going. The same held for Antonin Scalia, who pejoratively labeled the Voting Rights Act a "racial entitlement" as if protecting the right to vote from racial discrimination was an unworthy endeavor.[17] He deemed the overwhelming vote to reauthorize the law simply an example of how hard it is to use the normal political process to end those entitlements.

As the senior justice in the majority Roberts had the right to assign the opinion and he kept it for himself and basically tracked his *Northwest Austin MUD* opinion to find section 4 of the Voting Rights Act an unconstitutional infringement of what he repeatedly called the "fundamental principle of equal sovereignty" of the states covered.[18] By striking down section 4, he emasculated preclearance in section 5. The conditions that justified singling out certain states "no longer characterize voting in covered jurisdictions ... African American voter turnout has come to exceed white voter turnout in five of the six states originally covered."[19] The law was unfair to covered jurisdictions. "While one State waits months or years and expends funds to implement a validly enacted law, its neighbor can typically put the same law into effect immediately."[20] For Roberts this departure from the basic structure of our governments was justified in 1965 and for some years thereafter, but changed circumstance means it no longer can be justified. Sections 4 and 5 of the Voting Rights Act have been so successful that they are no longer necessary.

Roberts closed by blaming Congress. In Blum's prescient forecast *Northwest Austin MUD* had flagged the problems with the coverage provisions of the Voting Rights Act four years earlier when the Court told Congress that it isn't 1965 anymore in the Deep South. "Congress could have updated the coverage formula at that time, but did not do so."[21] With political polarization in the Capitol nothing was done to fix the Voting Rights Act.

The four liberals dissented in an opinion by Ruth Bader Ginsburg, who had been the Thurgood Marshall of the gender equality movement in the 1970s. It is a solid opinion although it lacks the fire she demonstrates when gender discrimination is at issue. She closed with an analogy to the majority's claim that the act was so successful it is not needed. "Throwing out preclearance when it has worked and is continuing to work to stop discriminatory changes is like throwing away your umbrella in a rainstorm because you are not getting wet."[22]

III

Blum achieved his goal of ending preclearance and believed he had moved another step closer to the color-blind Constitution he sought. But he had one more goal with respect to voting change. He wished to change the way equal population was determined so that future congressional and legislative districts would be more white. Rounding up Sue Evenwel from Titus County in northeast Texas and Edward Pfenninger from Montgomery County north of Houston, and handing them to former Thomas clerk William Consovoy, Blum called on the Court to address the actual meaning of "one person, one vote." Why doesn't it mean "one eligible voter, one vote"? This necessarily meant that districts with large numbers of nonvoters—noncitizens, minors, prisoners—were overrepresented. This was especially true of Hispanics, where the number of eligible voters was far less than the number of people, because of both noncitizens and high birthrates. If accepted, the claim would weaken the legislative power of urban districts and enhance that of most rural districts.

Justice Ginsburg made short-shrift of the plaintiff's claim, finding that constitutional history, the Court's precedents, and legislative practice all pointed to the allowable use of equal population districts regardless of voting eligibility. The most telling point was a quotation from Senator Jacob Howard during the debates on the Fourteenth Amendment: "The basis of representation is numbers ... and this is the principle upon which the Constitution was originally framed, that the basis of representation should depend upon numbers.... Numbers, not voters; numbers, not property; this is the theory of the Constitution."[23] Tellingly Ginsburg followed with: "Appellants ask us to find in the Fourteenth Amendment's Equal Protection Clause a rule inconsistent with this 'theory of the Constitution.'"[24] All the reapportionment decisions of the previous half century had used total population, and finding the Constitution barred it "would upset a well-functioning approach to districting."[25] (Of course, Ginsburg, unlike her good friend Nino Scalia, was scarcely a friend of originalism, which might well be fatal to protecting women under the Fourteenth Amendment.)

Thinking of the future, Texas had asserted: "States generally do not violate the [Equal Protection] Clause by selecting total, citizen, or voting-eligible population."[26] Ginsburg's majority declined to reach this issue. Justice Samuel Alito's concurring opinion did; it noted there were two theories of "one person, one vote" and the states were free to implement either one.

IV

In retrospect the equal voter issue was probably a sideshow (although the future may prove that wrong). The real beneficiaries of Blum's victory in *Shelby County* were states where Republicans controlled both branches of the legislature as well as the governorship, because on the state level the Republican Party had become obsessed with the fear of voter fraud. The Court, in a short opinion handed down just two weeks before the 2006 elections, had stated: "Voter fraud drives honest citizens out of the democratic process and breeds distrust of our government. Voters who fear that their legitimate votes will be outweighed by fraudulent ones will feel disenfranchised."[27] Three years later, in an opinion by John Paul Stevens, the Court approved an Indiana voter ID law despite the fact that there was no evidence of any in-person impersonation at any time in the history of Indiana.[28] Voter fraud exists, but in-person voter fraud where one person votes multiple times or an ineligible person votes is exceptionally rare (and the consequences of getting caught are unpleasant).

The Court's statement about legitimate voters feeling disenfranchised accurately summed up Republican concerns that arose during the second term of President George W. Bush. Thus Republican "activists grew increasingly frustrated that the Justice Department could not find the immense voter fraud party followers had been assured was afoot."[29] Karl Rove and others in the White House even contemplated asking for the resignations of all U.S. attorneys in the ninety-three districts. Instead, nine were cashiered for failure to bring charges in cases where they believed there had been no crime committed. Still, Royal Masset, the political director of the Republican Party of Texas, stated: "Among Republicans, it is an article of religious faith that voter fraud is causing us to lose elections."[30]

Where did that faith come from? One source was a book by John Fund, a former *Wall Street Journal* editorial writer, entitled *Stealing Elections: How Voter Fraud Threatens Our Democracy*. It was published in 2004, with a revised edition coming out in 2008. Fund did show examples of fraud with absentee ballots, but not with in-person voting. He also went conspiratorial by claiming eight of the 9 / 11 hijackers were registered to vote—without a shred of evidence. Other evidence of voter fraud came from former Republican majority leader Dick Armey with his assertion, like Fund without evidence, that three percent of all votes cast were fraudulent—by Democrats. Fox News also stoked the fires with its own "Voter Fraud Watch," and during the early Obama administration could not air often enough a picture of two African Americans (who looked very threatening) who were supposedly intimidating voters in Philadelphia. Fox commentators could not understand why the two had not been indicted and seemed to lay the blame on new attorney general Eric Holder, an African American.

Republicans intended to do something to prevent fraudulent voters from undermining faith in the democratic process. The typical, but not exclusive, means was voter identification, and in 2009 the business-backed conservative American Legislative Exchange Council drafted a model voter ID bill. Democrats had a less benign view of the Republican efforts and labeled them "voter suppression" because around 11 percent of voters lack ID and most of them would vote Democratic—if they bothered to vote at all. A senior vice president of the Metropolitan Milwaukee Chamber of Commerce asked about an election for the state supreme court: "Do we need to start messaging 'widespread reports of election fraud' so we are positively set up for recount regardless of the final number? I obviously think we should."[31] The majority leader of the Pennsylvania house gave the Democrats ammunition when he stated the state's new voter ID law "is gonna allow Governor [Mitt] Romney to win the state of Pennsylvania, done."[32] Jim Greer, former chair of the Florida Republican Party, stated that voter ID was designed to suppress Democratic votes: no one "came to see me and tell me that we had a fraud issue. It's all a marketing ploy."[33] The Fourth Circuit, in a North Carolina case decided in the summer of 2016, gave voice to the Democrats' concerns when the panel concluded that the state's new voter law (with ID provisions) deliberately "targets African-Americans with almost surgical precision."[34]

The laws the Republicans were adopting would never have received preclearance, but *Shelby County* held they didn't have to. One aspect of that case held true: the North and the South looked more alike. While Alabama, North Carolina, and Texas passed voter ID (and made other changes that impacted minorities), so did Ohio and Wisconsin. What they had in common was the professed Republican concern that in-person voter fraud was stealing elections. (This did not explain why some states cut back on early voting on Sundays when African American churches would often bus their parishioners to the polling station—the "souls to the polls.")

V

In-person voter fraud is truly rare. A recent study from Loyola University of Los Angeles found thirty-one cases out of one billion votes cast in this century. In Texas there were two successful prosecutions out of 20 million votes cast in the first decade of the century. Rare or not, Republicans were sure it was a problem and the Texas legislature got to work on the solution in the 2005 session. A voter ID bill passed the House, but died in the Senate in the end-of-session push to pass the most important bills.

Two years later the story was similar. The bill passed the House but died in the Senate under the then-applicable rule whereby two-thirds of the Senate must agree before considering a bill on the merits. The failure to gain the two-thirds was only possible because Lt. Governor David Dewhurst accepted a Democratic senator's word that he had been on the floor at the time of the vote and was not counted. With him actually there the Democrats had the eleven necessary votes to block.

In 2009 the story but not the outcome was a little different. The bill in the previous two sessions had authorized employer- and university-issued photo identifications to count as the requisite ID for voting. Both of those were dropped, the latter presumably because college students were likely to vote the wrong way. The Senate eliminated the two-thirds rule for any legislation relating to voter ID. This allowed the Republicans to push the bill through by majority vote. In the House, Democrats got creative and "chubbed" the bill to death. Chubbing is when a legislator uses his ability to speak on any bill for ten minutes.

When multiple representatives combine their speaking privileges across multiple bills, they are able to run the clock out on target legislation slated to be considered late in the session.

The fourth time was the charm. In light of the tactics—all legal—used by the Democrats, the Republicans decided to respond in kind. The bill was prefiled as SB 178. Then sponsors of the bill obtained Dewhurst's consent to refile it with a new lower number reserved for the lieutenant governor's priorities. It became SB 14. Governor Rick Perry then designated voter ID as an "emergency matter for immediate consideration," thereby allowing consideration of the bill during the first sixty days of the 140-day session as well as letting the legislature know he would call a special session if necessary.[35] The Senate adopted the same rules as the previous session, meaning that the two-thirds remained inapplicable to voter ID. In the House the bill was placed on the emergency calendar to assist quicker passage. With the procedural hurdles cleared, SB 14 became law effective as of January 1, 2012.

As passed, SB 14 states several types of photo ID are acceptable (provided they have not expired more than sixty days previously): driver's license, concealed handgun license, military ID, a passport, a certificate of citizenship if it carries a photo. Student ID and employer ID are not acceptable. If people lack any of the above they can go to a Department of Public Safety office and obtain a Election Identification Certificate upon proof of identity (typically a birth certificate). Over a half-million Texas voters lack the requested ID. The legislature appropriated very little money for educational outreach, and many Texans did not know of the legislative changes in 2012.

During the lengthy process of enacting voter ID, supporters of the measure offered three rationales. Naturally they claimed it was designed to prevent voter fraud (although if that were a concern one might have expected something to be done about absentee ballots). After all, one illegal vote is one too many. Related to this they wished to restore confidence in the integrity of Texas elections. With so many people convinced of fraudulent voting, the law assured them it would stop. At an earlier point in time supporters also claimed that the law would prevent noncitizens from voting. That rationale evaporated when opponents pointed out that noncitizens can obtain driver's licenses and concealed carry permits, both acceptable ID under the new law.

Such a drastic change in election procedures required preclearance. Knowing that Attorney General Holder would not preclear such a law, the state tried its luck with the District of Columbia three-judge district court. It denied preclearance.[36] Then came *Shelby County,* and immediately thereafter Texas attorney general (and gubernatorial candidate) Greg Abbott hailed the decision and announced that SB 14 was in effect.[37] Now the burden fell on those who opposed the law. They were going to be faced with a hostile Fifth Circuit with its nine Republicans to only five Democrats, but at least they could pick the district judge they wanted. That turned out to be Nelva Gonzales Ramos, a UT law grad and Obama appointee (with the consent of Senators Kay Bailey Hutchison and John Cornyn) in Corpus Christi.

After extensive discovery Ramos held a nine-day trial. The most compelling testimony came from Sammie Louise Bates by video. She grew up in Mississippi in the 1940s and began voting regularly as soon as she turned twenty-one. In the 2013 election she was turned away for lack of proper ID. To get that ID she would have to pay Mississippi $42 for her birth certificate. She didn't because she lives on $321 monthly from Social Security. "I had to put $42 where it would do the most good. It was feeding my family. We couldn't eat the birth certificate."[38] Others rely on public transportation and are several hours' round trip from the nearest Department of Public Safety office.

Ramos gave the challengers a complete victory. She found the preventing fraud rationale for the law to be the same as Texas had always used to deny the vote to African Americans. The other rationales were pretextual. The law was intended to discriminate against African Americans and Hispanics. Despite all discovery, there was no smoking gun of an elected Republican or a staffer who said "we're doing this to disenfranchise minorities." Democrats made that claim after SB 14 passed, but had no direct evidence to back the claim. Yet given Texas's past history, the pretextual justifications, and the clear effects on minorities, Ramos held SB 14 was unconstitutional under the Fourteenth and Fifteenth Amendments as well as the amendment outlawing the poll tax (given the cost of obtaining proper ID). If that were not enough it also violated section 2 of the Voting Rights Act that prohibits imposing a qualification which results in denying or abridging the right to vote. Ramos issued her opinion on October 9, 2014, and a final order two days later.[39] The elections would have to be held under the old law without voter ID.

Not surprisingly Texas went to the more fertile venue, the Fifth Circuit, with the request to stay the judge's order, and the state was not disappointed. Relying on Supreme Court decisions cautioning against courts changing the rules for elections on the eve of an election, the court issued a stay. The court found Texas would be irreparably harmed if the district court were ultimately reversed because there would be no way to rerun the election. If the stay were granted, those denied the right to vote because of lack of ID would be harmed, but not as much as the state—because the state was likely to prevail on the merits, a point underscored by the court's dismissal of the Ramos opinion; rather than saying the opinion held SB 14 unconstitutional, the court said it "opined that SB 14 is unconstitutional."[40]

The Supreme Court refused to vacate the Fifth Circuit's stay with Ginsburg (joined by President Barack Obama's two appointees, Sonia Sotomayor and Elena Kagan) dissenting. She found the Texas case different from the other decisions refusing to change the rules on an eve of an election for several reasons: the case involves a decision on the merits by a district court; state elections officials are familiar with the pre-SB 14 rules; the state made no serious effort to inform voters of the new rules; and most importantly, "the greatest threat to public confidence in elections in this case is the prospect of enforcing a purposely discriminatory law, one that likely imposes an unconstitutional poll tax and risks denying the right to vote to hundreds of thousands of eligible voters."[41]

If SB 14 had an effect on the 2014 elections, Democrat Pete Gallegos was the victim. The freshman congressman from West Texas was defeated by 2,200 votes. Otherwise the people most affected by the lack of photo ID are those statistically less likely to vote in the first place. Hence, attributing real world effects to the law is difficult.

In the real world of judges, however, a panel of the Fifth Circuit affirmed Ramos's decision that the law ran afoul of section 2 of the Voting Rights Act, even though after oral argument Texas eliminated the charge for a birth certificate for purposes of getting voter ID.[42] The panel concluded she misapplied existing law in finding the legislature had a discriminatory purpose and remanded for reconsideration on the point. Otherwise the panel concluded that she had been wrong on the constitutional issues. The state needed a complete victory and didn't get it. So it asked the Fifth Circuit to rehear the case en banc where the Republican super-majority could work its will. The en banc court found the Republicans split with four (including one Reagan appointee) voting that SB 14 violated section 2 and five voting to reverse the Ramos decision completely. The Republican split meant the decision was controlled by the Democratic-appointed judges and they voted unanimously that SB 14 violated section 2 and affirmed the panel decision.

Writing for the dissenters, Edith Jones saw the case as impugning Republicans rather than disenfranchising minorities. Her opinion made three points. First, African Americans and Hispanics were not significantly hurt by SB 14 even if they were more affected by it than Anglos. Second, the extraordinary legislative features in 2011 were necessary because Republicans were committed to passing voter ID no matter what. Third, "the law reflects party politics not racism."[43] It was just good old fashioned politics—trying to increase Republican turnout while simultaneously decreasing Democratic turnout by making it harder for some Democrats, who happened to be African American and Hispanic, to vote. To suggest otherwise, as Ramos and the majority did, was "perniciously irresponsible racial name-calling."[44]

On day three of Donald J. Trump's presidency, the Court declined to review that Fifth Circuit's decision.[45] That made sense. With Antonin Scalia's seat vacant, if the four Republicans had voted to hear the case, the likely outcome would be a 4–4 decision affirming the Fifth Circuit. And there was always the risk that Anthony Kennedy would vote with the liberals. Chief Justice Roberts wrote that the Fifth Circuit had remanded the case for further consideration on discriminatory intent and that there was yet to be a final remedial order and so the Court could take up the case in a different posture later (presumably with a full nine members).

After the 2016 presidential election Donald Trump claimed he won not only the Electoral College but the popular vote as well (even though Hillary Clinton led in the popular vote by just under 3 million votes) once one subtracted all the illegal votes. He offered no evidence to support his claim. Vice President–elect Mike Pence refused to state Trump's claim was false, and both House Speaker Paul Ryan and Republican National Committee chair Reince Priebus either ducked or said it was possible. They may know better, but they are speaking to Republican voters who don't. Yet one could build on Trump's claim. If there is massive voter fraud, then ID laws that suppress votes may be valid as proportional to the problem. But if there is de minimus voter fraud, then ID laws, like Texas's, that impact large numbers of voters are not proportional and should not be valid.

In one of his first acts as attorney general, Jeff Sessions overruled the career attorneys working on the case and reversed the Justice Department position on the Texas voter ID law. The DOJ no longer claimed the Texas law was passed with the intent to discriminate against minority voters. Judge Ramos nevertheless reaffirmed her earlier decision that SB 14 was passed with the intent to discriminate against minorities, highlighting that many photo IDs acceptable in other states were omitted from the Texas law.

The same legislature that passed SB 14 also redistricted the state and congressional delegations. So its members knew that Republicans were going to control everything in Texas and could enact any item on the Republican agenda. (If anyone wanted proof, all they had to do was look at the way the legislature crammed "campus carry" down the throats of unwilling public universities.) So they didn't have to depress minority turnout. This suggests that contrary to Judge Ramos, the reasons offered were not pretextual. Republican voters believe that in-person voter fraud exists even if it doesn't. In 2017 Republicans can point to Rosa Maria Ortega as proof that it does exist. She was brought from Mexico as an infant, got a green card as an adult, and is mother to four American children. Thinking she was eligible to vote, she registered in Dallas County and voted in the 2012 and 2014 elections. On moving to Tarrant County she tried to register and checked the noncitizen box, so she was rejected. She called election officials and said she had previously voted in Dallas. On receiving a new application she checked the box affirming citizenship.

That raised questions and she was arrested on fraud charges. Attorney General Ken Paxton was willing to let her walk in exchange for legislative testimony, but Tarrant County criminal district attorney Sharen Wilson wanted a trophy to "showcase her office's efforts to crack down on election fraud."[46] After a jury convicted Ortega, she was sentenced to eight years with a likely deportation when the sentence is complete. Paxton subsequently asserted that the case "shows how serious Texas is about keeping its elections secure."[47]

This "religious faith" causes Republicans to worry about elections being stolen and our democracy being undermined and may even discourage them from voting. SB 14 remedies all these problems—albeit at the disproportional cost to a half million otherwise eligible voters. And Republicans can respond that the problem is real by pointing to Ortega. In 2012 she voted for Mitt Romney; two years later she voted for, of all people, Ken Paxton—who never claimed she was part of an effort to steal the elections by fraud.

THREE

From Discrimination to Affirmative Action

Most of the black scientists in this country don't come from schools like the University of Texas.

—Antonin Scalia at oral argument in
Fisher v. University of Texas

In the first half of the twentieth century, Texas segregated its schools, like all other Southern states. A case involving the University of Texas School of Law produced a major stepping-stone toward *Brown v. Board of Education*.[1] In the current century, another case involving UT's undergraduate admissions reaffirmed a state's right to implement affirmative action policies.[2]

I

Barely six months after the win in the all-white primary case in 1944,[3] the Texas NAACP called for the integration of Texas's flagship university in Austin (there being no comparable school for African Americans). Some months later Thurgood Marshall wrote a letter to Austin's only African American lawyer asking for information about how to apply to the University of Texas School of Law. Before tackling primary education, Marshall intended to create good law in the more fertile area of professional education, where there also might be less resistance from whites.

Having decided on a target, the NAACP needed a plausible plaintiff, but after some months of searching it was coming up empty-handed. Then at a church meeting in Houston, following an NAACP presentation, thirty-two-year-old Heman Marion Sweatt volunteered. Finding the right plaintiff mattered. In litigation over law schools in Missouri, the plaintiff Lloyd Gaines had turned out to be very high-maintenance, craving publicity and then complaining it put him under excessive pressure. He won at the Supreme Court,[4] but while the remedy was being worked out he disappeared and was never heard from again.[5] As a result, his case was dismissed in state court.

Sweatt had attended Wiley College in Marshall. During his junior year Wiley gained its accreditation. Sweatt graduated in 1934 with okay grades, a few As, but mostly Bs and Cs. That was good enough to get him into UT—if he were white. At the time of his volunteering, he had been a postal carrier for some time. He was married, owned a home, and there is conflicting evidence about whether he wanted to be a lawyer.

With Sweatt's application, UT's acting president Theophilus S. Painter wrote state attorney general Grover Sellers asking what to do with it: "This applicant is a citizen of Texas and duly qualified for admission into the Law School at the University of Texas, save and except for the fact that he is a negro."[6] Sellers concluded that Sweatt should not be admitted until he made a good faith application to law school at the black Prairie View University (which did not have a law school). Three weeks later Sellers announced his (unsuccessful) candidacy for governor and opined that a suitable law course could be set up within forty-eight hours. The incumbent governor, Coke Stevenson, did him one better, saying that all Sweatt needed to be legally educated was one good lawyer, one set of encyclopedias, and one set of Texas statutes.

The model for handling a problem like Sweatt had been established in Missouri and Oklahoma. Faced with a qualified applicant for admission, the state would create a new law school for African Americans. When Sweatt filed suit in a Travis County district court, everyone knew that the judge would rule against him. And he did, giving the state six months to establish a new law school for blacks.

Five months later the Texas A&M regents passed a resolution to establish a law school at Prairie View. At the new hearing, Marshall argued that a resolution was not enough and that there would be no law school functioning the next semester. The lame-duck Sellers countered that the governor had promised funds and the school would in fact be functioning. As everyone knew he would, the judge ruled against Sweatt.

The 1947 legislative session authorized the UT regents to establish a temporary law school in Austin called the "School of Law of Texas State University for Negroes." The law also provided for its students to access the state law library in the capitol. UT's law school dean Charles McCormick would also serve as the interim dean for the new law school.

UT leased a thousand square feet in a building at 104 East 13th right by the capitol. The rooms were three steps below street level, and while not a basement, the law school was always called the "Basement School" by the NAACP. Sweatt refused to enroll, but two men and one woman did. The woman dropped out after a week, but the men met with UT professors in a single room where they could be expected to be called on daily, given the awesome—and undoubtedly the nation's best—faculty student ratio of 3:2. Corwin Johnson taught property in the Basement School and at UT, and stated he taught the same materials in each venue. This would support the state's claim, now made by the new attorney general Price Daniel (husband of the great-great-granddaughter of Sam Houston), that this school was substantially equal to UT.

That point was demolished by the cross-examination of McCormick conducted by Marshall's associate James M. Nabrit, Jr. McCormick agreed that "one of the basic elements of a great law school is the history and traditions which have been built up over years of time, including graduates who have become famous in the State of Texas."[7] Left unsaid, because it need not have been said, was that the new Texas governor, Beaufort Jester, as well as Supreme Court Justice Tom Clark, were UT law grads and the Basement School had not a single alumnus. When

Nabrit asked about moot court, McCormick stated it "of course, has not been instituted. It can't be instituted until you get some students."[8] He then referred to honors like Order of the Coif and Law Review as "extraneous" even though they propel early legal careers. Once again Judge Roy Archer ruled against Sweatt, finding the school substantially equal in facilities, courses, instructors, and graduation requirements and opportunities for the study of law substantially equivalent to UT.

The conclusion of Judge Archer was also the conclusion of the court of appeals, and the Texas Supreme Court chose not even to hear the case. The United States Supreme Court agreed to hear the case along with two others, one involving a graduate school in Oklahoma,[9] the other segregation in interstate railroad dining cars.[10] During this time a permanent all-black law school opened in Houston, but, like the Basement School, it had no alumni.

The attorneys general from all of the former Confederate states (save Alabama) filed an amicus brief on behalf of Texas. Accurately seeing the case as a threat to white supremacy, they stressed racial violence and offered the Court the helpful conclusion that "Negro men do not want their daughters, wives, and sweethearts dancing, dating, and playing with white men any more than white men want their women folk in intimate social contact with Negro men."[11] (As if law students were unaware of the unwritten social codes of the South.)

An amicus brief on behalf of law professors called the quickie Jim Crow law schools of Texas and the existing ones in Oklahoma and Missouri "a mockery of legal education and of the equal protection of the laws."[12] The brief went on to argue that the Reconstruction Congress intended the Fourteenth Amendment to outlaw all forms of racial segregation.

Price Daniel grumbled for local consumption that this was not the first time "northern professors have tried to tell us how to run out schools."[13] His assistant Joe Greenhill, a future chief justice of the Texas Supreme Court, who genuinely respected Thurgood Marshall, took the law professors seriously. He produced a brief showing there was no relation between the intent of the Reconstruction Congress in the Fourteenth Amendment and school segregation. A rarity, this history produced for constitutional litigation was more than mere lawyers' advocacy. Four years later, after ordering *Brown* reargued on the issue of the intent of the Framers, the Court stated that history was irrelevant (because it did not support the conclusion that segregation was intended to be unconstitutional from 1868 on).[14] The Court in *Sweatt* was not interested either.[15]

The time for an attack on segregation was propitious. *Smith v. All-wright*[16] had held the all-white primary unconstitutional. World War II had resulted in the total defeat of two racist regimes: Major League Baseball had been desegregated, and President Harry S. Truman had ordered the military desegregated. And perhaps most importantly, the 1948 Democratic Convention had adopted a civil rights plank for the first time. Furthermore, after argument Justice Tom Clark sent a memo to his Brethren listing seven reasons why separate but equal should be abandoned at the graduate level.[17] Clark was the only Texan ever to sit on the Court and a UT law grad, so his memo in favor of Sweatt probably helped (if help had been needed).

Dripping in sarcasm Thurgood Marshall's oral argument framed the inequality argument perfectly. The state courts had held that the Basement School was substantially equal to UT. "Since the new Negro school in Houston was concededly superior to the [Basement] Austin school, it must be superior to the school for white students."[18]

Chief Justice Fred Vinson, a Truman appointee from Kentucky, kept the opinion for himself. In his undistinguished tenure as chief justice he was dwarfed by the appointees of Franklin D. Roosevelt. Thus Vinson is best known for Felix Frankfurter's observation on his sudden death from a heart attack when *Brown* was set to be reargued and Vinson was reluctant to overrule separate but equal: it was "the first indication that I have ever had that there is a God."[19] *Sweatt* and its companion case from Oklahoma were Vinson's sole important opinions.

In *Sweatt*, he easily accepted Marshall's argument and produced an opinion that was short and to the point. UT's School of Law "may properly be considered one the nation's ranking law schools."[20] Its facilities, faculty, and opportunities dwarf the Houston school opened during the litigation. Law school is interactive; thus "the proving ground for legal learning and practice cannot be effective in isolation from individuals and institutions with which the law interacts."[21] Bluntly, if a students could choose between the two institutions no one would consider "the question close."[22] And of course the Court was right.

In the companion cases of *McLaurin v. Regents*[23] there was a special seat for McLaurin in the classroom; he couldn't eat with others in the cafeteria, and had a special table in the library. These impaired his ability to engage in discussion and exchange views with others and so violated equal protection.

Sweatt and *McLaurin* signaled the path to *Brown v. Board of Education*.[24] For Heman Sweatt it was not such a happy ending. It had been too many years since he had been a student and his writing abilities were horrible; furthermore, the pressures of being famous and first have always been enormous. His health was bad and his marriage was falling apart. He flunked out in his second year. Henry Doyle, one of the two students who lasted beyond the first week at the Basement School, became the first graduate of the black law school in Houston and then the first African American to be appointed to the state's appellate courts. The other, Heaullan Lott, could not (or would not) relocate to Houston and graduated from UT in 1956. The first African American to graduate from UT School of Law was Virgil Lott (no known relationship to Heaullan). A few black undergraduates were admitted to UT in 1955 and other public universities started accepting blacks a year later. The action had moved to *Brown* and K–12 education.

In Texas there was a reluctant acceptance of the decision, with state officials noting that it applied only to graduate education. Perhaps the muted reaction was because *Sweatt* was part of what the *Dallas Morning News* called "two body blows" to the state.[25] In the other decision (discussed in chapter 5), the Court ruled that the federal government, not Texas, owned the tidelands and therefore the oil revenues from offshore drilling. The state NAACP, focusing on *Sweatt* alone, pronounced itself "jubilant" over the decision.[26]

II

Unlike most of the Confederacy, Texas did not formally adopt the policy of "Massive Resistance," which would have involved using every possible means to preclude any form of school desegregation. But Texas was certainly a fellow traveler, as illustrated by the events in Mansfield, the first desegregation case. Mansfield was a community of 1,100 whites and 350 blacks just south of Fort Worth. After *Brown,* local African Americans asked for improvements in the black elementary school and a bus for teenagers attending school in Fort Worth (there being no black high school in Mansfield). The school board did nothing.

Three African Americans were denied admission to Mansfield High School for the 1955–56 school year, resulting in the filing of a lawsuit to force the issue. The white community was outraged and offered the comforting thought that it all was the result of outside agitators. The school board retained Fort Worth lawyer J. A. "Tiny" Gooch, a former All–Southwest Conference tackle for the Longhorns. The six-foot, seven-inch Gooch, a future president of the Fort Worth Chamber of Commerce, donated his services pro bono. He was successful in November 1955 in federal district court. The judge found the board to be "struggling with breaking the tradition of generations; opening their meetings with prayer for solution; studying articles in magazines and newspapers ... appointing a committee to work on a plan for integration—making the start toward 'obeying the law' which their abilities dictated ... the trustees now assure the Court that they are continuing their efforts and will work out desegregation."[27] Even though a board member had testified that there was no plan beyond the present year.

The Fifth Circuit unanimously reversed and ordered the three African Americans admitted to the high school for the 1956–57 school year, bluntly stating that the fact whites did not like desegregation was not a legal reason for preventing it.[28] Mansfield then anticipated the Little Rock crisis by a year (although with the blacks victorious the Supreme Court denied review).[29] In the two weeks before school opened, there were two cross burnings, three separate effigies of blacks hung (one on the flagpole of the high school), and threats as the Anglo community made clear that violence would be the order of the day if blacks attended the school.

Governor Allan Shivers stepped in by announcing he was sending the Texas Rangers to Mansfield and urging the school district to "go ahead and transfer out of the district any student whose attendance or attempt to attend Mansfield High School would reasonably be calculated to cause violence."[30] On the first day of school the captain of the Texas Rangers said he expected no trouble because "I do not think any Negroes will try to enroll."[31] He was right; the three went to Fort Worth.

President Dwight Eisenhower appeared unconcerned that a federal court order had been defied. He thought it was just an example of local governments acting to stop violence. "Before anyone could move, the Texas authorities had moved and order was restored. So the question became unimportant."[32] A year later, in Little Rock, Ike was forced to act, and in 1958 the Court reaffirmed *Brown* in the strongest language, holding that all state officials nationwide were bound by the decision.[33] But in fact desegregation was at a halt, although 122 school districts in the state were desegregated (somewhat). Desegregation would not recommence until the mid-1960s. Mansfield High School was desegregated in September 1965 without incident.

The 1957 legislative session under the new governor, Price Daniel (who as a United States senator had signed the infamous "Southern Manifesto" attacking *Brown* as usurpation), saw a number of bills introduced that could have led to Massive Resistance. The Texas House refused to adopt the typical Southern strategy of "interposition"—the theory that a state has the right to interpose its own laws between its citizens and the federal government, with the state's laws prevailing,

The only bills that made it to the governor's desk allowed whites to transfer out of integrated schools and put to the voters whether they wished their schools integrated. Compared to other Southern states, the Texas response was tepid, but it was enough to do the intended job of keeping desegregation at bay.

III

In 1971 in *Swann v. Charlotte-Mecklenburg Board of Education*[34] the Supreme Court unanimously affirmed a massive bussing order in an urban school district. *Swann* meant that neighborhood schools would not be the constitutional solution in the urban South. Urban school boards in Texas, like those elsewhere, were hostile to bussing because Anglos were very hostile to bussing.

Right after *Swann,* litigation commenced in Dallas, where eventually a federal judge adopted a plan that had some bussing, though nothing like *Swann*.[35] The NAACP, which saw massive bussing for racial balance as the holy grail (believing it would improve race relations), appealed and prevailed at the Fifth Circuit.[36] The Dallas school board was successful in getting the Court to grant a writ of certiorari (the means of discretionary review at the Court). At this point, the Dallas Alliance, a tri-ethnic civic organization, retained me to write an amicus brief defending the decision of the district court because the plan adopted by that court had been one presented by the Dallas Alliance.

I was clerking at the Court when *Swann* was decided, and I favored massive bussing. But a decade's experience had caused me to change my mind. White flight was much greater than I (and other liberals) expected. For example, Dallas lost half its Anglo students during the 1970s. (When Austin was hit by a bussing order, Round Rock was a sleepy community to the north. All of a sudden there were ads on television showing a white couple in their thirties in a backyard. The voice-over proclaimed, "Good fences make good neighbors." It was for a new housing development in Round Rock.) I also believed that the better solution was more resources for minority schools because it turns out there are only two options: move the green ($) or move the whites to desegregated schools. Except that if one tries to move the whites, they may move to a suburban district or private schools.

The brief I wrote emphasized the district judge and the task he faced, considering that this rapidly growing urban school system, the eighth largest in the nation, was in a city bisected by a river and downtown, and there was a sizeable Hispanic population added to the typical white-black desegregation. The judge had been presented with a maximum bussing plan by the NAACP and a minimal one by the school district. I asserted that both were unconstitutional and the judge, understanding the complexities facing Dallas, wisely exercised his discretion to adopt a constitutionally workable plan, the one offered by the Dallas Alliance. The plan had the added feature of businesses, churches, and civic organizations adopting schools (144 at the time of the brief) and providing the support to pass an $80 million bond issue.

I had two concerns about the case. First, it might have been too soon to pull the plug on *Swann*. Second, I wasn't sure it offered the best facts to take on urban bussing in the South. *Swann* stated, "it should be clear that the existence of some small number of one-race, or virtually one-race, schools within a district is not in and of itself the mark of a system that still practices segregation by law."[37] Dallas's sixty-two such schools didn't seem to be a small number. After oral argument, the Court dismissed the writ of certiorari as improvidently granted.[38] So I was right about the second point and may have been right about the first, too; though it took another decade and a half for the Court to give up.[39]

Justice Lewis Powell, a former local and state school board member from Virginia, along with Potter Stewart and William Rehnquist, dissented. His opinion tracks my brief, but he had been on the record as opposing bussing for years.[40] As Michael Graetz and Linda Greenhouse observe, Powell "abhorred any sacrifice of quality education by whites in pursuit of desegregation."[41]

The NAACP was happy with its win and ready to support the "extensive bussing" that would be necessary.[42] A column in the *Dallas Morning News* two days later observed that there had been "no wave of protest" to the decision, something unlikely five or six years earlier.[43] Yet over the subsequent decades Anglos have continued their exodus from the Dallas Independent School District. In the 2012–13 school year a mere five percent of the students were white.

IV

Two years earlier Powell had written one of his most famous opinions in *Regents v. Bakke.*[44] With the Court split 4–4 on the validity of affirmative action in higher education, he cast the decisive vote. His biographer noted that he was "faced with two intellectually coherent, morally defensible, and diametrically opposed positions [any affirmative action program is valid or all such programs are unconstitutional] ... [and he] chose neither."[45] Supporters of affirmative action offered several important reasons for the programs: remedying societal discrimination, increasing the number of minorities in the professions, increasing the number of people serving the minority community. Powell rejected them all. Instead he latched on to Harvard College's admissions program with its goal of creating a diverse student body. His opinion in *Bakke* garnered no other votes, but for years was taken to be the law by everyone.

It was hard to believe that a soft concept like diversity could rise to the level of a compelling state interest as required by the strict scrutiny standard that applied when laws specifically mention race. But if reciting the magic word "diversity" would make a program valid, so be it. College administrators turned diversity into the rage and affirmative action programs were unassailable (even though the Reagan Justice Department thought otherwise, adopting what was the post-1965 Southern view that the Constitution was color-blind).

UT's law school began efforts to recruit more minorities under Dean Ernest Smith (1974–79), but the program changed in the early 1980s into an aggressive affirmative action program to remedy societal discrimination and to add to the numbers of black and Hispanic lawyers. It did not comply with Powell's opinion—there was a separate subcommittee for minorities—but otherwise it looked like law school programs at all the elite schools. In a reverse *Sweatt* (but for the fact that Anglos made up the overwhelming number of students and were on top of Texas society), four Anglos denied admission in 1992 challenged the law school program. They lost at trial,[46] but scored a complete victory on appeal.[47]

The named plaintiff, Cheryl Hopwood, was at the time of application a twenty-eight-year-old mother of a child suffering from a muscular disease. Hopwood and the other three plaintiffs had better combined GPAs and LSATs than 36 of the 43 admitted Hispanics and 16 of the 18 African Americans. It wasn't clear that they would have been admitted in the absence of an affirmative action program, but it was clear that race mattered—a lot. The way Powell wrote *Bakke* made affirmative action a privilege of the university but accorded no rights to minorities. But it did leave rejected whites with a claim that they had been discriminated against because of their race, and that was the *Hopwood* claim.

Given UT's history, minorities claimed the law school had encouraged Hopwood's suit and by hiring its own Anglo lawyer intended to lose. As the twenty years following the litigation illustrate, that claim was completely false—but it hurt.

Besides diversity, the law school argued that its program was necessary because of perceptions in minority communities that UT was an unwelcoming white school. And naturally UT—represented by Harry Reasoner, a spectacularly good litigator with Vinson, Elkins—wrapped itself around *Bakke*.

The Fifth Circuit opinion by Jerry Smith, a very conservative Reagan appointee, treated Powell's *Bakke* as that of a single justice who could not garner a second vote and happily observed that " 'diversity' is mentioned nowhere except in Powell's single-justice opinion which "is not binding precedent on this issue."[48] Once he was there the case was over: "Finally, the classification of persons on the basis of race for the purpose of diversity frustrates, rather than facilitates, the goals of equal protection."[49] The court had adopted the Republican Party's color-blind Constitution (an anti-affirmative action stance adopted in the first years of the Reagan presidency).

The Fifth Circuit during the late 1950s through the early 1980s had been the most progressive Southern court. But with Reagan ideologues like Smith and Edith Jones followed by George H. W. Bush appointees, the court became the most conservative federal court in the nation, a position it has never relinquished.

In a tactical error the law school had changed its admissions policy after the litigation commenced. It thus did not defend its prior policy while simultaneously complaining about the court's opinion. In the brief opposing a grant of certiorari, Theodore Olson (who would go on to argue and win *Bush v. Gore*[50]) took advantage of the error: UT is "thus in the untenable position of asking this Court for an advisory opinion concerning an admissions program that is not the subject of this litigation, is nowhere set forth in the record, was not considered by either of the courts below, and which—if petitioners' latest public pronouncements are truthful—they do not intend to implement."[51] The Supreme Court denied certiorari with Justices Ruth Bader Ginsburg and David Souter writing a one-paragraph statement offering their reasons for voting to deny cert. They asserted that disagreeing with the Fifth Circuit's rationale was not a sufficient reason to hear the case in the circumstances where UT was no longer defending the specific policy under attack.[52]

If that tactical mistake could have been overcome, UT may have made another. At the stage of certiorari, Reasoner was replaced by Harvard law professor and Supreme Court advocate Laurence Tribe. But the optics of an Anglo UT law grad defending UT's affirmative action program were lost and those optics could have been valuable had the Court agreed to hear the case.

At the law school there was major consternation because it feared *Hopwood* would become a self-fulfilling prophecy that blacks and

Hispanics were unwelcome at UT. If there were too few blacks, probably none would attend and if there were one class without blacks it was likely future classes would be the same. Furthermore, *Hopwood* was only the law of the Fifth Circuit—Texas, Louisiana, and Mississippi. As the *Austin American-Statesman* editorialized, "The disheartening decision means that the three states with a history of Jim Crow segregation are the only ones in the nation legally prohibited from using affirmative action in higher education. This puts the states' universities at a disadvantage in recruiting the best minority faculty and students."[53] It would be hard to find a bigger comparative disadvantage in recruiting African Americans who could successfully handle the law school's workload. The law school's Dean M. Michael Sharlot (1994–2000) labeled *Hopwood* "the bane of my existence" throughout his deanship.[54]

Alums were split, Anglo students may have been afraid to speak out, and while most of the faculty supported affirmative action, my friend and colleague Lino Graglia, a longtime opponent of affirmative action, was especially outspoken and became a lightning rod for both sides of the debate (appearing twice on NBC's *Today* show). The president of UT called Graglia in, and was shocked that a faculty member could express such views. A member of the Board of Regents met with Sharlot to demand Graglia be fired (only to learn about tenure).

The law school had a preexisting prelaw program with the University of Texas El Paso to accept a few of their students and that idea was geographically expanded to other areas of Texas that were deemed to be historically underrepresented at the law school. The outreach was more successful with Hispanics than African Americans. Despite the hard work of a number of my colleagues, the anticipated drop-off in minority admissions occurred. African Americans enrollment plummeted from 29 to 4; Hispanics 46 to 31. UT itself was not lucky either; Hispanic enrollment dropped 4.3% but black enrollment dropped by 33.8%. At Texas A&M the declines were 12.6% and 29%.

Eventually minority enrollment increased, exceeding pre-*Hopwood* numbers for Hispanics by 2003 while African American numbers held about the same. Then in 2003 the Supreme Court, in an opinion by Justice Sandra Day O'Connor formally adopted Powell's diversity rationale in her most important opinion, *Grutter v. Bollinger*,[55] a case involving the University of Michigan Law School. President Ronald Reagan had promised to appoint the first woman to the Court and O'Connor, a former Arizona legislator—the last justice to hold elective office—and intermediate appellate court judge got the nod. After a decade on the Court she began to display an uncanny knack to sense the midpoint of the American people on contentious issues and then vote that position. *Grutter* was one such example.

Michigan's law school used a "holistic approach" in deciding which students to admit, with race being but one factor among several (or many). The advantage of a "holistic approach" is that outsiders can never know how big a factor race is; universities love the phrase. With *Grutter*, UT's law school once again created an affirmative action program.

V

The Texas legislature had responded to *Hopwood* by passing its famous "10% rule." Irma Rangel was the sponsor of HB 588 and she and other legislators saw it as creating opportunities for minorities to attend state universities. If students graduate in the top 10% of their high school class they are guaranteed admission into a state university regardless of standardized test scores or academic preparation. The legislators knew that a good number of Texas high schools were segregated by race— because housing patterns in many communities concentrated minorities together. So the 10% law would broaden the applicant pool (because those with low test scores might not have applied) and increase minority enrollment. Its intended beneficiaries, African Americans and Hispanics, were obvious. But there are ample schools, especially in the Panhandle, where the law created unintended beneficiaries—poor whites with the opportunity to attend UT and A&M.

The law has had its intended effect, although another unintended and unanticipated consequence was to constrict the number of places for students with special abilities—a tuba player for example—because so many of the available slots are filled with the automatic top 10% admits. Eventually this was solved by capping at 75% the numbers admitted under the top 10% (now functionally 7%) law. Because *Grutter* allows it, the undergraduate program also has an affirmative action dimension to admit additional minorities on top of those automatically admitted. The goal was to obtain a "critical mass"—another term from the Michigan law school litigation—of minority students. What a "critical mass" is has never been defined because to do so might make it look like a quota, held unconstitutional in *Bakke*.

In 2008 Abigail Fisher of Sugar Land was rejected for admission to UT where both her father and older sister had graduated. That year 29,501 students applied for admission; 12,843 were admitted and 6,715 enrolled. Once the top 10% were admitted there were 17,131 applicants including Fisher for the remaining 1,216 slots for Texas residents in the freshman class. Looking solely at that, UT was one of the most selective universities in the nation.

Fisher was found by Ed Blum, whose Project for Fair Representation is discussed in the previous chapter. Blum knew Fisher's father and had been aching to find a plaintiff to challenge UT's use of race in the admissions process. If Cheryl Hopwood was a good plaintiff, Fisher was not. According to ProPublica, her credentials, a 3.59 GPA and an 1180 SAT, were only better than 47 admitted freshman, 42 of whom were white, and 168 minorities with better credentials had been rejected.[56] But no matter. She brought suit, lost at both the trial court[57] and the Fifth Circuit,[58] but prevailed 7–1 at the Supreme Court in an opinion by Anthony Kennedy, who occupied the middle ground (previously held by the now-retired O'Connor) on a bench otherwise divided 4–4 between conservatives and liberals.[59]

Fisher was a muddled opinion because, as Justice Stephen Breyer later observed, "That opinion by seven people reflected no one's views perfectly."[60] Instead of holding that because of its use of race affirmative action was a violation of the Equal Protection Clause, the opinion determined that the Fifth Circuit "did not hold the University to the demanding burden of strict scrutiny articulated in *Grutter*."[61] The university was entitled to deference in its decision to pursue diversity as a goal, but a university is entitled to no deference as to whether its program is narrowly tailored to achieve its goal. When a university gives "a reasoned, principled explanation" deference must be given "based on its experience and expertise."[62] Yet in testing the means "strict scrutiny must not be strict in theory but feeble in fact."[63] The court below erred on giving the university deference on narrow tailoring and thus its judgment was vacated and the case remanded.

O'Connor's *Grutter* opinion offered the thought that affirmative action should be safe for twenty-five years, and during the *Fisher* oral argument Stephen Breyer observed, "I know that time flies, but I think only nine of those years has passed."[64] But what was more relevant was that O'Connor had been replaced by Samuel Alito, a staunch believer in the Republican Party's color-blind Constitution. Many observers, myself included, believed that the Court granted certiorari to end affirmative action because the *Grutter* dissenters now had Alito as a fifth vote (with the switch of William Rehnquist to John Roberts being a wash).

The Fifth Circuit panel, whose judgment had been vacated, consisted of Carolyn King, Patrick Higginbotham, and Emilio Garza, all senior judges. UT could not have found a better panel. King was the lone Democrat, having been appointed by Jimmy Carter. Higginbotham was an intelligent conservative appointee of Gerald Ford. Garza was appointed by the first Bush and he had concurred in the court's opinion solely because he felt he was bound by *Grutter*. Otherwise he stated that affirmative action was "ruinous behavior."[65] His vote was lost, but King and Higginbotham carefully assessed the record and once again held for UT. Unsurprisingly, the Court granted certiorari. It only takes four justices to grant cert and it is a near certainty that Chief Justice Roberts and Justices Antonin Scalia, Clarence Thomas, and

Alito did so because they were dead set against affirmative action. The unanswered question was whether Kennedy joined them; if he did, Texas was going to lose by at least a 5–3 vote (Elena Kagan again would be recused).

Oral argument pitted Bert Rein for Ed Blum's organization against Gregory Garre, George W. Bush's last solicitor general, for the second time at the Court. The argument demonstrated what everyone knew. Roberts, Scalia, and Alito were contemptuous of UT's position and the underappreciated Clarence Thomas as always was silent.[66] The fireworks came from Scalia, who claimed affirmative action could leave minority students worse off. "Most of the black scientists in this country don't come from schools like the University of Texas. They come from lesser schools where they do not feel that they're being pushed ahead in classes that are too fast for them."[67]

Scalia's assertion was based on the book *Mismatch* by UCLA law professor Richard H. Sander and Brookings Fellow and important legal journalist Stuart Taylor, Jr.[68] Among the conclusions of *Mismatch* are that although blacks are more likely to enter college than whites with similar backgrounds, they are less likely to graduate; that blacks are four times more likely to fail the bar exam than whites; and that elite universities do not produce black scientists because of the rigor of the majors. These findings are controversial to say the least and they go to whether affirmative action, as practiced, is a wise policy. They don't make it unconstitutional.

Scalia had been the darling of conservatives since he joined the Court in 1986. He spoke regularly before conservative groups like the Federalist Society (and also Koch brothers' gatherings) and his dissenting opinions in culture war cases were aimed at a general audience of believers. Besides the results, what conservatives liked about Scalia was his reliance on the original understanding of the Constitution and his demand that it be applied today as it had been understood in 1789 (or, with the Bill of Rights, 1791). Scalia could be confident—and was he ever—that the Due Process Clause—no one shall "be deprived of life, liberty, or property, without due process of law"—did not guarantee a right to abortions or protections for gays as a matter of original meaning.

But affirmative action was different. Reconstruction was in part about giving the freedmen a boost. Congress created a Freedman's Bureau and discussed giving the newly freed slaves forty acres and a mule. And, of course, Congress passed and the states ratified the Thirteenth, Fourteenth, and Fifteenth Amendments. A study of Reconstruction, like studies of other periods surrounding constitutional change, will find ambiguities and contradictions. It would be unlikely, however, to find that the original public meaning of the Equal Protection Clause was that "the constitution is color blind"—a phrase dating from 1896 in Justice John H. Harlan's *Plessy v. Ferguson* dissent.[69] In any event, there is no record of Scalia ever devoting time to searching for the original meaning of the Equal Protection Clause, perhaps because he knew it would not support the position that the Reagan Justice Department and he so thoroughly desired.

In any event, Scalia was found dead in West Texas in February 2016. With his death the outcome in *Fisher* was still in doubt and still in the hands of Anthony Kennedy. Roberts, Thomas, and Alito were going to vote against UT; Ginsburg, Breyer, and Sonia Sotomayor would support UT. As on the full nine-justice Court Kennedy was the controlling vote. He seemed anxious to be rid of a case about UT's 2008 admissions, where the biggest factor in the chance of getting in was the unchallenged 10% rule, that had been in the courts for eight years, and whose plaintiff had long since graduated from Louisiana State University. (She was harassed extensively for her participation in the lawsuit, showing once again that being a plaintiff is hardly cost-free.)

Kennedy complained of "a record that is almost devoid of information about students who secured admission to the University through the [10%] Plan. The Court thus cannot know how students admitted solely based on their class rank differ in their contribution to diversity from students admitted through holistic review."[70] He stated that the university should be compiling such data. On the record in the case,

Fisher's less restrictive alternatives—such as more outreach to minority communities—had been shown ineffective in the immediate post-*Grutter* world. The opinion closed with a mild warning. "The Court's affirmance of the University's admissions policy today does not necessarily mean the University may rely on that same policy without refinement. It is the University's ongoing obligation to engage in constant deliberation and reflection regarding its admissions policies."[71] The opinion did not cite *Bakke,* but its message was "back to *Bakke.*"

Reaction to the decision was predictable. Fisher expressed disappointment and hoped "that the nation will one day move beyond affirmative action."[72] UT president Gregory L. Fenves was "thrilled and very gratified" by the decision.[73]

The three oldest justices were in the majority and there was a vacancy due to the death of Scalia. With the election of Donald Trump as president and Senate confirmation of his choice of Neil Gorsuch to the Court, it is not clear that the *Fisher* decision will last until the year 2028 (as O'Connor had forecast in *Grutter*).

When UT won its twenty-plus years of battling for affirmative action, the Court was allowing federalism to control. In both California and Michigan voters amended their state constitutions to ban affirmative action. By contrast the Texas government aided the universities with the 10% law and never put to its voters the option to end affirmative action. Texas isn't often seen as a progressive state, but on this issue it is and California is not.

PART II

Texas the Western State

During the Progressive Era Texas tried to shake its image as a Southern state for a new one as a Western state (the same transformation that was necessary for Lyndon B. Johnson to become a serious presidential contender). Texas had a good claim to be part of the West. It had the two longest frontiers in the country, the southern one with Mexico and a more typical Indian frontier to the west, each stretching hundreds of miles. Furthermore, these frontiers lasted decades longer than the typical nineteenth- century frontiers. The cattle industry with its famous trail drives was quintessentially Texan and Western even if it were in the past.

In the shift from being a Southern to a Western state, Texas was led by Governor Oscar Colquitt, who emphasized the Texas Revolution. Stephen F. Austin was disinterred from his grave in Brazoria County and reburied on the Hill of Heroes in the state cemetery in Austin. The Alamo received money for necessary restorations. The Civil War and the "Lost Cause" were downplayed.

The American West has had a need / resentment relationship with the federal government. States need federal assistance—transportation, water projects, public lands, border security—while resenting federal intrusion into how resources (especially land) are developed. This latter point is well illustrated by Justice Sandra Day O'Connor in her memoir of youth on the family ranch. She (and her family) seethe with contempt at the Bureau of Land Management decisions affecting the ranch. Not surprisingly, O'Connor proved more sympathetic to federalism limitations on the federal government than her Brethren. She was a Westerner.

The railroad and oil cases are not only Western; along with the racial cases in Part I they bring the Texas story—and the economic issues that dominated the Court's constitutional jurisprudence—to the middle of the twentieth century.

Texas should not have had issues about public lands because of the terms of annexation, but it did. As a Western state Texas enjoys federal aid when it assists in the exploitation of its advantages, but resents federal interference even though they are two sides of the same coin. In no other area touched by Texas litigation are the issues of congressional legislative power so prevalent. When issues turn to state power, the key is the ability of a state to order its economy and there are few limitations in the Constitution.

Like New Mexico, Arizona, and California, Texas shares a border with Mexico. Like the other states Texas has been ambivalent about the advantages and disadvantages of that border and the extent of the federal government's control over immigration.

FOUR

Railroads

Should corporate power or the State control?
— Texas attorney general (and gubernatorial
candidate) James Hogg advocating a
constitutional amendment to create a
railroad commission

The Republic and then the state encouraged railroad construction. Prior to the Civil War, Texas had chartered sixty-three railroads and had given away five million acres of land. Yet only 468 miles of track, serving ten roads, existed. Most of that little track was in the Houston-Galveston area with a few miles in northeastern Texas. There was no construction in the western two-thirds of the state until the mid-1870s.

In 1880 there were 3,025 miles of track and ten years later 8,667 miles. Around the turn of the century the Southern Pacific ran from Beaumont to Houston to San Antonio to Del Rio to El Paso. The Texas and Pacific went from Longview in the northeast, to Dallas, Fort Worth, Abilene, Midland, and El Paso. The Panhandle was served by the Fort Worth and Denver City running through Wichita Falls and Amarillo. The International and Great Northern went from Longview to Austin, San Antonio, and Laredo. The Houston and Texas Central went from Galveston to Houston, Dallas, and north. Finally, the Gulf, Colorado, and Santa Fe connected Galveston to Fort Worth. Northeast Texas and the Gulf ports remained the best served parts of the state.

Railroads were a capital-intensive industry where a mile of track cost upward of $30,000, well over a half million today. Beyond the track, locomotives and railcars had to be obtained and engineers, crews, and depot agents hired and trained. Stock watering and graft added to the costs and this was all before a single dollar of revenue could be generated. It is no wonder that bankruptcies were so common, even without the economic downturns in 1873 and 1893.

Railroads priced shipping rates based on volume, distance, and alternatives. The ideal shipper was one who shipped heavier goods over longer distances (and with some frequency). By contrast short hauls of typically lighter goods (and less frequency) cost the railroads more to service. Short hauls defined the farmers' business and railroads drew the farmers' anger for charges that seemed (and probably were) excessive compared to long hauls. This was a special problem for smaller towns served by a single line. The long haul / short haul dichotomy also "made St. Louis more attractive than Dallas as a marketing center."[1]

Every town wanted a railroad because without one there was no connection to the emerging economy. Yet once the local boosters got their railroad connection they turned into critics. High shipping rates, poor and erratic service, injuries, and the corruption of public officials created the urge and need to tame this overly powerful industry.

I

Texas's existing statutory framework was inadequate. A railroad's main office had to be on its line, dividends could not be paid if the road was insolvent, schedules had to be publicly displayed, there had to be sufficient accommodation for freight and passengers, and the latter should not be endangered. There was nothing about rates, and in any event the laws were unenforced.

A catalyst for change was Attorney General James S. Hogg, briefly a young sharecropper after the Civil War (or, as my daughter learned it in a Texas public school, the War of Northern Aggression), then a lawyer and a justice of the peace with a reputation for enforcing all laws (including the Sunday closing of saloons). He served as the Wood County attorney and two terms as district attorney before returning to private practice and moving to Tyler, the center of East Texas politics. In 1885 he was elected to his first of two terms as attorney general.

Hogg's most prominent action as attorney general was a suit to break up the Texas Traffic Association for violating laws prohibiting combinations of competing or parallel lines. He won a Pyrrhic victory and became convinced Texas needed to regulate shipping rates. Running successfully for governor in 1890, he championed a constitutional amendment to authorize the legislature to create a railroad commission. He framed the issue succinctly: "Should corporate power or the State control?"[2]

As the Democratic candidate Hogg was elected with 262,452 votes. The commission amendment passed 181,954 to 73,106.[3] When the next legislature implemented the amendment Texas had a three-person commission with the power to regulate rates.

The first person Governor Hogg appointed to the Railroad Commission was seventy-two-year-old John H. Reagan, who at the time was a United States senator. While it might seem like a comedown, Reagan explained that he was motivated by his love of Texas and duty to her: seeking "just and proper regulation of her system of internal transportation ... [is] of the first importance ... and should command the consideration and service of her best and ablest citizens."[4] Reagan was an old friend of the much younger governor and he probably intended to run for governor at the end of Hogg's second term (which he did unsuccessfully), and his reelection to the Senate by the Texas legislature was by no means certain.

Born in Tennessee, Reagan arrived in the Republic in 1839. He held numerous jobs—assisting an Indian agent, surveyor, lawyer—and elective offices—county judge, road overseer, state representative, member of Congress—all before the Civil War. Although he was a Unionist, once Texas left the Union, he supported the South and became the postmaster general of the Confederacy. As an ex-Confederate official, he was initially banned from holding office, but after his disabilities were ended by President Ulysses S. Grant, he was elected to Congress in 1876 and the Senate a decade later.

In the House, especially as chairman of the Committee on Interstate Commerce, he championed railroad regulation with a moral indignation against what he deemed to be monopolies. His pet bills would have outlawed pooling—agreements among completing lines on how to divide up traffic—and prevented charging short hauls a higher rate than long hauls over the same line. It took the better part of a decade, but teaming with Iowa senator Shelby Collon, the Interstate Commerce Act passed (while Reagan was in Texas securing his Senate seat). When the Railroad Commission went from appointive to elective, Reagan won his election. At the end of his six-year term, he retired at age eighty-two.

The Railroad Commission immediately went to work on shipping rates. The commissioners tried to ensure that the rate would yield enough to give a sufficient rate of return (but not to give revenue to pay interest and dividends on stock in excess of the actual cost of the road). This was an impossible goal because the Railroad Commission did not know the actual cost of the roads. The commission lowered rates between 10 and 75 percent from their unregulated levels with the result of stimulating the local economy. Governor Hogg wrote: "Instead of ... Texas people buying Kansas corn and flour, they have used Texas corn and flour. This has been the case also of Texas beef."[5]

Shortly after Hogg's statement the trustees of seven railroads sued the three commissioners and the attorney general for an injunction against the rates and a further injunction against any future rates. The court agreed with the railroads, causing the Grange publication, *Texas Farmer*, to compare the decision with the infamous *Dred Scott*[6] case. The ruling temporarily ended any rate regulation as the commission decided not to enforce rates on the railroads that had not sued.

Heading to the Supreme Court the commissioners and Attorney General Charles A. Culbertson, who would defeat Reagan for governor in 1894, decided not to defend the reasonableness of the rates. Instead the attorney general took the position that the federal courts had no jurisdiction because the suit violated the Eleventh Amendment prohibition against suing states in federal court. Another attorney made a very cursory response that everything the commission did was fine.

John F. Dillon, lawyer, judge, and author of the famous *Municipal Corporations*,[7] argued for the railroad trustees. He talked of magna carta, socialism, the destruction of the values of the railroad properties, and wrapped them all up in the Fourteenth Amendment. "It may be that the oppressions of the freedmen by the States in which they had been slaves was the immediate cause of the amendment, but its language is not confined to color or to class. It is general and unlimited."[8] The key was sanctity of private property, which unreasonable rates could destroy. The Fourteenth Amendment "is, in fact, a reaffirmation, in the most impressive and solemn form, of the sacredness and stability of private property, as one of the fundamental and indestructible rights of the people of the United States."[9]

After complementing the oral arguments, Justice David Brewer's unanimous opinion in *Reagan v. Farmers' Loan and Trust Company*[10] reached the issue of the Eleventh Amendment. He disposed of it in two ways. First, anticipating *Ex parte Young*[11] but without much explanation, the opinion held that a suit to recover for acts of wrong injuring property rights under an unconstitutional statute "is not, within the meaning of the Eleventh Amendment, an action against the State."[12] Alternatively section 6 of the statute creating the Railroad Commission authorized suits against the commission "in a court of competent jurisdiction in Travis County, Texas."[13] The federal court was in Travis County, and Brewer overread the Texas statute to conclude it had waived objections to jurisdiction in the federal court.

The Court agreed with the lower court that the rates were unreasonably low. The Court perceived the situation as class legislation whereby "property without compensation [is] wrestled from him [one party] for the benefit of another, or the public" and thus "one class ...

[is] compelled to suffer loss that others may make gain."[14] This was the quintessential nineteenth-century constitutional violation—taking from A and giving to B. But unlike the court below, Brewer's opinion did not find rate-making an unconstitutional enterprise. The Court's order read in full: "It follows from these considerations that the decree as entered must be reversed in so far as it restrains the railroad commission from discharging the duties imposed by this act, and from proceeding to establish reasonable rates and regulations; but must be affirmed so far only as it restrains the defendants from enforcing the rates already established."[15]

Reagan laid the groundwork for both *Smyth v. Ames*[16] and *Ex parte Young*. In the latter the Court held that a suit against a state official claiming the law being enforced was unconstitutional is not an action against the state under the Eleventh Amendment. *Ex parte Young* breathed life into *Smyth*, where the Court offered a laundry list of considerations that were necessary to determine whether a given rate would provide a fair return on the value of a railroad's assets. *Reagan* had laid the seeds for a lot of work by federal judges over the next half century until the New Deal justices killed it.[17] But because the Court did not affirm the perpetual injunction against future rate-making, states could keep trying.

II

By the time Reagan retired, the commission was doing its job to the satisfaction of both carriers and shippers. Or if not to their satisfaction, close enough so that they weren't going to court with challenges. Instead it was the Louisiana Railroad Commission and the city of Shreveport that challenged Texas and led to the next Supreme Court case involving Texas rates.

Like all cities, Shreveport, in northwestern Louisiana, and its boosters wanted more commerce so that it could grow (and meet its supposed destiny). The city is strategically situated twenty miles from the

Texas border on the Red River, and by the end of the nineteenth century it was a regional distribution center with abundant rail, river, and wagon routes north, south, and into Texas. It was the midpoint on a line between Kansas City and the Texas Gulf ports, while another line went south to the capital at Baton Rouge and on to New Orleans. The Texas and Pacific connected it to East Texas. The hindrance to its growth, as its chamber of commerce and others claimed, was that it was cheaper for East Texas cities like Longview to ship west to Dallas or south to Houston. Shreveport was about half the distance from Longview to those cities. Yet the Texas Railroad Commission rates made it more economical to ship within the state. With Texas rates supposedly limiting its future, Shreveport cried foul.

The cry might have gone unheard had not Congress added to the powers of the Interstate Commerce Commission. The Hepburn Act of 1906 and the Mann-Elkins Act of 1910 gave the commission rate-making powers and created a Commerce Court to hear cases from the ICC. Shreveport and the Louisiana Railroad Commission petitioned the ICC to do something about what they claimed were discriminatory Texas rates. Texas was not a party to the case and the Railroad Commission intentionally chose not to participate, believing that its rates were reasonable—indeed, as noted, they were unchallenged by the railroads. Governor Oscar Colquitt, a former commissioner, also asserted that the Interstate Commerce Commission could not make the Railroad Commission do anything. He was right, but missed the key point that the ICC could supplant commission rates.

A majority of the ICC, using the annual reports of the Texas Railroad Commission, concluded that the intrastate rates were designed to protect Texas commerce. There was no doubt that the rhetoric was of protectionism, a necessity of local politics, and it was strong confirmation of the Shreveport claim. With an appeal to the Commerce Court forthcoming, the Houston law firm of Baker, Botts, Parker, and Garwood, which represented the railroads, asked the Texas Railroad Commission if it wished to join their appeal. Again the commission declined.

The Commerce Court agreed the Texas rates were discriminatory, that they interfered with interstate commerce, that only Congress had the power to regulate interstate commerce, and therefore the ICC could establish intrastate rates when they would affect interstate commerce. The result of the decision was that rates from Dallas to Longview were lower than the rates from Longview to Dallas. That absurdity flowed from the fact that the Texas Railroad Commission was right; its rates were reasonable (and unchallenged by the railroads) and therefore the interstate rates were too high.

The next stop was the Supreme Court where, in the *Shreveport Rate Cases*,[18] the railroads claimed that Congress did not have the power to regulate intrastate rates, and that if it did have the power, it had not exercised it. Rejecting the claim that Congress was reaching intrastate operations, the Court, in a forward-looking opinion by Charles Evans Hughes, asserted that when "intrastate and interstate operations are so related that the operation of one involves the control of the other, it is Congress, and not the State, that is entitled to prescribe the final and dominant rule."[19] Congress has "the power to foster and protect interstate commerce, and to take all measures necessary or appropriate to that end, although intrastate transactions of interstate carriers may thereby be controlled."[20]

The Supreme Court opinion did not end the case. The Texas Railroad Commission was formally named a party before the ICC in 1916, and the rates were not finally settled until 1922, somewhat before the highway system displaced rail as the prime method of moving people and commerce.

Two years after the *Shreveport Rate Cases* Hughes was drafted to be the Republican presidential candidate and he resigned from the Court. Then in 1930 President Herbert Hoover nominated Hughes to be chief justice. Because of his contempt for racial discrimination, Southern senators, including Texans Tom Connally and Morris Sheppard, created an unsuccessful opposition. The two Louisiana senators, Robert F. Broussard and Joseph E. Ransdell, voted "yea." If the Louisiana senators' votes for Hughes weren't enough irony, how about a case where a Southern state prevails by supporting an expansion of federal power?

III

The next Texas Railroad Commission case to reach the Court involved an entirely different type of discrimination—discrimination against Pullman sleeping car passengers riding on trains with but a single Pullman car. Trains with multiple Pullmans were in charge of a conductor while those with only one Pullman car were in charge of a porter (who was paid less). In 1939 the Texas legislature refused to enact a bill sponsored by the Association of Pullman Conductors to forbid operating a Pullman car without a Pullman conductor, a bill vigorously opposed by the railroads. Instead the Railroad Commission adopted the policy that the legislature had rejected, finding that the distinction between a train with one Pullman car without a conductor and a train with two or more Pullmans with a conductor to be an unjust discrimination. It ordered that a conductor be put in charge of all Pullman cars. The order was justified on the grounds that the problems that occurred in Pullman cars— intoxication and immorality—were better handled by conductors than porters.

This ruling was supported by testimony before the commission "that a Pullman conductor contributed to the safety and comfort of passengers."[21] A mother of two "testified that she was so fearful of Pullman porters that she would not ride in a Pullman car if it had no Pullman conductor and had only a porter in charge."[22] She was but one of several women who made identical assertions. Pullman conductors were white; porters were black, and "all in all, the order was a thoroughly racist diatribe."[23]

The Pullman Company challenged the order on statutory and constitutional grounds. It claimed that the statutory trigger of unjust discrimination did not reach this situation and that the commission order violated both due process and equal protection because it lacked a rational basis. "The contention that the order may be sustained on the assumption that the Pullman porter, being a negro [sic], is incapable of successfully policing the car, is also devoid of merit."[24] The Pullman Company asserted that it had years of experience of porters handling a single Pullman car successfully. Thus the "fact inquiry involved in the legislative determination that race or color renders them incompetent for the positon now held by them has been settled by the Fourteenth Amendment."[25] In their brief the porters objected to the order as racial discrimination in violation of the Fourteenth Amendment.

At the Supreme Court the Railroad Commission brief had two related flaws that reflected twentieth-century practice. First, it was written by attorneys in the attorney general's office with little or no Supreme Court experience. They treated the Court as simply another appellate court where the attorney general could appear to enhance his prestige. By contrast a private litigant, like the Pullman Company, could retain expert counsel as it saw fit. One of the Pullman lawyers was Austin attorney Charles L. Black (father of the justly famous Yale law professor Charles Lund Black, Jr., whose "The Lawfulness of the Segregation Decisions"[26] is the best contemporaneous defense of *Brown v. Board of Education*[27]). Second, Texas practice dictated addressing separately as many errors as possible. The result was a wordy, repetitious, unfocused brief and argument. The commission brief was eighty-four rambling pages filed with lengthy quotations covering a supposed twenty-one errors by the district court. In that mass of verbiage there was no mention of the facts that conductors were white and porters black. Indeed that was barely mentioned in the commission's reply brief: just two paragraphs near the end.

Although the Railroad Commission arguments went nowhere, constitutional doctrine on race was not as clear as the Pullman Company and its porters argued. Their position would soon become the law, but soon was not now, and the Court was not willing to let either side prevail.

The Court's opinion was written by Felix Frankfurter, President Franklin D. Roosevelt's third appointee to the Court following the rejection of his Court-packing plan in 1937. Frankfurter was the most qualified appointee to the Court in the twentieth century, and perhaps ever. An Austrian immigrant, he graduated from CCNY and then Harvard Law School, served under Henry Stimson in the U.S. Attorney's Office for the Southern District of New York, and then returned to his beloved Harvard where he taught the public law course on the Supreme Court. He helped found the American Civil Liberties Union, was associated with the *New Republic* and advocated for Sacco and Vanzetti. He was a confidant of the two most distinguished justices of the era (or any era)—Oliver Wendell Holmes and Louis D. Brandeis—and an advisor to Governor and President Roosevelt, populating the New Deal with Harvard law graduates—the "happy hot dogs." In a word, he was prepared. He should have been an all-time great, but he didn't get close because his views on the limited nature of the Court were ill suited to the changed climate of judicial review following the New Deal revolution—the great divide of constitutional law—and especially during the Warren Court era.

Frankfurter stated the claim of the porters was "more than substantial. It touches a sensitive area of social policy."[28] That should explain why the porters would prevail, but the sentence continued, "upon which the federal courts ought not to enter unless no alternative to its adjudication is open."[29] Here there was an alternative: "a definitive ruling on the state [law] issue would terminate the controversy."[30] The final meaning of the Texas statutes "belongs neither to us nor the district court but to the supreme court of Texas."[31] If that court holds the Railroad Commission lacks authority, "the constitutional issue does not arise."[32] Thus the Court remanded the case to the federal district court with directions to retain jurisdiction but allow first a determination of the state law issue by the state courts.

Pullman "abstention" was born. Unsettled issues of state law are to be decided first by state courts before a federal court reaches a constitutional issue. *Pullman* abstention has ebbed and flowed during the eight decades of its existence. Sometimes the Court has been eager to reach constitutional issues—viz., the Warren Court after Frankfurter's retirement—sometimes, as in *Pullman,* it has been reluctant.

The "definitive ruling" on Texas law never came. Indeed, no ruling ever came. The case was set for trial, but at the request of the commission it did not proceed (and the federal court's injunction remained in place). Requiring conductors or separate but equal facilities was an expense to railroads whose fortunes were in decline. Furthermore, troop transportation during World War II dramatically increased the number of black passengers and the War Department demanded equal treatment of black and white soldiers. As the 1940s ended, the commission's "resolve to enforce the state's Jim Crow laws completely collapsed" basically because of the railroads' "hostility to the cost of enforcing segregation statutes."[33] Finally, on May 7, 1955, Ireland Graves, who had argued *Pullman* fourteen years earlier, wrote a letter to the attorneys and general managers of the larger Texas railroads stating that "at long last, as an abdicating king once said," the commission had rescinded its unenforced 1939 order on April 11.[34]

FIVE

Oil

I know that when lands become valuable somebody wants
them.
—Governor James Allred on the new claim by the
federal government to own mineral rights in the
tidelands

In the first half of the twentieth century the Texas economy was transformed by the discoveries of mass oil fields, first at Spindletop in southeast Texas, then the Yates field in West Texas, and shortly thereafter by
the East Texas fields.

I

With oil at three dollars a barrel, Texas voters, in a 1917 addition to the
state constitution, declared that the legislature had the power to pass
all necessary legislation to conserve and develop the natural resources
of the state. Two years later, probably because the Railroad Commission was functioning well, the legislature gave it broad powers over
conservation to prevent waste, but by 1929 it was clear that waste "shall
not be construed to mean economic waste."[1]

At that time the Yates field was a couple of years old and the huge
East Texas field was a year from discovery. The crude in these fields, as
well as its smaller pools like Corsicana, exists along with gas and water
in porous rock formations, "shaped by the forces exerted by the rock

and sedimentary formations, gravity, natural gas and salt water. These elements remain essentially in balance until a drill bit breaks into them."[2] After that, the crude flows up the casing to the wellhead. If the well is not maintained properly, there will be waste because when the gas escapes too rapidly, the oil becomes sticky and eventually unrecoverable. The Railroad Commission could regulate this waste.

The oil industry lived on a feast or famine basis. When demand exceeded or matched supply everyone made money. A persistent problem was the "rule of capture," which is a common law rule developed for deciding who could kill game legally. The rule's answer was that the landowner could kill anything on his or her land. When the rule of capture was applied to oil it meant that there was no liability for capturing oil and gas that drains from another's land to a well on one's own land. The result was that everyone owning land over an oil field had the incentive to drill and pump as quickly as possible. But not all wells are created equally; in East Texas some would produce tens of thousands of barrels a day, others just ten. Furthermore, the costs of production varied. It was 52 cents a barrel in East Texas but $1.26 a barrel in North Texas. Still, the other oil-producing states had production costs almost twice that of the large Yates and East Texas fields. If a field were large enough, then the new supply would drive down prices. Thus when Spindletop was discovered, the price of a barrel of oil fell to three cents.

Economic waste could be avoided by proration in a single field where each well is allocated a production quota. This had been successfully accomplished in Yates and two smaller West Texas fields as well as Van, near Tyler. But each of these fields was dominated by major oil companies so there were fewer wells and the proration had been justified on the ground that it prevented physical waste. All this would be tested when, in October 1930 after drilling two dry holes, C. M. "Dad" Joiner brought in a gusher in an East Texas field.

The majors had not believed East Texas was oil land, and so most of the mineral rights were held by independents. That meant hundreds of wells would be drilled—3,612 by the end of 1931. The field eventually measured 40 miles long by 4–12 miles wide. At the time, this was the world's largest field—by far. The existence of a single field was shortly confirmed after Joiner's gusher when three other independents brought in gushers of the same high-quality crude at the same depth.

The black-gold rush was on. Wells could be drilled for $20,000. By March 1931, 36 had been completed with 176 being drilled. By April, 96 were producing, a number that jumped to 700 by the end of June when the field was producing 600,000 barrels per day. In January the price of a barrel was $1; by June it had fallen to 20 cents and would be halved in a month.

In East Texas the independents thought the majors cut prices to drive thinly capitalized independents out of business in the hope of becoming even more powerful. The majors, in turn, thought small operators working with short-term loans were compelled to realize returns too rapidly. An observer stated: "everyone is suspicious of everyone else."[3]

Governor Ross Sterling, responding to pressure to do something, called the legislature into special session in the summer. Sterling was a multimillionaire former president of Humble Oil and Refining. He thought proration to meet market demand was unconstitutional price-fixing. He believed that if there was physical waste, then there was economic waste. But he also believed that if there was no physical waste, then there was no economic waste. Not only was the latter wrong, East Texas proved it was wrong.

On August 4, while the legislature was in session, the Oklahoma governor declared martial law to cut production in the state's oil fields. He suggested that Sterling should do the same, but Sterling believed that the legislature was making progress. He was wrong on this, too. All the special session did was reaffirm that state power went only to the prevention of physical waste.

The Friday, Saturday, and Sunday of August 14–16 saw production in East Texas jump to one million barrels a day, three times the Railroad Commission allowance. On Friday at Tyler, 1,500 oilmen held a meeting to complain about "stealing" oil from the field by either exceeding allowances or never agreeing to any limits. A resolution stated conditions "have already resulted and caused threats of violence [and] may, in all probability, result in actual destruction of property and a reign of lawlessness."[4] The resolution and a delegation of five operators urged Sterling to declare martial law and shut down the field until a new commission order could be implemented.

On Sunday Sterling signed the order for martial law. After reciting provisions of the state constitution, the decree cited the existence in East Texas of "an organized and entrenched group ... of producers ... who were in a state of insurrection against the conservation laws ... and open rebellion against the efforts of the constituted civil authorities to enforce the law."[5] Sterling withheld the decree for a day so that General Jacob F. Wolters of the Texas National Guard could move his troops into place. The troops met no resistance in ordering operators to shut down. Between Oklahoma and Texas, martial law took a million barrels a day off the market and by the end of the month prices were stable at 68–71 cents a barrel.

Martial law hurt small refineries. These were thinly capitalized and initially lacked crude. Then, as the price rose, their margins narrowed. They believed martial law had been engineered by the majors, but were wrong. Despite Sterling's background, he had declared martial law because he believed something had to be done and he was the only one who could do something, especially in light of the Oklahoma example.

At the end of August, the Railroad Commission ruled that all well production was to be capped at 225 barrels a day. Sterling felt this was unfair to independents who could only afford a single well. When the commission acted without notifying the governor, he stated, "That order won't go into effect until I put it into effect."[6] But he did put it into effect, having the National Guard enforce it, because he feared a return to waste and threats of violence.

The Railroad Commission expected its order to limit the field to 400,000 barrels per day. Yet after only six days, the 400,000 was exceeded and hundreds of new wells were being drilled. On September 18, the commission lowered the rate to 185 barrels per day to put production back under the 400,000 barrels a day. But by October 4 that was exceeded again and the commission dropped the allowable to 165 barrels a day. Eugene Constantin, who was both a producer and a small refiner, where the orders hurt him in the latter capacity, sued as a producer, claiming an unconstitutional interference with his property rights.

Sterling was undeterred. "State's rights is involved and the federal court should not be permitted to throttle the will of the people."[7] As if the people had spoken. He would not comply with a federal court order to open the wells. "I guess I have more men than they have."[8] Indeed, instead of complying with a preliminary injunction, he ordered the allowable cut to 150 barrels a day per well without even consulting the commission. But when the federal district court issued a permanent injunction, he did comply while appealing to the Supreme Court.

When the Court heard oral argument in mid-November of 1932, Sterling had lost the governorship after a rematch with Miriam "Ma" Ferguson, whose strength in East Texas had been augmented by antipathy to Sterling. ("Ma" was the wife of James E. "Pa" Ferguson, Jr., who was governor from 1915 until his impeachment and removal in 1917. This was her second term, having initially served from 1925–27. She became the second of three governors to serve nonconsecutive terms, the others being Elisha Pease, 1853–57 and 1867–69, and Bill Clements, 1979–83 and 1987–91.) It was the closest primary to date with only three thousand votes out of 951,000 separating the two.

By the time the Court heard arguments three important legal events occurred affecting Texas oil. In an Oklahoma case, the Court upheld a proration statute limiting production to market demand.[9] A Texas civil court of appeals upheld a Railroad Commission proration order as it applied to preventing physical waste. And in a special session the legislature passed the Market-Demand Act, where waste was defined as "the production of crude petroleum oil in excess of transporting or market facilities or reasonable market demand."[10]

So Sterling's loss in *Sterling v. Constantin*[11] was anticlimactic, although profoundly important for constitutional law. Sterling argued that his decision to declare martial law was unreviewable. "Appellants assert that the court was powerless thus to intervene and that the Governor's order had the quality of a supreme and unchallengeable edict, overriding all conflicting rights of property and unreviewable through the judicial power of the Federal Government."[12] The argument was untenable, but it was the only one available on the facts. There was no insurrection in East Texas; there were no riots or destruction of property or breaches of the peace; and the only civil authority being ignored was by Sterling and Wolters in not complying with the preliminary injunction.

Chief Justice Charles Evans Hughes's unanimous opinion bluntly rejected Sterling's claim. "If this extreme position could be deemed to be well taken, it is manifest that the fiat of a state Governor, and not the Constitution of the United States, would be the supreme law of the land."[13] The Court acknowledged there was room for good faith actions. "The nature of the power also necessarily implies that there is a permitted range of honest judgment as to the measures to be taken in meeting force with force, in suppressing violence and restoring order, for without such liberty to make immediate decisions, the power itself would be useless."[14] Continuing in the same vein the Court concluded: "In the place of judicial procedure, available in the courts which were open and functioning, he set up his executive commands which brooked neither delay nor appeal ... .The assertion that such action can be taken as conclusive proof of its own necessity and must be accepted as in itself due process of law has no support in the decisions of this Court."[15]

II

By the time of *Sterling v. Constantin*, Franklin D. Roosevelt had been elected president. By the time of his inauguration, oil prices were once again collapsing. Despite the new Texas law authorizing proration, operators cheated in a variety of ways, sending so-called "hot oil" into the marketplace so that production quotas existed in rules, but not in fact. The 1931 claim of "stealing" was true as well in 1933. On May 5, the price of a barrel of oil was four cents, once again well below the price of water.

Of course oil was not alone in being battered. The Great Depression had sent the entire economy reeling. The cornerstone of the New Deal's First Hundred Days was the National Industrial Recovery Act (NIRA), which authorized the president to regulate industries. Roosevelt called the NIRA the most important statute in American history. The keys to the NIRA were codes of fair competition that were written by the industries affected. All but one was under the delegated jurisdiction to the National Recovery Administration led by General Hugh Johnson. Section 9(c) of the NIRA dealt with oil, giving the president authority to "prohibit the transportation in interstate and foreign commerce of petroleum and the products thereof produced or withdrawn from storage in excess of the amount permitted" by state law. FDR placed the industry under the jurisdiction of Secretary of the Interior Harold Ickes, a man who believed petroleum production was a national problem and therefore should be under national control. As historian John G. Clark notes, "Ickes harbored no deeply embedded belief in the capacity of the states or industry, acting unilaterally or jointly, to bring production under control by means of state prorationing laws."[16]

As federal regulation of some sort loomed, the majors / independents split had the majors favoring state control, with the federal government aiding but not controlling the industry. Independents were more sympathetic to national control, fearing industry self-government gave the majors too much sway. There was no doubt where Texas stood. Politicians raised "fears of concentrated federal power."[17] One Railroad Commission member invoked "Southern honor, populism, progressivism, and Texas nationalism" in supporting state control.[18]

Ickes's policy was aid without control, possibly because of the strength of Texans within the New Deal. If hot oil could be eliminated, prices would likely rise. Regulations targeting hot oil demanded extensive record-keeping and inspections of producers, shippers, and refiners with (minor) criminal penalties attached. Federal agents were dispatched to East Texas to stop the flow of hot oil, which was estimated at 85,000 to 200,000 barrels a day. A week after implementation Texas production dropped by 174,000 barrels a day. The *Oil and Gas Journal* observed, "These men evidently mean business."[19]

Before Ickes acted, the severance royalties per day to Kansas were $20,000, to Oklahoma $102,000, and to Texas $365,000. In October that had risen to $112,000 for Kansas, $406,000 for Oklahoma, and $995,000 for Texas. The price of oil was 89 cents a barrel.

Ickes imposed quotas on the oil-producing states, and to comply the Railroad Commission ordered a production cut of 130,000 barrels a day in East Texas. The field nevertheless exceeded its allowance each month even excluding hot oil. The illegal oil was estimated at 30,000 barrels a day, but better enforcement cut it to about 10,000 barrels by the end of 1934 because over time "only the diehard hot oil runners continue[d] to defy national authority."[20] The result was the sought-after higher prices, $1 per barrel at the end of 1933, $1.12 a year later. With national average production costs at 77.5 cents a barrel, the industry was turning a profit.

Still, not everyone was happy. Surveying the industry in April 1934 Ickes offered a resounding thumbs down. It was "one of the most ruthless, arrogant and haughty industries in the United States [responsible for] the most reckless and extravagant exploitation of a natural resource in the history of the world."[21] Ickes went out of his way to ridicule operators. "One rugged individualist stealing oil from a brother rugged individualist .... This industrial behemoth brought to its knees, came to Washington begging for help ... a far cry from 'less government in business.'"[22]

But within a year Ickes was brought to his knees. Six months earlier Panama Refining Company had taken Ickes to court by suing Archie D. Ryan, a special agent in the investigating division. The suit asked for an injunction against everything the agents were doing: gauging tanks, digging up pipelines, and prosecuting individuals for failing to file the required daily affidavits.

Panama Refining was represented by Fletcher "Big Fish" Fischer, a small-town East Texas lawyer. At the Supreme Court he filed a twelve-page brief in sharp contrast to the extensive brief filed by the government. Normally such a lawyering mismatch would overwhelmingly favor the federal government, but not this time. At oral argument he brought down the Courtroom with laughter when he claimed, "This heah Section 9(c) [which he pulled from his coat pocket] is inside some kind of pamphlet. Nobody really had notice of it. I had trouble finding this. This is the only place it is! That's the law, Your Honors. It's carried around in the pocket of a deputy administrator. And nobody else knows what it is!"[23] It was a devastating critique leading to his assertion that "after ten years of the NRA, a dictatorial president could very well tell Congress he didn't need it any more, and send it home."[24] While the claim seems over-the-top, in his inaugural FDR asserted that he would need "broad executive power to urge war against the emergency, as great as the power that would be given to me if we were invaded by a foreign foe."[25] It was the speech's top applause line, and with Walter Lippman, among others, suggesting FDR should consider a dictatorship, Fischer's claim found receptive ears.

Hughes, writing for all but one justice, found 9(c) an unconstitutional delegation of legislative power to the executive. The Court had previously mentioned excessive delegation, but *Panama Refining v. Ryan*[26] was the first case to hold a statute was an excessive delegation. The Court repeatedly stated that 9(c) evinced no congressional policy whatsoever even though "the question whether the transportation shall be prohibited by law is obviously one of legislative policy."[27] Yet there was no such policy. First, "it does not attempt to control the production of petroleum or petroleum products within a State. It does not seek to lay down rules for the guidance of state legislatures or state officials."[28] Second, it "does not state whether, or under what circumstances, the President is to prohibit the transportation."[29] Third, it "declares no policy as to transportation of the excess production."[30] Fourth, "the Congress did not prohibit that transportation. The Congress did not undertake to say that the transportation of 'hot oil' was injurious."[31] The opinion concluded that "there are limits of delegation which there is no constitutional authority to transcend [and 9(c)] goes beyond those limits."[32]

Congress reacted within a month, passing the Connally Hot Oil Act, named for Texas senator Tom Connally. The act prohibited the shipment in interstate or foreign commerce of "illegal petroleum" which was defined as crude produced or withdrawn from storage in violation of state allowables. Hot oil was not much of a problem at the time and never was again.

Correcting the hot oil problem of the NIRA foreshadowed by four and a half months *United States v. Schechter Poultry*,[33] where the Court unanimously struck down the NIRA as an excessive delegation and a violation of the Commerce Clause. The decision led to FDR's famous "horse and buggy" press conference where, thumbing a copy of the decision, he decried the federal government being denied "powers which exist in the national Government of every other Nation .... We have been relegated to the horse-and-buggy definition of interstate commerce."[34] *Schechter Poultry* was thus the second time a statute fell as an excessive delegation of legislative power to the executive; it was also the last time.

III

In the same year that the NIRA met its demise, an assistant attorney general named Ralph Yarborough wrote the legal opinion under which Texas started issuing its first leases for drilling in its offshore lands. California had been leasing its offshore lands since the 1920s. Now Texas followed suit, although the first well would not be drilled until 1940.

In 1937, for the first time, officials in the federal government questioned state ownership of offshore lands. This caused Texas governor James Allred to state: "I know that when lands become valuable somebody wants them."[35] Texas's claim, however, looked ironclad. Texas had been an independent republic and could claim what Mexico claimed on independence from Spain—three leagues (10.35 miles) offshore. (California only claimed three miles.) The 1845 Joint Resolution on Annexation stipulated that Texas retained all its public lands, and Texas had not subsequently ceded them.

On the eve of World War II advocates for state ownership sought congressional action to secure a federal release of any claims—a quitclaim deed (whereby one quits any claim to the property). The federal government saw oil as a national security issue and thought that the issue should be settled in the courts. If the federal government did own the land, it would be under the jurisdiction of the Interior Department and Harold Ickes. World War II then put everything on hold.

After the war, the Eightieth Congress passed a joint resolution ceding the federal claim. The vote reflected no party lines. But President Harry S. Truman vetoed it on the ground that the issue was pending before the Supreme Court. It was there because his Justice Department had filed an original action against California, a strong indication that the veto was on the merits.

United States v. California[36] was a 5–3 decision in favor of the federal government. The Court's split, like that of Congress, reflected no ideological lines. Hugo Black's majority opinion relied on the well-settled doctrine of the equal footing of states. Under the doctrine all new states enter the Union with the same rights as the original thirteen. As typically used, it meant new states acquired title to land under navigable rivers because the original thirteen had title. But looking to the law at the end of the eighteenth century the Court concluded that the original thirteen did not have title to their offshore lands; therefore, California didn't either.

Texas politicians saw *California* as an ominous sign. Governor Beauford Jester claimed it was a "further invasion of state's rights."[37] Land Commissioner Bascom Giles looked ahead: "If they try to apply it to Texas, I'm in favor of seceding before giving up our property to the federal government."[38] But, again, Texas entered the Union as its own nation; no other state had.

In 1948 the House once again passed a quitclaim bill, but no action was taken in the Senate. With a presidential election coming, the party platforms offered a peek into the future. The Republicans were unequivocally favoring "restoration to the states of their historic rights to the tides of submerged lands."[39] The Democrats, split so many ways, were also split on the tidelands. Accordingly, they said nothing. With Thomas Dewey expected to beat Truman, things looked good for Texas, and even Truman acknowledged that Texas "is in a class by itself."[40]

After Truman won and before the year was out, Attorney General Tom Clark, himself a Texan and UT law grad, filed a motion at the Supreme Court seeking permission to file an original suit against Texas. Texas politicians were aghast. Clark's motion especially affected those with their eyes on the governor's mansion in the near future: Jester, the reelected incumbent; Giles, the land commissioner; and two young rising stars, Lt. Governor Allan Shivers and Attorney General Price Daniel. It especially affected Daniel. With tidelands as *the* state issue, if he won, the stepping-stone should easily place him at the top. But if he lost . . . Well, he had better look like he fought the battle of his life, and he promised to fight "in the same spirit that caused our predecessors to win those lands by blood and valor at San Jacinto."[41]

In Congress there was stalemate with the overhanging threat of Truman's veto. Shivers and House Speaker Sam Rayburn favored a compromise because otherwise Texas would be "turned over to the mercy of the courts."[42] Jester, Giles, and Daniel opposed it as betraying Texas's heritage. Tom Clark told Rayburn that the federal government's paramount rights were not subject to compromise. Then Jester died unexpectedly of a heart attack and the forty-one-year-old Shivers became the first and only lieutenant governor in Texas history to assume the governorship due to the death of the incumbent. And on becoming governor, Shivers reversed his position and also came out against compromise.

So litigation it was, and Daniel did a masterful job in assembling experts to bolster Texas's historical claim. After oral argument in *United States v. Texas*[43] assistant attorney general J. Chris Dougherty (who would join with Ireland Graves of the *Pullman* litigation to found an excellent Austin law firm) publicly predicted victory. Privately, Daniel did, too. There was ample reason for optimism. *California* was readily distinguishable because Texas had been a republic and the United States had recognized that Texas retained title to its public lands. But a 4–3 opinion by William O. Douglas, the one legal genius on the Court, rejected Texas's claims to 2.6 million acres in the Gulf. It was a bad day for Texas government; earlier that morning the Court ordered Heman Sweatt admitted to UT's School of Law. The state's papers reflected that fact that the tidelands defeat was by far the greater loss.

The *Austin American-Statesman* had the headline "Tidelands Taken."[44] Senator Tom Connally asked, "is there nothing beyond the reach of arbitrary power?"[45] Congressman Ed Gossett of Wichita Falls, a UT alumnus and UT law grad, saw the decision as "another long shove on the road to national socialism."[46]

Douglas was the most liberal justice in Court history but also a strong believer in federal power and had once harbored (and perhaps still did) ambitions to become president (although he had rejected Truman's entreaties to run with him in 1948). Like *California, Texas* relied on the equal footing doctrine but in a novel way. The original thirteen did not own the tidelands; therefore Texas did not. Never before—or since—has the equal footing doctrine been used to strip a state of ownership.

The Texas house called for Douglas's impeachment with only eleven dissents. (Texas was there first; three years later there were calls for his impeachment when he stayed the execution of convicted atomic spies Julius and Ethel Rosenberg; and in 1970 House minority leader Gerald R. Ford used trumped-up charges to again try to impeach Douglas.) Years later, in retirement, Daniel called the case "the most criticized lawsuit and decision up to that time in the Supreme Court this century."[47] In Texas, perhaps, but nowhere else. One should be wary of old men praising their younger selves.

Texas made congressional action the only game in town, and a quit-claim bill passed. Truman's unequivocal veto message was a mirror to the Texas reaction to Douglas's opinion: the bill was "robbery in broad daylight on a colossal scale."[48] The veto was denounced throughout Texas, but if Texas was to prevail, a new president was essential.

The 1952 Democratic nominee, Adlai Stevenson, held a four and a half hour meeting with Shivers devoted to the tidelands issue. Afterward Stevenson issued a statement agreeing with the Court, but claiming he would favor "legislation providing for an equitable arrangement for administration of these lands, and the distribution of their proceeds."[49] That was not enough when the Republican nominee, Dwight D. Eisenhower, had already stated he would sign a quitclaim bill. Then in October, campaigning in Texas, Ike asserted that Stevenson "wants to take over the tidelands and dole out to the states whatever Washington decides you ought to have. That isn't what I can a fair shake, I call it a shakedown."[50] With Shivers and Daniel supporting the Republican ticket, Ike carried the state, and in 1953 signed the Submerged Lands Act giving coastal states like Texas title to their tidelands.

The act was sustained in a per curiam opinion written by Felix Frankfurter in 1954 by simple recitation of Article IV, Section 3, Paragraph 2: "The Congress shall have the power to dispose of ... Property belonging to the United States." In a note to his majority attached to the initial circulation, Frankfurter wrote: "We ought not be responsible for any delay in throwing these cases out of court."[51] Black and Douglas dissented, with Douglas complaining that states were no longer on an equal footing when some got more than others.[52] In 1960 the act was construed to give Texas its three leagues offshore.[53] Douglas dissented alone. His votes against Texas were becoming a habit; he never supported the state in a constitutional case.

The Texas congressional delegation was elated, with House Speaker Sam Rayburn asserting it was "a very just decision."[54] This was echoed in the editorial "Justice at Last" in the *Dallas Morning News*: "Few good words can be said for the arguments that have been advanced by the Department of Justice in the tidelands fight. It has had to argue with a straight face for breach of faith."[55] Governor Price Daniels, who had been involved as both attorney general and then senator, named the seven lawyers involved in the victory "Admirals of the Texas Navy."[56]

IV

Daniel had urged Shivers to oppose Tom Connally for the Senate in 1952, but Shivers liked being governor. So Daniel went for the Senate instead and bested Connally in the primary. In both 1952 and 1954 Ralph Yarborough challenged Shivers in the Democratic gubernatorial primary and lost. In 1956, with Shivers retiring, Daniel and Yarborough were pitted in a runoff, which Daniel won; he then won two more terms. In 1957, with Daniel's Senate seat open, Yarborough finally won an election and then a couple of terms before being defeated by Lloyd Bentson in 1970.

In 1967, in the only book about a single state among the thirty he wrote, Douglas had good and bad extrajudicial words about the lands of Texas that were not offshore. He praised the beauty of canyons, waterways, forests, and grasslands, but lamented that private development threatened them because Texas had no public lands. In the half century since *Farewell to Texas: A Vanishing Wilderness* was published, a considerable amount of that beauty has been acquired by the state. Perhaps not enough to have met Douglas's plea, but probably more than he expected.

SIX

School Finance

A lot of Anglo guys used to argue with me; they didn't like it.
They thought I was a Communist. I told them, I'm no more
Communist than you are. I'm using the judicial system and I
don't care what you say. I told them, You know why I'm doing
this? Because I've been the victim of discrimination.

— Demetrio Rodriguez on why he filed suit over
school financing

As the University of Texas experience shows, Hispanics, too, enjoy the
benefits and the burdens of affirmative action. In Texas, one cannot talk
minorities without thinking of Hispanics. That was a prime reason that
the NAACP bussing plan in the Dallas litigation made no sense. How
could Hispanics be left out or treated as Anglos? Texas has a long and
rich history of second-class treatment of Hispanics, even if it was culture and norms rather than law that perpetuated the situation. The
same discrimination against African Americans in the first half of the
twentieth century operated on Hispanics as well. Texas was an Anglo-
ruled state with two minorities as second-class citizens.

I

Pete Hernandez was a cotton-picker in Jackson County just northeast
of Victoria. He got into a fight with several men in a tavern and lost. He
went home, picked up his .22 caliber rifle, walked back to the tavern,

and shot one of his assailants before forty witnesses. After being convicted of murder he claimed that all persons of Mexican descent were systematically excluded from jury service. There was no doubt that if he had been black and all blacks were systematically excluded, his conviction would have been reversed as unconstitutional. Hernandez's lawyers, Carolos Cadena and Gus Garcia, became the first Hispanics to argue a case before the Court and they showed how the attorney general's office was overmatched.

The brief by the state of Texas was shockingly bad. It consisted of three pages of argument, boiled down to a single point. "The defendant in this case is a white man. The jury was composed of white men. No actual exclusion of the white race or any other race therefrom is shown. No discrimination against the white race or based on race or color is shown."[1] The brief then reprinted in full the opinion of the Texas Court of Criminal Appeals as if that would instruct the Supreme Court that discrimination against Hispanics was okay because they weren't black. During this era, briefs out of all state attorneys general were weak, but this one would win a prize for being as weak as possible. It gave embarrassment a bad name.

In a very short unanimous opinion—Tom Clark had initially voted the other way[2]—delivered two weeks before *Brown v. Board of Education*,[3] Chief Justice Earl Warren bluntly rejected Texas's claim.[4] "It taxes our credulity to say that mere chance resulted in their being no members of this class [Hispanics] among the over six thousand jurors called in the past 25 years. The result bespeaks discrimination."[5] So did the Texas courthouse where Hernandez had been tried. "There were two men's toilets, one unmarked, and the other marked 'Colored Men' and 'Hombres Aqui' ('Men Here')."[6] Hernandez's "only claim is the right to be indicted and tried by juries from which all members of his class are not systematically excluded—juries selected from among all qualified persons regardless of national origin or descent. To this much, he is entitled by the Constitution."[7] The decision when read side by side with *Brown* shows that *Brown* was not about a color-blind constitution but rather one that prohibits the subordination of a group.

Hernandez was promptly reindicted. He took a twenty-year sentence on a guilty plea and was paroled in 1960. He subsequently married and had a son, and apparently had no more run-ins with the law.

Hernandez and the history of discrimination against Hispanics fully explain why any desegregation remedies had to consider Hispanics as well as blacks. That was the holding in *Cisneros v. Corpus Christi Independent School District*,[8] the first suit to press the issue. Yet the major case involving Hispanics was not litigated as racial discrimination but rather as a wealth discrimination case.

II

In the late 1960s the Edgewood Independent School District on the west side of San Antonio was a predominantly Hispanic area where less than ten percent of the adults had completed high school. It had formed its own school district right after World War I, but in the 1950s it made three separate attempts to join the San Antonio Independent School District. The efforts were rebuffed because the low property values in Edgewood would mean that the larger district would be subsidizing Edgewood. In addition to low property values Edgewood was the home of Kelly Air Force Base, a federal entity paying no property taxes at all.

The Edgewood ISD was cash-strapped and its residents had a median family income of $4,686, the poorest in the city. Despite the highest property tax rate of the seven school districts within metropolitan San Antonio, the low values of property produced only $26 per student in a district with over 20,000 students. State funding added $222 and another $108 came from the federal government. But the result of the minimal funding was no air conditioning, crumbling buildings, few supplies, and a thirty-plus percent turnover of teachers each year. That matched the student dropout rate between grades seven and twelve.

After a student strike in 1968, Edgewood High School parents formed the Edgewood District Concerned Parents Association with Alberta Snid as its leader. The group was sure that corruption and kickbacks by the school board were responsible for the conditions of the schools and were placed in contact with Arthur Gochman, a thirty-seven-year-old University of Texas law school grad who had been active in civil rights causes. Gochman quickly figured out the board members were honest and that the problem was that Edgewood could not raise enough money via property taxes. He recommended suing, said he would handle the case pro bono, and replaced Snid with the Hispanic-surnamed Demetrio Rodriguez, a navy and air force veteran, as the lead plaintiff. The case was not popular with the Anglo community in San Antonio. Thus Rodriguez noted "A lot of Anglo guys used to argue with me; they didn't like it. They thought I was a Communist. I told them I'm no more Communist than you are. I'm using the judicial system and I don't care what you say. I told them, You know why I'm doing this. Because I've been the victim of discrimination."[9]

To make the case that Edgewood was been discriminatorily treated under the Equal Protection Clause that had been so successful in *Brown,* the litigation would always contrast Edgewood with Alamo Heights, an affluent community on the north side of San Antonio with a median family income of $8,001 and where 50% of the male workers had executive or professional titles (compared to 4% in Edgewood). Unlike Edgewood which had tried to join the San Antonio ISD, Alamo Heights had refused to join it. Edgewood schools were 50% more crowded, with one-fourth fewer counselors and one-fifth of its teachers lacking a college degree. Alamo Heights had eight times the assessed property value as Edgewood, taxed itself at the lowest rate in San Antonio and still generated $333 per student to which the state added $225 and the federal government $26. Edgewood would have had to tax itself at twenty times the Alamo Heights rate to generate equal money. That would have been illegal under the Texas Constitution which limits the maximum property tax rate.

Although Gochman avoided making the case about race because both districts had Anglo, Hispanic, and African American students, the issues of race and class were not far (if at all) below the surface. Edgewood schools were 90% Hispanic and 6% African American. Alamo Heights schools were 81% Anglo, 18% Hispanic, and less than 1% black.

In preparing for the litigation Gochman relied on a decision of a District of Columbia District Court that had demanded ending segregation once again but intertwined issues of funding.[10] But to some extent events in California overtook that case. There was already a case working through the California courts that challenged school funding by local property taxes. In 1970 John Coons and colleagues William Clune and Stephen Sugarman published *Private Wealth and Public Education*, challenging state reliance on local property taxes and arguing instead that the state should provide additional funds so that the same property tax rate in affluent and less affluent districts produces the same amount of revenue for each district, something they called "power equalizing." A year later in *Serrano v. Priest*[11] the California Supreme Court had generously cited the book while striking down the way the state's schools were funded.

Back in Texas, Gochman and the lawyers on the other side traded motions before the federal district court for a year. During that time the state legislature passed HB 240, which authorized the formation of a committee charged with recommending "a specific formula or formulae to establish a fair and equitable basis for the division financial responsibility between the state and the various local school districts of Texas."[12] In October 1969 the district court issued a stay order to hold off proceedings until the next legislative session met, believing that a legislative solution would be superior to a judicial one. In January 1971 the session began. It ended 140 days later having taken no action on school finance.

Later that summer, Mark G. Yudof, a University of Pennsylvania law grad, joined the UT law school faculty as an assistant professor, having spent the previous two years at Harvard at the newly established Center for Law and Education. His specialty there was school finance litigation, so he was more familiar with *Serrano* than was Goch-man (whom he had met there once). Upon arriving in Austin, Yudof wrote Gochman a letter, hoping he would remember him, and offering to assist (pro bono, of course) with the *Rodriguez* litigation. A trip to San Antonio sealed the deal and Yudof became the principal draftsman of the *Rodriguez* briefs. (He would later get a letter of reprimand from the Board of Regents because he used the law school address, but not name, on the briefs. The reprimand was purely political in opposition to his being on the plaintiffs' side; all of us at UT used the law school address, but not its name, on the briefs we signed.)

In December the district court issued its opinion finding the Texas system violated equal protection. The court found the system to be wealth discrimination, which would require Texas to show a "compelling state interest" for justification—an all-but-impossible task. It went on to conclude that the Texas justification—offering enhanced local control—did not even satisfy the lenient "rational basis" test because districts like Edgewood, with low tax basis, had little or no autonomy. Furthermore, Alamo Heights received more state money than Edgewood because state aid "tends to subsidize the rich at the expense of the poor rather than the other way around."[13] Implicit in the decision was the idea that money equated with quality. The more you had the better the education. Gochman's decision to play down race in favor of class (wealth) paid off.

III

The decision, rendered by a three-judge district court, gave Texas the right to appeal directly to the Supreme Court without going through a circuit court. Texas attorney general Crawford Martin turned to UT law professor Charles Alan Wright to handle the state's appeal. Martin could not have made a better choice. Forty-six years old, Wright was already an experienced Supreme Court advocate. Six feet three inches tall, he literally and figuratively towered above everyone else. He was authoritative because he was so knowledgeable. He was the nation's leading authority on the law of the federal courts, having authored a wonderful hornbook and co-authored the leading treatise. He was a member of the council of the prestigious American Law Institute—the council being the body that really controlled the ALI—and federal judges across the board respected him (and wanted his advice). As Carolyn King, then chief judge on the Fifth Circuit, stated: "Charlie was the quintessential preceptor for the federal courts.... And when it came to coaching federal judges, I can testify, as one, that Charlie was the Vince Lombardi of our coaches."[14]

Charlie told me he was prouder of his *Rodriguez* brief than any other brief he wrote. The idea came to him on a flight from D.C. to Austin and he outlined the brief on the inside cover of the mystery paperback that he was reading. The forty-eight-page brief reached the middle of page 25 before beginning a section entitled "The Flaw in the Legal Argument." That was the first time the brief had mentioned any law. The first half of the brief discussed the ruling below, the Coons, Clune, and Sugarman thesis, with the section right before the legal argument entitled "The Unsound Factual Assumptions." Wright noted that the trio's thesis was new and that it deserved a gestation period before the Supreme Court would announce that it was the supreme law of the land. It was a terrific and compelling brief which candidly, if necessarily, acknowledged that the Texas financing system was far from perfect, but it is designed "to provide an adequate education for all, with local autonomy to go beyond that as individual school districts desire and are able.... It leaves to the people of each district the choice to go beyond the minimum and, if so, by how much."[15]

The brief Yudof wrote tracked the district court's decision. Education was so important to voting and citizenship that it was a fundamental right necessitating strict scrutiny. So, too, did classifications based on wealth. But even if the Court chose to apply the rational basis test, Texas failed that as well because of the real lack of autonomy facing districts with a low property tax base.

Wright's oral argument began with Coons, Clune, and Sugarman and the state's fear that it would impose a constitutional straightjacket on the states. He noted how little was known about district power equalizing and asserted that the state's contribution to local districts assured that what was needed for an adequate education was provided. This was an interesting point because there was nothing in the record to either support or refute it. And he went back to his brief to stress the implicit judgment of the district court that money equaled quality.

Gochman in his first and only Supreme Court argument faced questions about money and quality, the correlation between poor people and poor districts and why education, rather than food, shelter, or access to public health, was a fundamental right. Furthermore, local control is "the one thing that the Texas system does not have ... because those that tax at the highest rates have the lowest expenditure per pupil and those that tax at the lowest rates have the highest expenditure per pupil. That is just the reverse of local control."[16]

In his rebuttal Wright praised Coons, Clune, Sugarman, Gochman, and Yudof for opening the nation's eyes to the problems of school financing. He claimed the true difference between the parties was the choice of venue to deal with the issue. For Wright the solution was in the various state legislatures, not a single judicial fiat.

Lewis Powell, a courtly "Southern gentleman,"[17] finishing his first Term since President Richard Nixon appointed him, had shown an interest in *Rodriguez* even before the Court agreed to hear the case. His experience as a school board member in Richmond and then on the state board of education made him exceptionally uneasy about the decision below. He told two of his law clerks to put the case on their summer study list and one of them, Larry Hammond, to write an extensive memo for Powell to study before oral argument. Hammond, a UT law graduate, had gone to school in a small, property poor district in West Texas and was initially sympathetic to the plaintiffs, but later changed his mind. The other clerk who helped on the case was J. Harvie Wilkinson III, a conservative University of Virginia law grad and the son of a good friend of Powell's.

The discussion of the justices at their Friday Conference revealed that the four appointees of Richard Nixon—Warren Burger, Harry Blackmun, Powell, and William Rehnquist—plus Eisenhower Republican Potter Stewart favored reversing the court below. The four Democrats— William O. Douglas, William J. Brennan, Byron White, and Thurgood Marshall—would affirm. In that and subsequent discussions it was obvious that the Republicans were horrified by the plaintiffs' claims. Powell saw in them a whiff of totalitarianism. Centralizing control of education was a hallmark of authoritarian states. "I have in mind the irresistible impulse of politicians to manipulate public education for their own power and ideology—e.g., Hitler, Mussolini, and communist dictators."[18] Even if control stopped at the state level he foresaw trouble because with the purse strings comes control, and local control "has been the most dynamic force behind the overall effectiveness of our public school system."[19] He questioned "the relationship between expenditures and the quality of public education."[20] But it didn't matter. In his notes he described the plaintiff's theory as a "'communist' doctrine that had no place in a country based on the principle of free enterprise."[21] In 1895 Joseph Choate argued against the income tax, which he claimed was "communistic in its purposes and tendencies, and is defended here upon principles as communistic, socialistic … as ever have been addressed to any political assembly in the world."[22] In striking down the law Chief Justice Melville Fuller saw it as "an attack upon accumulated property by mere force of numbers."[23] Powell was channeling this earlier era.

If the Court affirmed the lower court's holding on school finance there would be "a distressing equality with no one getting anything that is very good. This smacks of the type of thing that emerged from the French Revolution."[24] So the reluctance of districts with high property values was really in everyone's interest.

All of the Republicans worried about the problems of judicial intervention into school financing. Entering an "educational thicket would be far worse than the reapportionment area" because the Court would be overhauling "the fiscal and taxation structures across the land."[25]

Because of Powell's obvious interest and expertise, Burger assigned the majority to him and Powell, with the help of Hammond and to a lesser extent Wilkinson, produced the most important opinion of his tenure on the Supreme Court, an opinion that is never mentioned in the sympathetic 600-page biography written by another former Powell clerk.[26]

IV

Powell's task was threefold. He had to show that education was not a fundamental right, that wealth was not a suspect classification, and that the Texas system was rationally related to local control. The latter point would be the easiest because the rational basis test was essentially toothless. The former two would require dealing with (and perhaps ending) two emerging trends in the jurisprudence of the late Warren Court.

The opinion begins with a rather tedious discussion of school funding in Texas going back well over a century. It notes the disparities—although not as starkly as I presented them earlier. But an explicit theme later in the opinion is that Texas has been trying. "[W]e think that, in substance, the thrust of the Texas system is affirmative and reformatory."[27] It's not perfect, of course, and Wright admitted that the system could not withstand strict scrutiny, but Texas has improved its financing over time. Implicitly the opinion seems to suggest that Texas will continue to do so.

Then Powell turned to the issue of wealth discrimination as a suspect class. *Harper v. Virginia Board of Elections*[28] stated that "lines drawn on the basis of wealth or property, like those of race, are traditionally disfavored."[29] That decision along with several others had established that the right to vote (or run for office) was fundamental and a person did not lose the right because of indigency. There was a separate line to the same effect involving various aspects of the criminal justice system from counsel,[30] to transcripts,[31] to incarceration because of inability to pay a fine.[32] As Powell read those cases the individuals affected "shared two distinguishing characteristics: because of their impecunity they were completely unable to pay for some desired benefit, and as a consequence, they sustained an absolute deprivation of a meaningful opportunity to enjoy that benefit."[33] The Court noted that the "argument here is not that children in districts having relatively low assessable property values are receiving no public education; rather, it is that they are receiving a poorer quality education than that available to children in districts having more assessable wealth."[34] But that was equating money with quality and the Court would not go there. At best more money seemed to mean higher salaries for teachers and a lower teacher:pupil ratio.[35]

Accepting Wright's argument, the Court found no absolute deprivation as required by the prior cases. "Nor, indeed, in view of the infinite variables affecting the education process can any system assure equal quality of education except in the most relative sense. Texas asserts that the Minimum Foundation Program [of state aid] provides an 'adequate' education for all children in the State.... No proof was offered at trial persuasively discrediting or refuting the State's assertion."[36] Going back to the Warren Court cases Powell noted the "Court has never heretofore held that wealth discrimination alone provides an adequate basis for invoking strict scrutiny."[37] With emphasis on "alone."

The claim that education was a fundamental right had both a practical and a doctrinal basis. Education is, as Gochman and Yudof asserted, tied to citizenship and freedom of speech and the right to vote. Education makes those rights meaningful (which is perhaps why Wright kept asserting that the state did guarantee to every child an adequate education). The doctrinal claim goes straight to the most important decision in the Court's history—*Brown v. Board of Education*—where the Court recognized that "education is perhaps the most important function of state and local governments."[38]

The Court struck two themes in rejecting the claim that education was a fundamental right. First, the importance of the service provided is not relevant to whether something is fundamental; instead it is the relationship of the claim to the Constitution itself. Second, given the complexities involved, the Court should not sit as a super-legislature.

"The importance of a service performed by the State does not determine whether it must be regarded as fundamental for purposes of examination under the Equal Protection Clause."[39] The Court will not weigh the significance of education against that of housing. "Rather the answer lies in assessing whether there is a right to education explicitly or implicitly guaranteed by the Constitution."[40] Like, say, the right to travel interstate. The plaintiffs' claim was too much in forcing the Court to choose between housing, food, or education—or perhaps worse, holding all were fundamental.

Essentially the majority saw the plaintiffs' arguments as mandating that the Court sit as a super-legislature.[41] But the justices "lack both the expertise and familiarity with local problems so necessary to the making of wise decisions."[42] Complexity "of financing and managing a state-wide public school system suggests that there will be more than one constitutionally permissible method of solving" the problems.[43] Thus at the conclusion of the opinion Powell returned to the theme. "We are unwilling to assume for ourselves a level of wisdom superior to that of legislators, scholars, and educational authorities in 50 States, especially where the alternatives proposed are only recently conceived and nowhere yet tested."[44]

With its holdings that wealth was not a suspect classification and education was not a fundamental right, the need for strict scrutiny and a compelling state interest vanished. All that was necessary was finding local control was a rational state interest and Texas would prevail. The statements about the Court not becoming a super-legislature because of the complexities of the problems were sufficient to demonstrate that Texas had a rational basis for its system. The compelling state interest requirement might demand that states try to achieve perfection, but the rational basis test does not. A law must be crazy in the extreme (if that) to fail the test.

In a single opinion Powell and the Republicans brought to a halt two emerging doctrinal trends of the Warren Court. There were hints and holdings—and language from *Harper*—that indicated the Warren Court was going to make wealth something of a suspect classification guaranteeing at least a real minimum adequacy. Had Hubert Humphrey won the 1968 election and been able to appointee four justices in his first term, this likely would have come to pass.[45] But Richard Nixon won and he appointed four justices who could join with Stewart to end this movement once and for all.

The Warren Court was also talking about fundamental rights, not only in voting, but with marriage and interstate travel. That Court likely would have done something similar for education if the justices thought it necessary for justice. Furthermore, the rejection of education as a fundamental right seems odd, coming as it did just two months after the Court found a constitutional right to an abortion in *Roe v. Wade*.[46] There the Court held that the right of privacy was broad enough to encompass an abortion even though it was not relying on constitutional text (because privacy appears nowhere in the document). But the Republicans meant what they said in *Rodriguez*.

Thurgood Marshall, the great and inspiring lawyer who won *Brown,* wrote the principal dissent. He had been appointed by Lyndon B. Johnson at the height of the Warren Court and doubtless expected to be a member of the majority that advanced the rights of minorities under the Constitution. *Rodriguez* was a very early indication that that was not going to happen.

Marshall's lengthy dissent emphasizes the harm done to the Edgewood children and condemned the "unsupportable acquiescence in a system which deprives children in their earliest years of their chance to reach their full potential as citizens."[47] He decried the "cruel irony" that the state offers more aid to rich districts like Alamo Heights than it does to tax poor districts like Edgewood.[48] And he rejected the idea that adequacy could erase "unjustifiable inequalities."[49]

Turning to doctrine, Marshall condemned the all-or-nothing classification of two-tier equal protection. "We must consider the substantiality of the state interests sought to be served, and we must scrutinize the reasonableness of the means by which the State has sought to advance its interests. Differences in the application of this test are, in my view, a function of the constitutional importance of the interests at stake and the invidiousness of the particular classification."[50] Not only was it a dissent; his position was a losing proposition.

Marshall ended by noting that the majority "seeks solace" from its decision because of the possibility of future legislative action.[51] He didn't believe that would be forthcoming.

The *Dallas Morning News* provided blanket coverage of the decision and editorialized "Cheers for the Court."[52] State officials, echoing Wright, acknowledged there was a problem and there was work to do, but Marshall's prediction was better than Wright's as the state made minor funding changes in both 1975 and 1979 while large funding disparities remained. Speaker of the House Price Daniel, Jr., focused elsewhere and saw the decision as meaning passage of the two-year budget without tax increases. The president of the Dallas School Board proclaimed "ain't it wonderful" and the Dallas school superintendent said it was "the best news I've heard in many a week."[53]

Representatives of Edgewood ISD promised to take the fight to the state legislature. Gochman and Rodriguez were dismayed. The former predicted a two-class school system, one for the rich, the other for the poor. The latter was terse: "The poor people have lost again."[54] Superintendents of the victorious districts acknowledged a new funding system should be enacted by the legislature. The Alamo Heights superintendent was silent. His constituents, as Justin Driver would wryly note, were dancing in the cul-de-sacs.[55]

V

In 1984 Edgewood parents including Demetrio Rodriguez brought a suit against funding in the Texas courts relying on the Texas Constitution. Section 1 of Article VII states: "A general diffusion of knowledge being essential to the preservation of the liberties and rights of the people, it shall be the duty of the legislature of the State to establish and make suitable provision for the support and maintenance of an efficient system of public free schools."

In seven decisions over twenty-seven years the Texas Supreme Court rejected the state's claim that the legislature had absolute (and therefore unreviewable) discretion to provide whatever public education it chose. Delegates of the 1875 constitutional convention "spoke at length on the importance of education for all the people of the state, rich and poor alike."[56] Disparities in "public school finance were not contemplated."[57] Thus in *Edgewood I* the court held that the school funding failed a test of financial efficiency because of the wide disparities in property wealth, tax rates; and spending per student; and perhaps most importantly the 700 to 1 ratio between property wealth per student in the richest and poorest districts.[58] Unlike Lewis Powell's beliefs, the court noted that equalizing funding would enhance local control because it would give poorer districts more options.

The legislature responded with SB 1, creating two tiers of schools, a scheme still in existence. Tier 1 guaranteed funding to all districts that taxed property at or above a specified minimum. Tier 2 guaranteed a certain level of funding for each cent of taxation above the minimum. In a concession to wealth, SB 1 excluded the wealthiest five percent of school districts. *Edgewood II* held the exclusion unconstitutional: "To be efficient, a funding system that is so dependent on local ad valorem property taxes must draw revenue from all property at a substantially similar rate."[59]

In response the legislature passed SB 351 which, in effect, constituted a statewide ad valorem tax, that is, a tax on real or personal property assessed according to the value of the property. This violated an absolute prohibition in Article VIII, Section 1(e) of the Texas Constitution and *Edgewood III* so held.[60] The ruling came at the end of January 1992 and the legislature was not scheduled to meet until the following January. Hence the court chose to defer the effect of its ruling for seventeen months to avoid disruption of public education and to enable the legislature time "to consider all options fully."[61] The court also held that its decision could not be used as a defense to payment of the 1991 and 1992 taxes.

Several taxpayers filed suit in federal court to enjoin the collection of a tax, claiming it was a violation of due process to collect a tax that the state supreme court had held violated the state constitution. The district court held that the 1991 taxes were acceptable because *Edgewood III* was decided after they were collected, but collecting the 1992 taxes would violate due process (although the court declined to enjoin their collection).[62]

With both sides appealing the district court's ruling Douglas Laycock, the most accomplished member of the UT law school faculty after Charlie Wright, quickly wrote an amicus brief arguing that the federal courts lacked jurisdiction to hear the case because the 1937 Tax Injunction Act[63] precluded jurisdiction when a like suit could be brought in state court. Doug then asked Charlie and me to sign the brief and we did. (Amicus, or friend of the court, briefs are usually anything but, being written by parties and organizations strongly interested in the outcome. Laycock's brief, by contrast, was a true amicus.) At the end of the oral argument at the Fifth Circuit, the judges did what judges virtually never do; they rendered judgment from the bench. Doug's argument was accepted; the federal courts had no jurisdiction.[64]

Another ramification of *Edgewood III* was that for the first time the voters were asked to weigh in. Proposition 1 on the May 1993 ballot was a redistributive scheme and the voters didn't like it. It went down by a 63–37 percent vote. Broken down by race, Anglos voted no, while African Americans and Hispanics voted yes.

With the ability to collect taxes and fund schools at issue the legislature adopted SB 7, popularly (or unpopularly) known as Robin Hood. It kept the two-tier scheme of SB 1, but added a cap on taxable property greater than $280,000 per student. Districts whose wealth exceeded that were given five options, three of which involved consolidation that all rich districts found unacceptable. Realistically almost all rich districts took the option of purchasing from the state daily attendance credits that then were redistributed to poorer districts. *Edgewood IV* upheld Robin Hood over the complaints of the wealthier districts, noting the 700 to 1 ratio of wealth per student had been reduced to 28 to 1.[65]

When adopted, Robin Hood redistributed money from 34 mostly rural districts that had large industrial plants in their tax base. With the rise of property values during the first decade of this century more districts—142 in 2006—had to give money to less fortunate ones. A decade later, with Austin and Houston now giving money, 257 districts were covered, sending $2 billion to property poor districts and unhappy about the whole thing.

Meanwhile in 2016 the Texas Supreme Court, while acknowledging that the "State can do better," signaled an end.[66] In 2004 it had found that the wealthiest to poorest ratio of 200 to 1 was not inefficient. In the 2016 case the ratio had jumped to 330 to 1, but the court concluded that 330 was closer to 200 than it was to the 700 to 1 (*Edgewood I*) and therefore it was not financially inefficient.

There is no doubt that Texas can do better; that is always true. There is a lot more money going into education than there was a quarter century ago and the vast disparities of money available to districts have eroded. Whether the children of the state are getting a better education is less certain. Twenty-five years earlier Yudof offered an analogy: "School finance reform is like a Russian novel: it's long, tedious, and everybody dies at the end."[67]

VI

Neither Arthur Gochman, nor Mark Yudof, nor Charles Alan Wright (with the exception of signing the Laycock brief) had any further involvement with school finance litigation. But all had very successful post-*Rodriguez* careers. Gochman left the law right after the case to join his father's business that sold military surplus, Academy Surplus Stores, which he then transformed into one of the largest sporting goods retailers in the South.

Yudof published an important book, *When Government Speaks*, in 1983. This put him in the forefront of First Amendment scholars who realized that the government as speaker represented an important issue. He had already become the associate dean for academic affairs at UT School of Law. A year after the book's publication he became dean and enjoyed a successful nine-year run until he became UT's provost. From there he left to become president of the University of Minnesota. Then it was back to UT as chancellor of the entire UT system. Finally he went to the flagship state university system—the University of California—to run it until he retired. During that stretch he served under governors Arnie Carlson and Jesse Ventura in Minnesota, George W. Bush and Rick Perry in Texas, Arnold Schwarzenegger and Jerry Brown in California. It was quite a ride.

Charlie Wright was already distinguished when he won *Rodriguez*. He continued to be the towering figure in the law of the federal courts with his hornbook and treatise and talks to judges at the various federal judicial conferences (at which he was a prized speaker). He moved from the council at the American Law Institute to its vice presidency to its presidency. He also continued to argue at the Court where he only had lost three times, and in each case the Court eventually came around to the position he had advocated.[68]

Powell's two law clerks who worked on *Rodriguez* also enjoyed successes. Larry Hammond became an outstanding white-collar criminal defense lawyer in Phoenix. Beyond that he helped found the Arizona Justice Project, which offers representation to poor defendants in capital cases. In 2010 he won the Morris Dees Justice Award from the University of Alabama for his work. J. Harvie Wilkinson joined the Virginia law faculty and then was appointed to the Fourth Circuit Court of Appeals where he had a distinguished record and displayed an independent mind.

Demetrio Rodriguez continued to live in Edgewood until his death in 2013. His daughter Patricia teaches in the Edgewood school district as a third-grade bilingual teacher and was named teacher of the year several years before her father's death.

Despite the two decades of changes in the financing of Texas schools, the students in Edgewood and Alamo Heights face futures on leaving school that look much like they did during the *Rodriguez* litigation. Fewer than 10 percent of Edgewood students go on to college, while 96 percent of Alamo Heights students do.

SEVEN

Immigration

The problem is that I'm the president of the United States,
I'm not the emperor of the United States. My job is to
execute the laws that are passed. And Congress right now
has not changed what I consider to be a broken immigration
system.

> —President Barack Obama explaining why he could
> not do more for undocumented immigrants
> (February 14, 2013)

Undocumented immigrants pay in-state tuition at Texas's public universities. The state of Texas led the charge against allowing undocumented parents of American citizens to work legally. If Texas does it, it's okay; if the federal government does it, it isn't.

I

In his April 1975 reply to the commissioner of education, Texas attorney general John Hill issued an opinion stating that undocumented children were entitled to attend public schools. A month later legislation passed that allowed school districts to deny admission and therefore education to any student who could neither prove lawful residence in the United States nor pay the requisite tuition. It did so by providing that school districts could only apply for state reimbursement for citizens or those legally admitted from another country.

There is no legislative history for the law, but there is little doubt the legislature wished to deter illegal immigration if it could. There were also fiscal claims, although these were more amorphous: the limited money should be spent on those legally within the state, and there was a reluctance on the part of voters in districts like Brownsville to pass new bond issues for public schools.

There was no doubt the new policy would be challenged, and suits were filed first in state court and later in all four federal districts. The state case upheld the law and the state supreme court declined even to review it.[1] The first federal case was decided adversely to the law in Tyler where William Wayne Justice, the most liberal federal judge in the state, sat.[2]

Justice recognized that the immigration of Mexican nationals into the United States created problems for the public schools because of the linguistic special needs of the children, but most of the problems were caused by legal immigration. He doubted whether the savings from excluding undocumented children would "improve the quality of education" for the others.[3] As he saw it, the undocumented children were "[a]lready disadvantaged as a result of poverty, lack of English-speaking ability, and undeniable racial prejudice."[4] Without education they "will become permanently locked into the lowest socio-economic class."[5] He found the legislation lacked a rational basis and was in any event preempted by federal law.

The other three lawsuits were consolidated in Houston, where the court reached the same result by holding that the "absolute deprivation of education should trigger strict judicial scrutiny, particularly when the absolute deprivation is the result of a complete inability to pay for the desired benefit."[6] The state's interest in saving money was not a compelling interest.

Justice's decision reached the Fifth Circuit first and a unanimous opinion by the legendary Alabama judge Frank Johnson affirmed on equal protection while rejecting the preemption argument.[7] The other cases were then summarily affirmed. The Court took Texas's appeal from both decisions.

Realizing that rational basis review had been good enough to sustain Texas funding in *San Antonio Independent School District v. Rodriguez*[8] (and that the Court had grown more conservative) attorneys for the children argued that the Court should apply strict scrutiny to the Texas law and that in any event it conflicted with federal education law and should be invalidated on that basis. Their argument was easy to make, but lacked a grounding in the Court's decisions.

From the Texas perspective the goal was to show the law made sense and therefore survived rational basis scrutiny (as all laws normally do). To do so was remarkably easy. While the justifications weren't the best, saving scarce dollars for those legally in the country and deterring illegal immigration were certainly sufficient for the rational basis test. What was instead remarkable was what Texas did before it got there.

The Texas brief begins with an attack on the federal government for not securing the border, having underfunded the Immigration and Naturalization Service "to the direct detriment of Texas."[9] The brief quoted the director of the Dallas district of the INS that illegal immigration is "more or less ... out of control."[10] The Texas law had been on the books for six years "and not a murmur has been heard from Congress. Congress must decide whether these children 'should be educated ... or ... sent home.'"[11]

Texas next turned to attacking Mexicans. One of the state's witnesses had "testified to studies which show that 55.5% of illegal aliens have had no formal education and another 19.2% had less than a fourth grade education."[12] Another witness "testified that illegal aliens are generally lower in educational capabilities than legal immigrants. Others testified that illegal aliens are unusually 'overaged and oversized.'"[13] A study indicated that 25% of Mexican children between ages five and fifteen were not in school.[14] For Texas, that explained a sentence in its reply brief about the need to protect Texas's "resources from the indeterminable impact of educating the population of Mexico."[15]

Having satisfied itself that the federal government and Mexico were culpable, Texas turned to its prime legal argument—not about rationality, but instead about the Equal Protection Clause, which reads that no state shall "deny to any person within its jurisdiction the equal protection of the laws." Texas claimed that the undocumented children were not "within its jurisdiction." (Imagine if one of their parents killed someone and defended on the ground that they were not within the jurisdiction of Texas.)

Texas, under Attorney General Mark White, had filed a repulsive brief. It was maybe fit for a political argument about what to do about immigration, but it would not even persuade the already persuaded. Like so many other cases where the state was not represented by Charles Alan Wright at one time or a professional solicitor general at a later date, the attorney general's office unintentionally undermined the state's position.

In *Plyler v. Doe*,[16] like *Rodriguez,* the Court split 5–4, but this time against the state. Blackmun and White switched positions and Powell voted with the majority. In the nine years since *Rodriguez* Blackmun had been moving left and separating himself from his best friend, Chief Justice Warren E. Burger, while the irascible White—thought by President John F. Kennedy to be the ideal New Frontier judge and as a former All-American and National Football League star, the best athlete ever to sit on the bench—was moving right.

As the most senior justice in the majority William J. Brennan kept the opinion for himself. It was a wise decision because either Powell or Blackmun could change his mind and no one was better than Brennan at holding a majority together. The reasons were multiple. He was both smart and well liked. He famously coined the phrase "Five votes can do anything around here."[17] And he had proven again and again he would do anything to hold five votes. His problem, it turned out, was Powell, the author of *Rodriguez.* The two negotiated for three months, with Powell pulling Brennan away from calling the undocumented a suspect class or now declaring education a fundamental right, and Brennan pushing Powell into a more moderate stance on the issues in a way that *Plyler* would be more important than just its result.

The opinion begins by debunking Texas's argument that those who enter the country illegally are not within the jurisdiction "even if they are present within a state and subject to its laws."[18] To accept Texas's positon "would undermine the principal purpose for which the Equal Protection Clause was incorporated in the Fourteenth Amendment. The Equal Protection Clause was intended to work nothing less than the abolition of all caste-based and invidious class-based legislation."[19]

Next Brennan acknowledged that "[p]ersuasive arguments support the view that the State may withhold its beneficence from those whose very presence within the United States is the product of their own unlawful conduct."[20] But this case is about children and they "are not comparably situated" to the adults who illegally cross the border because the children "can affect neither their parents' conduct nor their own status."[21] Penalizing children for a "legal characteristic over which children can have little control" makes it "difficult to conceive of a rational justification" for the Texas law.[22]

Next the opinion moved to the importance of education to assist in leading an economically productive life and to absorb the values of society. "Illiteracy is an enduring disability. The inability to read and write will handicap the individual deprived of a basic education each and every day of his life."[23]

In a part where Powell's influence is quite present, Brennan acknowledges that undocumented children are not a suspect class nor is education a fundamental right. But that sets up the final attack on the Texas argument that the law is rational simply because the children are not legally in the state. The majority stated it was clear that "[c]harging tuition to undocumented children constitutes a ludicrously ineffective attempt to stem the tide of illegal immigration."[24] Indeed, it "is difficult to understand precisely what the State hopes to achieve by promoting the creation and perpetuation of a sub-class of illiterates within our boundaries, surely adding to the problems and costs of unemployment, welfare, and crime."[25]

That was it. It wasn't strict scrutiny by its own admission, but it was something more than rational basis review.

Both Blackmun and Powell joined the opinion but added short con-currences. The former noted *Rodriguez* was properly distinguished because this was an absolute deprivation of a right to education. The lat-ter stressed that the case was unique—so don't think of it as precedent—and, echoing Brennan's opinion, that Texas was close to irrational. "But it hardly can be argued rationally that anyone benefits from the creation within our borders of a subclass of illiterate persons many of whom will remain in the State, adding to the problems and costs of both the State and National Governments attendant upon unemployment, welfare, and crime."[26]

The thrust of Burger's dissent was that the Court was wrongly filling in a political vacuum. "[I]nstead of allowing the political processes to run their course—albeit with some delay—the Court seeks to do Con-gress' job for it, compensation for congressional inaction. It is not unrea-sonable to think that this encourages the political branches to pass their problems to the Judiciary."[27]

Everyone agreed that the Texas policy satisfied the minimal rational basis test. "I assume no Member of this Court would argue that prudent conservation of finite state revenues is *per se* an illegitimate goal."[28] The dissent took some solace from its belief the majority opinion had no legs. "In a sense, the Court's opinion rests on such a unique confluence of theories and rationales that it will likely stand for little beyond the results in these particular cases."[29]

All nine justices had agreed the law was unwise. Thus the dissent began by stating it "agree[d] without hesitation that it is senseless for an enlightened society to deprive any children—including illegal aliens—an elementary education."[30] The justices in the majority proved presci-ent when, just four years later, Congress passed the Simpson-Mazzoli Immigration Reform and Control Act,[31] which overhauled immigra-tion and provided for legal status to the students who Texas did not think deserved an education.

In Texas reactions varied, although the winning lawyer had the most obvious: "We're ecstatic—nothing lower than that."[32] While the Tyler superintendent expressed disappointment, he thought the decision would have little local impact. That was not the case elsewhere, as the *Dallas Morning News* reported the decision "sent shock waves through the state's education system."[33] The Dallas superintendent expected a doubling of undocumented children, but had set aside $2.5 million just in case. Brownsville expected to be the hardest-hit district because of its existing undocumented students, proximity to Matamoros, and low property tax base. In fact that number of Hispanics attending public schools in the county had jumped by over a third in the seven years between 1976 and 1983 and was expected to continue to rise at near that rate for the rest of the decade.[34] Some were undoubtedly undocumented; how many is unclear.

The decision may not have had legs, as Burger happily suggested, but it did restrain other states at future dates from copying the Texas law when the issue of undocumented immigrants became salient. Twenty-five years after the decision came down, James Plyler looked back and stated he was glad he lost because the costs of not educating the children would have been too great.

II

Presidential candidate Barack Obama favored comprehensive immigration reform—soothing words that meant a path to citizenship for immigrants who were undocumented. But with a solid majority in the House and a filibuster-proof majority in the Senate, President Obama had other priorities and never submitted comprehensive legislation to Congress.

There was one immigration bill in that Congress, one that had been around for almost a decade—the DREAM Act. It was a proposal to legalize undocumented immigrants who had been brought to the United States before they were sixteen, had no criminal record, and had lived in the country for a period of years. It passed the House by a 216–198 vote, but failed to avoid a filibuster in the Senate. Alabama

Republican senator Jeff Sessions led the opposition to so-called "amnesty." "This bill is a law that at its fundamental core is a reward for illegal activity."[35] As if the children had the choice of not coming with their parents. The vote in the Senate was 55–41, thus falling five votes short of the necessary 60. Five Democrats voted in the negative. Had all Democrats supported the bill it would have become law. Obama called it "maybe my biggest disappointment" during those first two years.[36]

After the Democratic wipeout in the 2010 mid-term elections, Obama never again had a Democratic majority in the House and never submitted an immigration bill to Congress during the remainder of his presidency. Instead he hoped that Congress would pass a bill on its own that he could sign. Because of this hope he initially limited the executive actions he took with respect to undocumented immigrants, frequently resisting the call to do something with the claim that he lacked power to do so because only Congress can pass laws and that he was not a king.

Then on June 15, 2012—the thirtieth anniversary of *Plyler v. Doe*—the Obama administration announced Deferred Action for Childhood Arrivals (DACA). Using the criteria of the DREAM Act, DACA offered two-year periods whereby someone who qualified under the policy would not face deportation and would have work authorization. DACA covered about 1.4 million immigrants without prior authorization and four years later 742,000 had been approved.

House Republicans howled and tried to defund the program. But the program was self-funding from a $465 application fee. Just as Republicans believed DACA went too far, many Democrats believed it did not go far enough.

Obama, however, claimed he had reached the limits of presidential authority. In a presidential debate with Mitt Romney he stated, "I've done everything that I can on my own."[37] Three months later on Telemundo he was asked about the undocumented mother of three American children and said, "We simply can't ignore the law."[38] He stated, "The problem is that I'm president of the United States, I'm not the emperor of the United States. My job is to execute the laws that are passed. And Congress right now has not changed what I consider to be a broken immigration system."[39] His fallback was that the administration has "stretched our administrative flexibility as much as we can."[40] For the next sixteen months he kept saying the same thing.

Obama's hope was a bipartisan Senate effort—the "Gang of Eight"— that was searching for a filibuster-proof comprehensive immigration bill. The hope was rewarded when the bill passed the Senate. Then on June 9, 2014, House majority whip Kevin McCarthy stated that there were enough Republican votes in the House to pass the bill.

One day later in Richmond, House majority leader Eric Cantor was defeated in a Republican primary by a political unknown. Cantor's support for the Gang of Eight was a, and maybe *the*, key factor. Republicans reacted by fleeing from the Senate bill, and on June 30 House Speaker John Boehner announced that the immigration bill would not be brought up for a vote.

A few hours after Boehner's announcement, Obama, in impromptu remarks in the Rose Garden, promised to "fix as much of our immigration system as I can on my own without Congress."[41] He had been blasting gridlock in Congress and offered it as a justification for action.

Four months later, and two weeks after yet another resounding Democratic defeat at the polls, the Obama administration issued two memoranda on immigration and deportation. The first set deportation priorities: (1) security threats; (2) new immigration violators; and (3) other violators with removal orders. The second memorandum, Deferred Action for Parents of Americans (DAPA), copied DACA for parents. This action allowed four million more undocumented immigrants to work legally because otherwise there would be no lawful way for them to make ends meet. It did not confer legal status, but it did everything else. According to Politico, the White House viewed more than sixty iterations of the policy until it found what it wanted.[42] Obama announced, "I just took an action to change the law."[43] Yet DAPA was what Obama had consistently stated he lacked the power to do.

Had Obama believed what he had been repeating? Perhaps. But if he were telling the truth—and he had said he lacked the power often enough—what part of the Constitution had changed between the end of June and the end of November? My copy stayed the same and nowhere did it state that a failure by a Congress controlled by the opposition party to enact a law transfers to the president the power to do so.

One thing that did change was that Obama obtained an opinion from the Office of Legal Counsel saying that he had the powers in question. The opinion relied on generic statutes, because if there had been one even arguably granting authority Obama would not have spent six years denying he had the power to act. It shows what everyone knows— if a president is adamant about doing something, eventually his lawyers will find a way to say he can do it. That is why Justice Robert Jackson pooh-poohed reliance on his opinions as attorney general under President Franklin Roosevelt when faced with a similar issue on the Court.[44] And Obama's lawyers' opinion goes in the face of the Court's rather sensible observation that "[w]hen an agency claims to discover in a long-extant statute an unheralded power to regulate a significant portion of the American economy" the Court "typically greet[s the] announcement with a measure of skepticism."[45]

The administration noted that Congress only appropriated $6 billion for deportations and that forced the necessity to have broad discretion. But that goes to the priorities memorandum which no one challenged. DAPA went further by giving deferred action status to people "extremely unlikely to be deported."[46]

III

That Texas (and others) would sue was a foregone conclusion. Texas attorney general Greg Abbott started preparing the suit in the summer well before DAPA was finalized, and the suit was filed within two weeks after DAPA was announced. It was also a foregone conclusion that the suit would be filed in the Fifth Circuit that had been remade with the appointees of Ronald Reagan and the two Bushes. The real choice was which federal district court would be chosen. It was in Brownsville where Texas sought a nationwide injunction to prevent implementation of DAPA. The point of forum shopping—which every plaintiff who can does (just wait for challenges to the Trump administration in California)—is to get a court that is already inclined to believe the plaintiff is right. Texas could not miss.

Texas did not miss. Four days before DAPA was to take effect, Judge Andrew S. Hanen—a Baylor law grad who was initially nominated by George H. W. Bush but the nomination had lapsed, so a decade later George W. Bush nominated him successfully—issued the nationwide preliminary injunction, concluding that Texas would prevail on the merits. He then refused to stay his order or limit it to just Texas.[47]

Three months later Jerry Smith, a Reagan appointee, and Jennifer Walker Elrod, a George W. Bush appointee, refused to lift the stay, finding that the immigration provisions cited by the government "cannot reasonably be construed, at least at the early stage of the case, to confer *unreviewable* discretion."[48] Stephen A. Higginson, a former clerk to Bryon White and an Obama appointee, would have granted the stay because he found the case nonjusticiable (meaning no court could decide it). Six months later, on the merits, Smith and Elrod again affirmed Hanen's decision, this time over a dissent by Carolyn King, a Carter appointee.[49]

The United States expeditiously filed its certiorari petition on November 20, 2015, to be sure the petition would be considered in January and if granted the case would be argued in April, normally the last month during which the Court hears arguments before the fall. Texas's response was due thirty days later, but Texas asked for a thirty-day extension, clearly designed to put the case over until the fall. The Court granted Texas nine days only and thus considered the petition in January when it granted cert and added to the questions presented, one under the Take Care Clause that attaches to the president's duty to faithfully execute the laws.

With the addition of the Take Care argument the Court was bringing *Youngstown Sheet and Tube v. Sawyer*[50] into play. The case is more popularly known as the *Steel Seizure Case* due to the fact that President Harry Truman ordered Sawyer, his secretary of commerce, to take over the nation's steel mills in order to prevent a union strike during the Korean War. An expedited appeal to the Court resulted in a 6–3 decision that the president lacked the power in question because Congress, not the president, makes the laws. This conforms nicely to Obama's statements prior to the end of June 2014.

Two concurring opinions were especially salient for DAPA. The first, by William O. Douglas, offered Obama a cautionary note, one I expressed with some frequency during his last two years. "If we sanctioned the present exercise of power by the President, we would be expanding Article II of the Constitution and rewriting it to suit the political conveniences of the present emergency…. Today a kindly President uses the seizure power to effect a wage increase and to keep the steel furnaces in production. Yet tomorrow another President might use the same power to prevent a wage increase, to curb trade-unionists, to regiment labor as industry thinks it has been regimented by this seizure."[51] It is a lesson that ought not be forgotten. A Harry Truman might find one of his successors to be a Richard Nixon and a Barack Obama might find one of his successors someone who could not be trusted with expanded Article II powers.

The second, by Robert H. Jackson, is considered by Constitutional Law professors to be one of the all-time greats. Its credibility is enhanced because Jackson had been there as attorney general in the months before American entry into World War II, justifying FDR's swap of aging navy destroyers for British bases in North America. He knew what enhanced presidential powers looked like.

In what he admitted was "a somewhat oversimplified grouping of practical situations" Jackson outlined three exercises of presidential power.[52] First, when the president acts pursuant to express or implied congressional approval, his powers are at the maximum because they have all the Article I and Article II powers working together. Second, "[w]hen the President acts in the absence of either a Congressional grant or denial of authority, he can only rely on his own independent powers, but there is a zone of twilight in which he and Congress may have concurrent authority, or in which its distribution is uncertain."[53] Third, when the president takes action incompatible with the expressed or implied congressional authority, his powers are at their lowest where he must rely on his own less any that Congress might possess.

Jackson undoubtedly thought that the destroyers for bases swap was a twilight authority situation and that "congressional inertia … may sometimes, at least as a practical matter, enable, if not invite, measures of independent presidential responsibility."[54] That was not the case with Truman's seizure of the steel mills. This was a number three, and Truman's authority could not block out the contrary congressional will.

The twilight zone, recognizing tugging and pulling between branches where authority is uncertain and responsibility rests squarely on the president when he acts, is but one reason why law professors have been so enamored with the eloquent, candid, and astute opinion—"emergency powers would tend to kindle emergencies."[55] My own view is that, however apt the twilight zone was at mid-century, its analysis has been overtaken by the changes in government. There is probably no domestic issue today where the president could credibly claim there is no relevant legislation. Given the incredible volumes of legislation, a court can always find something to say that authorizes the president's action or that forbids the president's action (and in domestic affairs that will be the final word). In other words, the twilight zone is a null set and no case will turn on the constitutional issue because all will become issues of statutory construction.

If my analysis is correct then the issue between Texas and the Obama administration was clearly whether some part of the immigration statutes authorized DAPA as the OLC opinion had concluded. The *New York Times*, however, was outraged at the case, believing it was "a naked political dispute masquerading as a legal one … [where Texas's claim] has never been more than a highly politicized anti-immigrant crusade wrapped in legal briefs."[56] As if no one could question a president's exercise of executive powers in the courts.

At oral argument the United States went first and the conservatives beat up on U.S. solicitor general Donald Verrilli, Jr. Texas followed and the liberals beat up on Texas solicitor general Scott Keller. Antonin Scalia had died between the cert grant and oral argument so an eight-justice Court decided the case. Or not. They split 4–4 and thus affirmed the Fifth Circuit. While the votes were not divulged there seems no doubt that it was a Republican-Democrat split. Had Scalia been able to participate the Fifth Circuit would have been affirmed on the merits. I say this not only because the other Republicans went that way, but also because Scalia attacked DACA four years earlier in *Arizona v. United States.*[57]

In summarizing his dissent that would have sustained all of Arizona's anti–illegal immigrant policies, Scalia gratuitously turned to DACA—which was not before the Court. He did not believe Arizona should be helpless before the "evil effects of illegal immigration."[58] He went on: "[T]o say, as the Court does, that Arizona contradicts federal law by enforcing applications of the Immigration Act that the president declines to enforce boggles the mind."[59] So does attacking a president for a policy not before the Court—something I cannot remember happening before.

Scalia was getting old and bored before our eyes, seemingly auditioning for FOX and Friends[60] and actually attending a private Koch brothers function in Palm Springs. In a 2013 interview he stated that he read two newspapers, the *Wall Street Journal* and the *Washington Times* and listened to talk radio during his commutes. He had canceled his subscription to the *Washington Post* because "it was slanted and often nasty" when dealing with conservative issues.[61] When in the Obamacare oral argument the issue of severability—does one unconstitutional provision render an entire statute void?—came up, Scalia was offended that the justices might be required to read and understand the entire statute. Better just to be rid of the whole thing.

He reminded me of William O. Douglas near the end. Both wrote opinions that anyone could read and played well to nonjudicial audiences. Neither was especially effective with their Brethren. But they sure knew where they stood.

IV

Judge Hanen's injunction against DAPA was but one of five federal district court injunctions issued in Texas that halted Obama administration executive policies in 2015 and 2016. Others included restroom access for transgendered students and a Labor Department rule that would have made over four million Americans eligible for overtime pay. These two came within a week of each other right after the November 2016 election. With conservative district judges and the ultra-conservative Fifth Circuit sitting on appeals (so that no injunction would be stayed), Texas found yet another way to be special.

While DACA remained, Texas attorney general Ken Paxton informed U.S. attorney general Jeff Sessions that the government had little more than two months to reverse it. Otherwise Texas would sue yet again, albeit this time against a Republican administration. Apparently litigious grievances against the federal government are unquenchable and / or good politics. The Trump administration let DACA expire. Whether this will create a future bargain on immigration is unclear.

PART III

Texas and Cultural Issues

Texas, like the rest of the South, turned Republican by the end of the twentieth century when the effects of the Civil Rights Act and the Voting Rights Act were fully realized. But Texas was concerned with issues of morality and order before the state turned Republican. *Roe v. Wade* was litigated at a time when Democrats were in as complete control of Texas as Republicans have been in this century. But as Texas became more Republican, issues of abortion, speech, and religion became more contested and salient. In addition to the already visited areas of federal power and equal protection, the cultural wars have brought to bear the Due Process Clause of the Fourteenth Amendment as well as the Speech and Religion Clauses of the First Amendment. They do this in no small part because civil liberties came to dominate the Court's constitutional docket once fights over economic issues were put to rest by the New Deal revolution.

EIGHT

Freedom of Speech and the Press

Texas license plate designs are often closely identified in the public mind with the [State].

—*Walker v. Texas Division, Sons of Confederate Veterans* (2015)

As you sat there watching these plates speed by, would you really think that the sentiments reflected in these specialty license plates are the view of the State of Texas and not those of the owners of the car? If a car with a plate that says "Rather Be Golfing" passed by at 8:30 am on a Monday morning would you think: "This is the official policy of the State—better to golf than to go to work"?

—Samuel Alito dissenting in *Walker v. Texas Division, Sons of Confederate Veterans* (2015)

Texas cases raising the First Amendment's freedom of speech have varied over the years from informing laborers about unions, to street corner disorders, to flag burning, to what can appear on license plates. But they have one commonality. Texas officials from the legislators to the cops on the beat have a strong penchant toward order.

I

Organized labor has always been weak in Texas. Business leaders like it that way and accommodating legislatures have helped them.

In the 1938 Democratic gubernatorial primary, radio crooner and flour salesman W. Lee "Pappy" O'Daniel overwhelmed a crowded field of twelve to win. O'Daniel ran on a platform of the Ten Commandments, higher pensions, no sales tax, and against professional politicians. He posed as a country boy, but was a wealthy business school graduate secretly backed by some of the richest corporate leaders in the state.

In the late winter of 1941, O'Daniel discovered that "labor leader racketeers," who were supposedly crippling Great Britain's war effort against the Nazis, threatened to take over Texas.[1] It was an interesting observation since not a single man-hour had been lost to strikes in the defense industries. He asked for an immediate joint session of the legislature to pass an anti-violence bill. Although no one had read it, it passed immediately. When read, the bill made picketers using violence against strikebreakers a felony, but strikebreakers using violence against picketers remained a misdemeanor.

After the April 1941 death of Senator Morris Sheppard, O'Daniel ran for the Senate. He claimed that after passage of his anti-violence bill "labor agitators ... , scurried out of Texas overnight. [Yet] radical wild-eyed labor leaders" were supporting his opponent, Congressman Lyndon B. Johnson.[2] After Johnson's only defeat in Texas, it was Senator O'Daniel.

In 1943 the Texas legislature passed the anti-labor Manford Act, named after Speaker Durwood Manford, by votes of 86–37 in the house and 16–7 in the senate. The bill became law without Governor Coke Stevenson's signature. The law's preamble made its purposes clear: "Because of the activities of labor unions affecting the economic conditions of the country and state, entering as they do into practically every business and industrial enterprise, it is the sense of the Legislature that such organizations affect the public interest and are charged with a public use. The working man, unionist or nonunionist, must be protected. The right to work is the right to live."[3] The Manford Act required unions and union agents to register, file comprehensive annual reports, including financial and organizational records, to be open for public inspection, and it forbid political contributions by unions.

The Manford Act was put to immediate use when R.J. Thomas, the president of the United Automobile, Aircraft, and Agricultural Implements Union and vice president of the Congress of Industrial Organizations, made a well-publicized trip from Detroit to Houston to address a mass meeting arranged by the Oil Workers Industrial Union to foster its organizing campaign against Humble Oil and Refining. A day before his speech the state attorney general went to a Travis County judge and obtained an ex parte temporary restraining order against Thomas for soliciting for union members without registering under the Manford Act, which barred solicitation by a paid union employee without prior registration with the secretary of state. The order was served on Thomas six hours before the meeting. He gave his speech anyway. Two days later he was found in contempt for violating the TRO.

The case split the justices and had to be reargued in the following Term. Thomas claimed that any speech by a union executive would necessarily encourage listeners to join a union and such speeches by union personnel were protected by the First Amendment. Texas claimed it was operating under the Police Power "for the protection of the general welfare of the public, and particularly the laboring class."[4] The claim was that it was regulating business activity, not speech, an activity to persuade people to join a union and pay dues. From its perspective, Texas wished to protect its citizens in dealings with those who held themselves out in some professional capacity. It was not a licensing scheme, like law or medicine, just a registration requirement for someone who is paid by a union to solicit membership.

The majority opinion was delivered by Wiley Rutledge, an avid New Dealer whose promising judicial career would be cut short from a stroke in 1949 at age fifty-five. Thomas's speech to some three hundred peaceful listeners discussed "the State's effort, as Thomas conceived it, to interfere with his right to speak and closed with a general invitation to persons present" who were not union members to join.[5] The speech did not address any specific individual, although Thomas did address one person afterward. Was the speech itself solicitation? Of course.

"Workingmen do not lack capacity for making rational connections. They would understand, or some would, that the president of the UAW and vice president of the CIO, addressing an organization meeting, was not urging merely a philosophic attachment to abstract principles of unionization, disconnected from the business immediately at hand."[6] Yet the TRO was anticipatory; it "was issued in explicit anticipation of the speech and to restrain Thomas uttering in its course any language which could be taken as solicitation."[7] Thomas "could avoid the words 'solicit,' 'invite,' 'join.' It would be impossible to avoid the idea."[8]

The TRO's "effect, as applied, in a very practical sense was to prohibit Thomas not only to solicit members and memberships, but also to speak in advocacy of the cause of trade unionism in Texas, without first" registering.[9] That violated the First Amendment's right of freedom of speech.

The fifth vote was provided by Robert Jackson, the finest writer ever to sit on the Court. He recognized the power of the state: "The modern state owes and attempts to perform a duty to protect the public from those who would seek for one purpose or another to obtain its money. When one does so through the practice of a calling, the state may have an interest in shielding the public against the untrustworthy, the incompetent, or the irresponsible, or against unauthorized representation of agency."[10] Licensing is usually the mechanism. He explained that was what Texas was doing. "Here, speech admittedly otherwise beyond the reach of the states is attempted to be brought within its licensing system by associating it with 'solicitation.'"[11] But on balance Thomas's was a public speech "rather than that of practicing a vocation as solicitor. Texas did not wait to see what Thomas would say or do."[12] It just assumed and issued the unconstitutional TRO.

The four dissenters joined an opinion by Owen Roberts, the sole remaining justice who acquired his current position without appointment by President Franklin D. Roosevelt. Unhappy as a Republican on a Democrat-dominated Court, he would retire at the end of the Term. For this case, he accepted and followed Texas's argument.

The winning counsel was Lee Pressman. During the CIO's purge of communists in 1948, he would be fired. As it turned out, he had been a Soviet agent as part of the Ware group (with Alger Hiss and Whittaker Chambers) in the Department of Agriculture in the 1930s.

II

During the hysteria of McCarthyism, in a 1954 special session Texas passed the Suppression Act, which complemented the 1951 Texas Communist Control Act (that had required members of the Communist Party to register with the Department of Public Safety). Among other offenses, the act criminalized (with a penalty of twenty years) the possession of writings relating to the Communist Party. Having labeled Communist activity similar to treason, Governor Allan Shivers stated his intent was "to crush them under our heel every way we can."[13]

After the 1951 law passed, John Stanford of San Antonio mailed a four-page open letter to Attorney General Price Daniel and Homer Garrison, Jr., director of the Department of Public Safety, declaring that he was a member of the Communist Party and that he had no intent to register. The rambling letter gave several reasons why he opposed the recently passed law, the most cogent being that it violated state and federal constitutional guarantees. The Communist Party decided it could not afford a legal defense and sent him into hiding in Alabama.

Years later, after moving back to Texas, local San Antonio law enforcement officers obtained a search warrant for Stanford's home and conducted a more than four-hour search, seizing around two thousand books, pamphlets, and writings, but nothing relating to Stanford being a member of the Communist Party. The officers seized books by Karl Marx, Fidel Castro, and former American Communist Party head Earl Browder (who Stalin had ordered replaced). They also seized books by Jean-Paul Sartre and Theodore Draper. Most tellingly, however, they seized writings by Pope John XXIII and Supreme Court Justice Hugo L. Black.

Stanford moved to suppress the warrant and for return of the books. The judge who issued the search warrant denied the motion and there was no available appeal to a Texas court, so Stanford, assisted by Maury Maverick, Jr. (who had cast a rare vote against the Suppression Act and against the call to impeach Justice William O. Douglas over his *Tidelands* vote) and the American Civil Liberties Union, went to the Supreme Court, which reversed. In a unanimous opinion Potter Stewart chose not to state the obvious—government has no legitimate interest in the contents of a private library—and instead attacked the legality of the search warrant.[14] Stewart analogized what was issued in San Antonio to the general warrants issued prior to the American Revolution. Those constituted a major reason for the Fourth Amendment's prohibition on unreasonable searches and seizures and that was enough to block the search of Stanford's home (which was his place of business).

Attorney General Wagner Carr expressed displeasure at the result, but only Stanford's local paper ran a story about the decision that in addition to noting Carr's opinion stated Stanford was pleased but not surprised by the result.[15] Stanford subsequently became secretary of what must have been a miniscule Texas Communist Party and continued that position into this century. He died at the age of eighty-eight in 2013.

III

Wiley Rutledge had emphasized the peaceful nature of the union rally Thomas addressed in 1943. When, three decades later, the Court next addressed a Texas labor dispute the issue was violence. It came during a farmworkers' strike in the lower Rio Grande Valley that commenced in June 1966 and was effectively over by the time Hurricane Beulah permanently ended it in September 1967 with no gains and no union contracts for the strikers.

There were many reasons why the strike failed.[16] It was led by Californians with no real knowledge of the Valley and called without the preparation that had gone into Cesar Chavez's California strike. "Green card" Mexicans came across the border as strikebreakers. Religious leaders who supported the strike turned it into a broader claim for equal justice and political status for Hispanics. Money and interest waned over time. Perhaps most importantly, the Starr County law enforcement officials called in the Texas Rangers, and they and local law enforcement officers used violence and intimidation on behalf of the growers. The sheriff's office regularly distributed an anti-union newspaper, and one Ranger told a striker that they had been called in to break the strike and would not leave until they had done so. Almost seven years after the strike ended, the Supreme Court ruled on the violence of the Rangers.

Not only was the strike gone, but by the time the Court decided *Allee v. Medrano*[17] several of the statutes at issue in the proceedings had been repealed. But the charges that law enforcement used illegal arrests and detentions, coercions and violence in order to prevent the strikers' exercise of First Amendment rights of free speech and assembly remained along with an injunction against several Rangers prohibiting them from engaging in the future in a number of unlawful practices: "using their authority as peace officers to arrest, stop, disperse, or imprison appellees, or otherwise interfere with their organizational efforts without 'adequate cause.'"[18]

The Rangers argued that the case was moot because the strike was long since over. Justice William O. Douglas answered that just because the Rangers' harassment had been successful in forcing the plaintiffs to abandon the strike did not moot the case. "There can be no requirement that appellees continue to subject themselves to physical violence and unlawful restrictions on their liberties throughout the pendency of the action in order to preserve it as a live controversy."[19] As that sentence indicated, the Court knew the Rangers' behavior had been unlawful and the injunction was appropriate because it "does no more than require police to abide by constitutional requirements; and there is no contention that this decree would interfere with law enforcement by restraining the police from engaging in conduct that would otherwise be lawful."[20]

Throughout the first two-thirds of the twentieth century the Texas Rangers had been strikebreakers. As one Ranger recounted in an oral history: "There was a cliché that people would always say to me, and that was 'Every Texas Ranger has Mexican blood' and then they would pause and add 'on the tips of their boots.'"[21] After *Allee v. Medrano* peaceful exercise of First Amendment rights by strikers was off-limits to the Rangers and their days as strikebreakers were at an end. In 1975, Allee's son tried to get the Rangers involved in breaking a strike in Presidio organized by Cesar Chavez, but his superiors flatly refused, telling him, "We saw what mess your dad got us into before."[22]

IV

In July 1975, during late-afternoon rush hour, there was a minor traffic accident on a busy street in downtown Austin. A driver pulled alongside and said, "Get your fucking car out of the way. You're blocking traffic." This upset the woman in the other car and she asked the driver to give her his car's license number and then leave. He did so, she noted, in a very civil manner.

Several weeks later, Louis C. Acker received notice that a criminal complaint had been filed against him for the incident. He was tried in municipal court and appeared pro se. When convicted he "appealed" to the county court-at-law for a trial de novo. There Judge Mary Pearl Williams of the Travis County Court-at-Law Number Two, and wife of UT law professor (and eventual Fifth Circuit judge) Jerre Williams, presided over Acker's trial for disorderly conduct, a Class C misdemeanor, for using "abusive, indecent, profane, or vulgar language in a public place, and the language by its very utterance tends to incite an immediate breach of the peace." She stated, "These are fighting words," convicted Acker, and fined him $75.[23] Under Texas law a Class C misdemeanor conviction cannot be appealed when the fine is less than $100. Accordingly, Acker appealed directly to the Supreme Court, claiming his First Amendment rights had been violated.

The risk was that the case would look so trivial that the Court would just ignore it. To show there was more to it, Acker's lawyer, William Allison, head of UT's Criminal Defense Clinic, urged the Court to take a look at the invisible part of the criminal justice system, decisions of municipal courts, where minor penalties are imposed and appellate review is absent.[24] Claims of abusive language as the case showed always have a potential to infringe on First Amendment rights. Extrapolating from Austin statistics Allison claimed, "it can reasonably be deduced that except for traffic offenses and intoxication charges, more people are brought to bar in our lower court systems to answer for 'speech' crimes than any other category."[25] Often the defendant will not have a lawyer and the judges themselves may not be attorneys.

Judge Williams's conclusion that Acker spoke fighting words was absurd in fact and wrong in law. The drivers never left their cars, and there was no chance of a fight. Furthermore, several years earlier, in *Cohen v. California*[26] the Court held that "fuck" without more could not be criminalized, and it followed *Cohen* with a handful of cases that made clear that offending the "sensibilities" of listeners was not enough to turn "fuck" into fighting words.[27] Accordingly Acker's convicted was summarily overturned without opinion.[28]

V

Ray Hill has been a gay-rights activist most of his adult life. He recalls coming out to his parents when he was eighteen. His mother's reaction: "What a relief. We noticed that you kind of dress up more than the other boys in the neighborhood and we thought you were pretending to be wealthy and we aren't. We were afraid you might grow up to be a Republican."[29] Hill was a big man who had several run-ins with the police. Indeed, he was arrested (but never convicted) four times under a Houston ordinance making it unlawful "for any person to assault, strike, or in any manner oppose, molest, abuse or interrupt any policeman in the execution of his duty." One of the arrests came when he saw two policemen confronting a friend who had stopped traffic on a busy street to allow another vehicle to enter. Although the testimony of one of the cops and Hill diverged (as often happens) they did agree the officer asked Hill if he were interrupting him in his official capacity as a Houston police officer. Hill responded yes and to the effect why didn't the cop pick on someone his own size, Hill being six feet tall and weighing two hundred pounds. After being acquitted in a nonjury trial, Hill sued in federal court to have the ordinance declared unconstitutional.

The district court rejected Hill's claim, but the Fifth Circuit reversed. The city then requested the Fifth Circuit hear the case en banc and the court agreed. It broke 8–7 in favor of Hill.[30] The city then appealed to the Supreme Court and after the Court agreed to hear the case Hill's attorney brought in Charles Alan Wright to brief and argue the case for Hill. With eleven Supreme Court arguments under his belt and huge victories like *San Antonio ISD v. Rodriguez*[31] Hill was in exceptionally good hands.

Justice William J. Brennan delivered the opinion affirming Hill's victory.[32] He found the Houston ordinance could reach too much constitutionally protected speech and gave too much discretion to the police to arrest or not (especially when the two sides would present conflicting testimony about the encounter). The ordinance had been "employed for making arrests for, *inter alia,* 'arguing,' 'talking,' 'interfering,' 'failing to remain silent,' 'refusing to remain silent,' 'verbal abuse,' 'cursing,' 'verbally yelling,' and 'talking loudly.' "[33]

Houston claimed that speech challenging police officers was not constitutionally protected. Quoting a 1949 case, the Court asserted, "Speech is often provocative and challenging."[34] The sweep of the ordinance, reaching speech that "in any manner ... interrupts" an officer was just too much. "The freedom of individuals verbally to oppose or challenge police action without thereby risking arrest is one of the principal characteristics by which we distinguish a free nation from a police state."[35] Thus in closing the Court, as it often does, praised the First Amendment, which "recognizes, wisely we think, that a certain amount of expressive disorder not only is inevitable in a society committed to individual freedom, but must be protected if that freedom is to survive."[36]

VI

Acker and *Hill* were minor cases affecting lots of people. *Texas v. Johnson*[37] was a major case affecting but a handful of people (if that).

During the 1984 Republican National Convention in Dallas, about a hundred demonstrators came to protest what they feared would be nuclear war. They staged "die-ins and on several occasions spray-painted buildings. At one such building a demonstrator took the American flag from a flagpole. He gave the flag to Gregory Lee Johnson who doused it with kerosene and set it ablaze while a crowd chanted 'America, the red, white, and blue, we spit on you.'"[38] Johnson was the only demonstrator charged with a crime. He was convicted of flag desecration under Texas law for the burning of the flag, not the insulting words about it.

In a shocker, the Texas Court of Criminal Appeals held Johnson's conviction was unconstitutional by a 5–4 vote. When the case went to the Supreme Court, the Dallas County district attorney's office continued to argue the case, but Johnson replaced his lawyers with the radical lawyer William Kunstler, who was well known for representing unpopular—to say the least—lefty clients and causes. David Cole, who would soon join the Georgetown University Law Center faculty, wrote the brief for Johnson, and Kunstler tracked its argument, having already watched a nervous Kathi Alyce Drew trying to defend the Texas law.

The flag had been a tricky issue for the Court, blurring the lines between liberal and conservative. Prior to *Texas v. Johnson* Justices William O. Douglas, William J. Brennan, Thurgood Marshall, joined by Potter Stewart, had protected abusing the flag in demonstrations. But Chief Justice Earl Warren, and Justices Hugo Black, Abe Fortas, joined by Byron R. White and conservatives Warren E. Burger and William

Rehnquist, voted the other way. If a justice saw a case as about the First Amendment, then he—Justice Sandra O'Connor had yet to participate in a flag case—would vote to favor the First Amendment. If he saw the case as being about the flag, then he would reject the First Amendment claim. That same confusing split and pull showed up again in the final 5–4 vote. Antonin Scalia was in the majority; John Paul Stevens was a dissenter. Brennan kept the opinion for himself.

There was little difficulty in determining that burning the flag was expression for purposes of the First Amendment. For the majority the question was the strengths of the two Texas justifications for the prohibition. The first was preventing breaches of the peace, but none occurred and the Court had consistently held mere fear of breach of the peace was not enough. The dissenters did not dispute this.

The second justification was preserving the flag as a symbol of nationhood and national unity. As Brennan rephrased the Texas concern: "The State, apparently, is concerned that such conduct will lead people to believe either that the flag does not stand for nationhood or national unity, but instead reflects other, less positive concepts, or the concepts reflected in the flag do not in fact exist, that is, that we do not enjoy unity as a Nation."[39] Texas also argued for a flag exception to the First Amendment: "Quoting extensively from the writings of this Court chronicling the flag's historic role in our society, the State emphasizes the 'special place' reserved for the flag in our Nation."[40] The Court, fearing a slippery slope, would not go there.

The opinion turned preachy as its end. "We are tempted to say, in fact, that the flag's deservedly cherished place in our community will be strengthened, not weakened, by our holding today. Our decision is a reaffirmation of the principles of freedom and inclusiveness that the flag best reflects.... The way to preserve the flag's special role is not to punish those who feel differently about these matters. It is to persuade them that they are wrong."[41] Good luck with that.

Chief Justice Rehnquist, joined by White and O'Connor, started his dissent with his conclusion. "For more than 200 years, the American flag has occupied a unique position as the symbol of our Nation, a uniqueness that justifies a governmental prohibition on flag burning."[42] Rehnquist noted that Johnson's act "obviously did convey Johnson's bitter dislike for his country," but that thought "conveyed nothing that could not have been conveyed … just as forcefully a dozen different ways."[43] Having said the message and noted alternatives, in the very next paragraph he called it "an inarticulate grunt or roar."[44] Rehnquist was so upset by Johnson's act he couldn't think straight.

Rehnquist also wrote the flag "does not represent the views of any particular political party, and it does not represent any particular political philosophy."[45] Perhaps he forgot that he served in the Nixon administration, which started the habit of wearing a small enameled replica of the flag in the suit lapel—to represent support for the administration's continuation of the Vietnam War.

Stevens dissented alone, calling the question "unique" and therefore previous precedents were "inapplicable."[46] He would create a flag exception to the First Amendment because "The value of the flag as a symbol cannot be measured."[47]

Stevens wrote a powerful closing: "The ideas of liberty and equality have been an irresistible force in motivating leaders like Patrick Henry, Susan B. Anthony, and Abraham Lincoln, school teachers like Nathan Hale and Booker T. Washington, the Philippine Scouts who fought at Bataan, and the soldiers who scaled the bluff at Omaha Beach. If those ideas are worth fighting for—and our history demonstrates that they are—it cannot be true that the flag that uniquely symbolizes their power is not itself worthy of protection from unnecessary desecration."[48]

There were three World War II veterans on the Court. All three were dissenters.

The reaction to the case was swift and overwhelmingly negative. President George H. W. Bush went to the Iwo Jima Memorial to denounce the decision and he proposed a constitutional amendment to overturn it. The Senate passed, by a 97–3 vote, a resolution expressing profound disappointment in the decision. The House passed a similar resolution 411–5. One might have thought that with such support a constitutional amendment would have been sent to the states. Instead, at the urging of people such as Harvard's Laurence Tribe, Congress passed the Flag Protection Act to overturn *Texas v. Johnson*.

A year later the federal act was at the Court with Kunstler again defending protestors and Solicitor General Kenneth Starr arguing for the government. Not a single vote changed as the statute was held a violation of the First Amendment.[49] With the right to burn a flag established, no one bothered to do so until Donald Trump was elected president. And Trump reacted—on Twitter of course—by suggesting a loss of citizenship for those who burn the flag.

VII

In 1917 Arizona became the first state to add a graphic on its license plates. Two years later Texas added the Lone Star emblem to its plates. In 1928 Idaho became the first state to add a slogan—"Idaho Potatoes"— to its plates. Subsequently, Texas followed, adding "Centennial" in 1936. In later years it has placed "Hemisfair 68," "150 Years of Statehood," "Read to Succeed," and "Texans Conquer Cancer" as well as "Keep Texas Beautiful." Finally, in the 1990s Texas began offering specialty plates that contain the state name, but have privately created designs for nonprofits that are approved by the state.

Walker v. Texas Division, Sons of Confederate Veterans[50] involved the rejection of a specialty plate with SONS OF CONFEDERATE VETERANS in bold script as well as the Confederate battle flag. The Department of Motor Vehicles Board, which considers specialty plates, twice denied the Sons their request, stating "that a significant portion of the public associate the confederate flag with organizations advocating expressions of hate directed toward people or groups that is demeaning to those people or groups."[51] The conclusion seemed inconsistent with a state holiday, Confederate Heroes Day, celebrating the birthdays of Robert E. Lee and Jefferson Davis.[52] On the capitol grounds there are monuments to Confederate Soldiers, Terry's Texas Rangers, and Hood's Brigade. Inside the capitol, on the floor under the rotunda, is an emblem symbolizing Texas's role in the Confederacy. And in the capitol gift shop one can purchase miniature Confederate flags and replica Confederate currency. But that's the capitol, not the DMV.

SCV brought suit, lost in the district court, but prevailed in the Fifth Circuit.[53] The case pitted R. James George, a UT grad, Thurgood Marshall clerk, and the top First Amendment lawyer in the state, against the much younger state solicitor general, Scott Keller, who was having a very active time arguing before the Court.

The Court's existing doctrine was procrustean. When the state speaks, the First Amendment is totally inapplicable. When the state opens up speech opportunities for private individuals, it must not discriminate among what is said except in a very few specific categories of which giving offense is not one. Keller's job was to make a license plate Texas's speech no matter what it said. George's job was to convince the justices that Texas had ceded control over specialty plates and opened a limited public forum in which it could not discriminate. Both men did what was necessary, but George was heavily criticized by Supreme Court correspondents for not offering a limiting principle to no discrimination. The criticism was unfair because the doctrine does not include one and if he suggested one it might be used to defeat his client. For both sides absolutism was the order of the day because it offered the path to victory. The problem for both was that the license plate partook of both government and private speech and the doctrines were all or nothing.

The key precedent was *Pleasant Grove City v. Summun*.[54] The city had accepted a number of private donations of monuments in its Pioneer Park including a Ten Commandments monument donated by the Fraternal Order of Eagles (celebrating the Cecile B. deMille film *The Ten Commandments* starring Charlton Heston as Moses) as part of an effort to combat juvenile delinquency. Summun, a religious group, wished to donate a monument to the Seven Aphorisms that it believed were presented by God to Moses. The city refused and the Court agreed, holding that permanent monuments in a public park were government speech. If it were otherwise the city would either be faced with an influx of clutter in the parks or else with removing long-standing existing monuments.

The Court's all-or-nothing doctrine set up the absurd question: is a license plate more like a monument in a public park or a speaker in that park? The Court split 5–4 on the question with Stephen Breyer's majority holding the former and Samuel Alito, the author of *Summun,* writing for the dissenters.

Breyer attended Oxford and then Harvard Law School, after which he clerked for Justice Arthur Goldberg. He joined the Harvard faculty and became one of the country's leading scholars of administrative law. In the Carter administration he became chief counsel of the Senate Judiciary Committee before moving to the First Circuit Court of Appeals. Back when Congress may have deserved respect, Breyer was the only justice who did respect the legislative branch because he was the only one with exposure to the congressional process.

Alito was from Princeton and Yale law, who after time with the Reagan Justice Department and as a federal prosecutor was appointed by George H.W. Bush to the Third Circuit Court of Appeals, where he became a tribune of the powerful. He adhered closely to culturally conservative views, which caused him to support First Amendment claims when they lined up with those views and oppose them when they did not.

Breyer stated that the majority's "reasoning rests primarily on our analysis in *Summun.*"[55] The history of license plates shows "they have long communicated messages from the States."[56] That is true for Texas, too, and Texas "license plate designs 'are often closely identified in the public mind with the [State].'"[57] That internal quote was interesting. Was Breyer quoting from the findings of fact at the trial court or from a witness at trial? The answer is neither; he was quoting from *Summun.* But whether "license plates are closely identified in the public mind with" Texas is a factual question that cannot be answered by stating that permanent monuments in a public park in Utah are identified with the government. Breyer went on to assert that a driver with specialty plates "likely intends to convey to the public that the State has endorsed that message."[58] Again there is no proof and one wonders why Texas would endorse the "University of Alabama," which is an available specialty plate as is "Rather Be Golfing." Indeed, if Texas officials were endorsing the University of Alabama a good bet would be that they would be replaced as quickly as possible. Texas is, after all, Texas.

Breyer's conclusion is also at odds with a 1977 opinion involving New Hampshire putting the state motto "Live Free or Die" on all noncommercial license plates. There the Court held that citizens could blot the message out because they did not wish to be associated with it.[59] Their rights not to speak prevailed over the state, even though no one would think that a slogan on all license plates would represent the views of all owners.

"The specialty plates here in question are similar enough to the monuments in *Summun* to call for the same result."[60] The license plates are not traditional public forums like streets and parks. They aren't a designated public forum because the state maintains final control. "Of course, Texas allows many more license plate designs than the city in *Summun* allowed monuments."[61] But *Summun* did not turn on numbers.

Alito took apart the twin pillars of Breyer's reasoning: that the messages are those of the state and that license plates are like monuments. Alito had great fun with "Rather Be Golfing." "As you sit there watching these plates speed by, would you really think that the sentiments reflected in these specialty plates are the views of the State of Texas and not those of the owners of the cars? If a car with the plate that says 'Rather Be Golfing' passed by at 8:30am on a Monday morning, would you think: 'This is the official policy of the State—better to golf than to work?'"[62] He then referred to a plate reading NASCAR -24 Jeff Gordon: "Would you think that Gordon (born in California, raised in Indiana, resides in North Carolina) is the official favorite of the State government?"[63]

Alito saw Texas plates as "little billboards."[64] The state sells them to raise money, and people pay that money not to spread a message of the state but to express themselves. The billboard analogy also received support from the facts. Until the 1990s Texas had controlled the messages on plates, but then made the financial decision to open up messages through private created specialty plates. With that decision "Texas crossed the line."[65]

As to *Summun*,[66] since ancient times governments and rulers "have used monuments as a means of expressing a government message."[67] They use government property to do so. The monuments are permanent not transitory. As operated by the DMV there does not appear to be the selective receptivity of cities accepting monuments when it comes to adding new specialty plates. And there are a limited number of monuments that a park can accommodate—far fewer than the potential of millions of Texas cars.

Besides Alito besting Breyer by miles there are two things that stand out in the decision. First, the vote. Breyer was joined by Ruth Bader Ginsburg, Sonia Sotomayor, and Elena Kagan. Makes sense. Alito was joined by Kennedy, Scalia, and John Roberts. Makes sense. When the Court splits like that, everyone knows Thomas will be there with his conservative Republican brethren. But he wasn't, raising the question of why he was with the majority and not with his natural allies? If there is an answer that is not antipathy to the Confederate battle flag, it escapes me.

This was Keller's first victory at the Court and Attorney General Ken Paxton congratulated him. Paxton observed that the decision "confirms that citizens cannot compel the government to speak just as the government cannot compel citizens to speak."[68] Congressman Al Green of Houston stated, "an endorsement of the Confederate flag has no place in office government speech."[69] Jim George had a solution to make the First Amendment work and keep the Confederate flag off license plates: "The answer is for the state to get out of the silly business of selling advertising on license plates in the first place."[70]

The Court's timing was as good as it gets. Shortly after the case came down, the horrific shooting killing nine in the historic black church in Charleston occurred. The revulsion against the Confederate flag was so intense that South Carolina's Republican governor, Nikki Haley, urged the legislature to bring down the Confederate flag from the state capitol grounds because it was a symbol of hate for too many of the state's citizens. Three weeks later the legislature agreed. One of those voting yes was longtime state senator Paul Thurmond, son of Strom Thurmond: "I found myself trying to defend it, as everyone else does. How do you defend it? And I just flat out couldn't."[71]

VIII

Two years after Lee Harvey Oswald assassinated President John F. Kennedy and was in turn murdered (on television) by Jack Ruby, the nation got a further look at the problem of whether too much publicity about a crime could preclude a defendant from receiving a fair trial. The so-called "fair trial–free press" issue dominated legal discussions well into the next decade.

Billie Sol Estes, a good-old-boy from West Texas, was a con man on a grand scale. His agricultural scams were incredibly complex, and he made the cover of *Time*, albeit not for positive reasons, while still in his thirties. The law caught up to him during the Kennedy administration and he was convicted in federal court for mail fraud and state court for swindling.

In Estes's state trial, photographers had been allowed in the courtroom, and parts of his pretrial hearing and the trial itself were televised. This, he claimed, had denied him due process of law. When his case came to the Court only the necessary four votes—Chief Justice Earl Warren plus Douglas, Harlan, and Brennan—wanted to hear the case. On the merits, dealing with what they saw as the brand new and powerful medium of television, the justices split along no recognizable lines.

Undoubtedly because of his duties as chairman of the commission looking into the Kennedy assassination, Warren had exceptionally strong views. He believed that cameras in a courtroom constituted a per se violation of the Due Process Clause. Douglas agreed. Harlan and

Arthur Goldberg refused to go that far, but nevertheless agreed that on the facts Estes had been denied a fair trial.

The odd combination of Black, Tom Clark, Brennan, Stewart, and White voted to affirm the conviction. They believed that with a sequestered jury no prejudice had been shown. Black saw the situation as "a new thing that's working itself out."[72] As senior justice in the majority he assigned the opinion to Stewart.

Warren in the meantime went to work on his own dissent—twice the length of *Brown v. Board of Education*[73]—and thereafter successfully persuaded Clark to switch, thereby creating a majority to reverse. Clark wrote an opinion for the Court which can be read to hold that cameras always denied the defendant a fair trial; but it did not, in fact, go so far (because Clark wished to save that issue for another day).[74] Warren's dissent, now a concurrence, did go all the way.

Despite his victory, Estes did not go free. His federal conviction for mail fraud stood, and he served six of his fifteen years, being released in 1971. At the end of the decade he was again convicted of mail fraud, sentenced to ten years but freed in 1983. He lived another three decades, and just like John Stanford, died in 2013 at the age of eighty-eight.

NINE

Freedom of and from Religion

This act reverses the Supreme Court's decision *Employment Division v. Smith.*
> —President Clinton on signing the Religious Freedom Restoration Act

Texans are a religious people. Religion has been the backbone of the state's position on abortion and gay rights. It has also been a force for keeping God out in the public. In 2011, with Texas mired in its worst drought in at least a century, Governor Rick Perry designated April 22 to April 24 as official days of prayer for rain. (That didn't stop the drought.)

Texas exempted periodical subscriptions from its sales tax. Then in a striking example of a preference for religion, the law was changed to exempt only "periodicals that are published or distributed by a religious faith and that consist wholly of writings promulgating the teaching of that faith." *Texas Monthly* paid the tax but sued for a refund, and while the Supreme Court split on why the exemption was unconstitutional a majority held it was, with a plurality concluding it violated the Establishment Clause by lacking a secular purpose.[1] What the Court should have said was there never should be a sales tax on, as every cover proclaims, "the national magazine of Texas"—especially its barbeque issues.

I

Alfred Smith and Galen Black were Native Americans who ingested peyote as a sacrament in the Native American Church even though use of peyote was criminalized by the state. They were fired from their jobs working for a private drug rehabilitation company and applied for unemployment compensation. That was refused because the commission deemed their firings were for cause. At the Supreme Court they claimed that on the facts Oregon lacked a compelling state interest and hence the denial of compensation was an unconstitutional infringement on their rights of free exercise of religion as protected by the First Amendment. The Court, through Justice Antonin Scalia, rejected their claim. "If 'compelling interest' really means what it says ... many laws will not meet the test. Any society adopting such a system would be courting anarchy, but the danger increases in direct proportion to the society's diversity of religious [beliefs]. Precisely because 'we are a cosmopolitan nation made up of people of almost every conceivable religious preference,' and precisely because we value and protect that religious divergence, we cannot afford the luxury of deeming *presumptively invalid,* as applied to a religious objector, every regulation of conduct that does not protect an interest of the highest order."[2] The state could enact a religious exemption to its general laws (if it wishes), but the Free Exercise Clause does not require it to do so.[3] Four justices objected to what they viewed as the Court's backing away from three decades of Free Exercise law.

Jewish groups, Protestant groups, and some civil libertarians like the American Civil Liberties Union and People for the American Way were taken aback by a decision using America's religious diversity as a rationale to limit religious freedom. These groups quickly coalesced in an umbrella organization called the Coalition for the Free Exercise of Religion and, working with New York congressman Stephen Solarz, produced the Religious Freedom Restoration Act (RFRA) designed to require courts to apply the compelling state interest test in cases where a party asserts a religious defense. RFRA was justified under Section 5 of the Fourteenth Amendment: "The Congress shall have the power to enforce, by appropriate legislation, the provisions of this article." Because the Free Exercise Clause was protected by Section 1 of the Fourteenth Amendment, Congress could enforce that protection by Section 5 legislation.

RFRA was introduced in the 101st Congress with bipartisan support in both chambers. Hearings were held by a subcommittee of the House Judiciary Committee, but no other action was taken before the Congress adjourned. One reason may have been the opposition of the Catholic Church, which was worried that the bill would allow women to seek exemptions from restrictive anti-abortion laws. It also had concerns over a long-running battle over tax-exempt status.

RFRA was reintroduced in the 102nd Congress along with a companion bill designed to meet the Catholic concerns. It was reported out of the House Judiciary Committee, but with the presidential election just weeks away no action was taken.

Unlike George H. W. Bush, Bill Clinton was an enthusiastic supporter of RFRA. Furthermore, the climate was better. Catholic opposition had lessened because the Court had reaffirmed *Roe v. Wade*[4] and so new restrictive anti-abortion laws would not be sustained.[5] Furthermore, the Coalition for the Free Exercise of Religion had grown and the act faced no serious opposition except for prison officials who wished to be exempted. No House member spoke against it. In the Senate the prison exemption came to a vote but failed 41–58. Then the bill passed 97–3. When President Clinton signed the law, he accurately noted, "this act reverses the Supreme Court's decision *Employment Division v. Smith.*"[6] The goal was achieved and the compelling state interest test restored when courts faced a free exercise defense.

Clinton was but one of those cheering RFRA. Vice President Al Gore called the act "one of the most important steps to reaffirm religious freedom in my lifetime."[7] The *New York Times* editorialized that the act "reasserts a broadly accepted American concept of giving wide latitude to religious practices that many might regard as odd or unconventional."[8] Few seemed bothered that, like the effort to recriminalize flag burning, Congress was brushing aside a constitutional decision of the Supreme Court by a simple statute. Those few, however, included the justices of the Court.

II

In the extensive testimony to the two judiciary committees the only active threat to religious liberties pointed out was historic zoning, and, fittingly, the case heard by the Court, *City of Boerne v. Flores,*[9] involved historic zoning. In 1992 Boerne, some thirty miles northwest of San Antonio, created a historic preservation district. St. Peter's Catholic Church, built in 1923 in a style that replicates the mission style from the region's earlier history, was within the district, and according to the chair of the city's Historic Landmark Commission, it was "a drawing card [to attract tourists] for the whole city."[10]

Just as San Antonio was gaining population, so was Boerne. St. Peter's could seat 230 people, but its congregation exceeded its capacity at mass each Sunday and Archbishop P.F. Flores of San Antonio gave the church permission to expand to hold 700. The proposal, presented to the Historic Landmark Commission and then city council, was to maintain the façade but demolish 80 percent of the rest of the church. The church's request was denied. The chair of the commission stated "We would like you to build a new church, but don't touch a rock of the old one."[11] With more practicing Catholics than seating capacity, the church moved mass to a former high school gymnasium that was a senior citizens center, hardly an optimal solution, but St. Peter's remained a tourist attraction aiding local businesses.

Flores then sued, relying on RFRA. A district court held RFRA unconstitutional, but the Fifth Circuit reversed. Flores was represented by Douglas Laycock, a UT law professor and more relevantly the nation's leading scholar on the Religion Clauses. His spontaneous amicus brief at the Fifth Circuit had abruptly ended litigation to prevent collection of taxes for public schools (as discussed in chapter 6). He had condemned *Employment Division v. Smith* and testified in favor of RFRA before both the House and Senate Judiciary Committees. He was also winning counsel in the one major post-*Smith* case. The City of Hialeah had passed an animal cruelty ordinance that banned "ritual slaughter" of animals and thus prevented members of the Santeria religion from sacrificing chickens as their sacrament. The Court held the ordinance was not neutral and was passed to single out one religious practice and therefore was a violation of the Free Exercise Clause.[12] You could eat a Chicken McNugget in Hialeah, but not sacrifice a chicken to your god. (And a chicken was sacrificed in Laycock's honor, surely the only law professor to achieve that distinction.)

Laycock was joined in oral argument with former Duke law professor and current acting solicitor general Walter Dellinger. Marci Hamilton, a Yeshiva law professor and former O'Connor clerk, argued for Boerne and she was joined by Jeffrey Sutton, a recent Scalia clerk who took the job as solicitor general of Ohio. (He is now on the Sixth Circuit.) This was real talent on both sides.

There were numerous amicus briefs filed on both sides. Given the behavior of subsequent attorneys general Greg Abbott and Ken Paxton in challenging the federal government at every turn, then-attorney general Dan Morales, a Democrat, opposed the City of Boerne and instead argued that RFRA was an appropriate exercise of congressional power. Religion trumped state's rights.

There were more anti-RFRA votes on the Court than there had been in the entire Congress. Seven justices explicitly rejected the assertion that Congress could overrule the Court. David Souter and Stephen Breyer, despite his deference to Congress, did not commit one way or the other, leaving the question for a future day (that has yet to come). Souter, Breyer, along with Sandra Day O'Connor, wanted to revisit (and overrule) *Smith,* but the passage of RFRA had made that outcome look like a capitulation to outside pressures. The Court does not like to be seen doing that.[13]

Hamilton and Sutton argued that RFRA put separation of powers at risk because Congress was exercising its remedial powers under Section 5 to change the meaning of a right under Section 1. Anthony Kennedy, for the majority, agreed. "Legislation which alters the meaning of the Free Exercise Clause cannot be said to be enforcing that Clause. Congress does not enforce a constitutional right by changing what the right is."[14] The superiority of the Constitution to legislation allowed the Court to bring the hallowed *Marbury v. Madison*[15] into the argument. "If Congress could define its own powers by altering the Fourteenth Amendment's meaning, no longer would the Constitution be 'superior paramount law, unchangeable by ordinary means.' It would be 'on a level with ordinary legislative acts, and, like other acts, ... alterable when the legislature shall please to alter it.' *Marbury v. Madison*."[16]

If the compelling state interest test were applied to all laws affecting religious activity, "Laws valid under *Smith* would fall under RFRA without regard to whether they had the object of stifling or punishing free exercise. We make these observations ... to illustrate the substantive alteration of its holding attempted by RFRA."[17]

Laycock and Dellinger had relied, as they had to, on cases involving the right to vote where Congress was able to declare unenforceable state laws that were nevertheless constitutional. The Court was unimpressed with the analogy. "The appropriateness of remedial measures must be considered in light of the evil presented.... Strong measures appropriate to address one harm may be an unwarranted response to another, lesser one."[18] There was a huge difference between voting discrimination and religious persecution as practiced in America. "In contrast to the record which confronted Congress and the Judiciary in the voting rights cases, RFRA's legislative record lacks examples of modern instances of generally applicable laws passed because of religious bigotry."[19] Furthermore the Voting Rights Act targeted state laws about voting; RFRA affected any state law in any area that impacted religion.

This led to the Court's test, as it explained "[t]here must be a congruence and proportionality between the injury to be prevented or remedied and the means adopted to that end. Lacking such a connection, legislation may become substantive in operation and effect."[20] RFRA failed the test; it "cannot be considered remedial, preventive legislation, if those terms are to have any meaning."[21] It put too many state laws at risk while not dealing with any serious current problem of religious discrimination. "Sweeping coverage ensures its intrusion at every level of government, displacing laws and prohibiting official actions of almost every description and regardless of subject matter."[22] What a difference this was from the test the Court offered in the 1966 case sustaining the Voting Rights Act.[23] There the Court adopted the test created by Chief Justice John Marshall in *McColloch v. Maryland*,[24] his greatest opinion: "Let the end be legitimate, let it be within the scope of the constitution, and all means which are appropriate, which are plainly to that end, which are not prohibited, but consist with the letter and spirit of the constitution, are constitutional."[25]

The Court concluded by telling Congress to know its place and stay there. Congress was well aware of *Smith* and had to know that "the Court will treat its precedents with the respect due them under settled principles, including stare decisis, and contrary expectations must be disappointed."[26] The Constitution works best "when each part of the Government respects both the Constitution and the proper actions and determinations of the other branches."[27]

Thus while the case was ostensibly about religious freedom, the opinion and result turned on separation of powers in the service of federalism by privileging the state's choices over those of the federal government. There was an irony in that the Texas attorney general supported federal law against the autonomy Texas had granted its own cities.

A five-sentence concurring opinion by John Paul Stevens deserves mention. He found RFRA unconstitutional under the First Amendment's prohibition of laws "respecting an establishment of religion." RFRA "provided the Church with a legal weapon that no atheist or agnostic can obtain. This governmental preference for religion, as opposed to irreligion, is forbidden by the First Amendment."[28] Stevens was a fan of irreligion. He was a Northwestern law school grad who went on to clerk for Justice Wiley Rutledge. He specialized in antitrust until appointed to the Seventh Circuit Court of Appeals in 1970. Attorney General Ed Levi, who knew Stevens well, recommended his elevation to President Gerald R. Ford, and Stevens joined the Court in 1975. As a justice he changed a number of his early positions but was consistent in his opposition to religion. He believed in minimal free exercise protection as in *Smith* but also in maximal Establishment Clause protection as with RFRA. Normally justices with a minimal free exercise position also have a minimal Establishment Clause position because they do not wish to hamstring governments. Those with a strong free exercise position have a strong Establishment Clause view because they believe this necessary to protect religion from government. Stevens was unique. (No justice has ever had a maximal free exercise position coupled with a minimal Establishment Clause view.)

Few people, outside of the historic preservation community, came out in support of the decision. And in what may be a first—and last—the Texas attorney general and the legal director of the ACLU both expressed disappointment in the result.

St. Peter's got its expansion. With the litigation over, the church and city reached an agreement that preserved 75 percent of St. Peter's while allowing for expansion to accommodate 800 parishioners. Laycock had two subsequent Supreme Court arguments, winning a free exercise case[29] and losing an Establishment Clause case.[30] He became the trailing spouse when his wife, Teresa Sullivan, became provost at the University of Michigan and president at the University of Virginia. Dellinger never got a vote on becoming solicitor general because his home state senator, Jesse Helms, blackballed him.

III

Contrary to John Paul Stevens's conclusion in *Flores*, the federal government almost never takes actions that implicate the Establishment Clause's supposed "wall of separation between church and state," to quote Thomas Jefferson whose language the Court adopted in its first state Establishment Clause case.[31] But states have been frequent targets of Establishment Clause litigation coming from issues of public schools—typically prayer—and religion in the public sphere—as when Summun wished to place a monument to its Seven Aphorisms in a public park.

The Court had been perfectly clear about prayer since the early 1960s. Organized prayer on school time in the classroom violated the Establishment Clause because of a duty of the state to remain neutral between religion and nonreligion.[32] The principle was extended a year later to organized Bible reading.[33] These cases met resistance in homogeneous communities in the South and Midwest but were otherwise not overly controversial because religion was not that much of a factor in political life; one scholar described the religious spirit of the age as "one of religious piety, but of a decidedly thin brand."[34] With the advent of the religious right the principle did become more controversial, but the Court nevertheless extended it in 1992 to a religious invocation at a high school graduation.[35]

The first Texas case involved prayer at a football game, a long-standing practice that occasioned no complaints prior to 1995. But the case, from Santa Fe (named for the Atchison, Topeka, and Santa Fe Railroad), a town of about 10,000 between Houston and Galveston, was about much more before it narrowed down to just prayer. The precipitating incident occurred in 1993 in a seventh-grade Texas history class. The teacher passed out fliers in class for a Baptist revival meeting. A student asked if non-Baptists could attend and the teacher asked her what her religion was. She was a Mormon, which caused the teacher to go on a ten-minute rant about the "non-Christian cult-like nature of Mormonism and its general evils."[36] Her parents complained, the teacher was given a written reprimand and directed to apologize to the girl, her parents, and his class.

Another Mormon girl in the system declined to accept a Gideon Bible, which were being passed out in her classroom. "Teachers got after me, students got after me, I was pushed into lockers. I was called a devil worshipper."[37] A Jewish student had similar troubles. Fellow students addressed anti-Semitic language like "Hitler missed one" to him.[38] The school district eventually settled a lawsuit with the family for the not insubstantial sum of $325,000. The family had already moved from Santa Fe.

The district also allowed teachers to lead classroom and lunchtime prayers, in clear violation of the Establishment Clause. The cumulative effect caused two students, one Mormon, one Catholic, along with their parents, to sue to put a stop to placing religion in the schools. The lawsuit was not popular. At a Baptist church one school board member denounced the complaining parents from the pulpit "as 'dim-witted' and 'bored' housewives with a void in their lives."[39] Elsewhere another board member saw the larger problem as being that "we as parents have allowed the expungement of Judeo-Christian teachings from our schools, allowing moral decay."[40] The students and parents, with good reason, had filed the lawsuit under assumed names—Jane Doe. School officials "engaged in strenuous efforts to undercover their identities."[41] This caused the federal judge to order them to halt and in block letters he wrote: "THE HARSHEST POSSIBLE CONTEMPT SANCTIONS FROM THIS COURT" would follow if they did not cease.[42] So instead their classmates tried to ferret out the plaintiffs—there were suspicions, and someone did kill the dog of one of the Does,[43] but to this day only their attorneys know who they were. The risks of physical, financial, and psychological retaliation were too obvious.

Faced with a lawsuit, the school board knew it was going to have to make changes in a policy that had students electing a student chaplain who would deliver a benediction at graduation and football games—the two most important events for high school students in Texas. The board kept changing its policies during the course of the litigation at the district court level, hoping to find the sweet spot where prayer would not run afoul of the Establishment Clause. The overriding idea was to create a cut-out so that the board's support for prayer would be deemed irrelevant. The board created a series of two-part elections. In the first the students would be asked if they wished to have an invocation or benediction at graduation. If the answer was yes, a second election would be held for the student to deliver the benediction. In one iteration the policy required the benediction to be nonsectarian and nonproselytizing. The board then dropped that restriction, but with the proviso that if a court found the new policy unconstitutional, the restrictions would automatically become effective.

The policy for graduation was then applied to football games under the title "Prayer at Football Games." When the students elected the person to deliver the prayer, that student could offer a sectarian prayer unless enjoined by a court. If there were such an injunction, the student had to offer a nonsectarian and nonproselytizing prayer. In a final modification, after the election for the student, the board changed the wording to delete prayer and instead refer to messages, statements, and invocations.

The federal district court approved the fallback policy, but not prayers that appealed to distinctively Christian beliefs. Both sides appealed and a divided Fifth Circuit sided with the Does. The board's petition for rehearing en banc was denied by a 8–7 vote. Then the Supreme Court granted certiorari limited to the question of prayer at football games.

Anthony Griffin, an ACLU lawyer from Galveston, represented the Does throughout the litigation. At the Court he added Douglas Laycock to write the brief and help prepare for oral argument. The board brought in Jay Alan Sekulow of the conservative American Center for Law and Justice. Texas attorney general John Cornyn also argued as amicus for the school district.

Sekulow asked the justices to mimic ostriches and stick their heads in the ground, so they would give deference to the sham secular purposes offered by the board, which "asks us to pretend that we do not recognize what every Santa Fe High School student understands clearly—that this policy is about prayer ... [it] further asks us to accept what is obviously untrue: that these message are necessary to 'solemnize' a football game and that this single-student year-long position is essential to the protection of student speech."[44]

Stevens's opinion for the Court relied heavily on the previous graduation prayer case. In rejecting Sekulow's assertion that the students were cut-outs, the opinion put the school district front and center. "These invocations are authorized by a government policy and take place on government property at government-sponsored school-related events."[45] As with the graduation prayer case, "the 'degree of school involvement' makes it clear that the pre-game prayers bear 'the imprint of the State and thus put school-age children who objected in an untenable position.' "[46] In the full context "the members of the listening audience must perceive the pregame message as a public expression of the views of the majority of the student body delivered with the approval of the school administration."[47]

The Court was obviously unimpressed with the elected student as a cut-out from the board's actions. Indeed the Court turned the election itself against the board. "One of the purposes served by the Establishment Clause is to remove debate over this kind of issue from governmental supervision or control.... . The [election] mechanism encourages divisiveness along religious lines in a public school setting, a result at odds with the Establishment Clause."[48]

The Court's opinion had touched on three Establishment Clause concerns: no coercion, no endorsement, and no promoting religious strife. Furthermore, as Chief Justice William Rehnquist would note in a subsequent case, the Court has been "particularly vigilant in monitoring compliance with the Establishment Clause in elementary and secondary schools."[49] The Does won because the Court saw a majority of the community trying to ram their God upon the minority. The losers saw it differently. They saw a minority demanding to prevail. Establishment Clause jurisprudence is a zero-sum game, but the Court had an answer for the wounded majority. "Nothing in the Constitution as interpreted by this Court prohibits any public school student from voluntarily praying at any time before, during, or after the school day."[50]

There were three dissenters, Rehnquist, Scalia, and Clarence Thomas, the justices most committed to allowing majorities to attach their religion to government activities. Writing for them, Rehnquist asserted that "even more disturbing than its holding is the tone of the Court's opinion; it bristles with hostility to all things religious in public life."[51] That seems over the top. But Rehnquist, a Stanford law grad and law clerk to Justice Robert Jackson, had two signature issues during his tenure. Both related to federalism and giving states more authority to act. One was deregulating capital punishment so that the states could execute those convicted as they pleased; he was unsuccessful. The other was weakening Establishment Clause barriers to more governmental participation in religious activities. He had started that as a lone dissenter, but had achieved considerable successes over time. The loss in *Santa Fe* hurt.

The decision was overwhelmingly unpopular in both Santa Fe and Texas generally as prayer often seemed as much a part of high school football games as halftime marching bands. In Santa Fe Reverend Joe Cota wondered, "If a government can say you can't pray at football games, what else can they tell us we can't say?"[52] Governor George W. Bush, the presumptive Republican presidential nominee, expressed "disappointment"—how often those who lose start with that—and went on to "support the constitutionally guaranteed right of all students to express their faith freely and participate in voluntary, student-led prayers."[53] Gary Bauer, a defeated presidential aspirant from the Religious Right, claimed the decision "drips with hostility to public religious expression ... a majority of the Court is at war with the religious tradition of America."[54]

Both the *Austin American-Statesman* and the *Houston Chronicle* editorialized in favor of the decision. The latter rebuked both Bauer and Bush. "It is not an anti-religious or anti-Christian ruling.... It is important to keep the ruling in perspective and understand that it does not prohibit students themselves from praying anything, anywhere."[55]

Sekulow continues to litigate conservative religious causes (and in 2017 became a member of President Trump's outside legal team). Cornyn, of course, went on to become the senior senator from Texas. For Griffin the ending was unhappy. In early 2015, faced with multiple disciplinary complaints, he turned in his law license.

IV

One of those Rehnquist dissents was in *Stone v. Graham*.[56] Kentucky ordered placing a copy of the Ten Commandments on the wall of every public school classroom in the state with the notation at the bottom: "The secular application of the Ten Commandments is clearly seen in its adoption as the fundamental legal code of Western Civilization and the Common Law of the United States." Without bothering with briefs, much less oral argument, the Court summarily held that there was "no secular legislative purpose behind the law."[57]

As mentioned in the *Summun* case from the previous chapter, the Fraternal Order of Eagles was offering governments monuments with the Ten Commandments. They saw—somehow—the monuments as a way to combat juvenile delinquency. Texas accepted the offer and selected a site on the capitol grounds 75 feet north of the capitol building and 125 feet from the Texas Supreme Court. The monument is six feet high and three feet wide. In addition to the text of the Commandments, there is an eagle gripping the American flag, two small tablets, and below the text are two Stars of David and the Greek letters chi and rho, which represent Christ. At the very bottom there is an inscription telling readers that it was donated by the Eagles in 1961. The monument is one of 17 (along with 21 historical markers) on the 22-acre capitol grounds. In 1986 the capitol grounds were designated as a National Historical Landmark.

No one seemed to care about the monument. But that may mean that members of a religious minority who would have objected never visited the capitol—or that they, like me, were completely unaware of the monument's existence. Then, in 2000, the very conservative and very religious Roy Moore was elected chief justice of Alabama. As soon as he took office he arranged for a huge Ten Commandments monument to be conspicuously placed in the state supreme court building. A federal court ordered it dismantled, but Moore refused. As a result a state commission removed him from office. Many Americans, however, thought Moore was right and they were enraged by the continual attack from the ACLU on any show of public religiosity by governments. The publicity of the Alabama battle had effects elsewhere.

Thomas Van Orden was a Vietnam vet and a Southern Methodist University law grad who worked as a judge advocate general, assistant city attorney in Tyler, and criminal defense lawyer until depression caused him to be suspended from practicing; he also lost his family and home. He spent nights in a tent and during the day he was either at the Texas Supreme Court library or the Tarlton Law Library at UT. For six years while walking between the capitol cafeteria and the supreme court library, he passed the Ten Commandments monument without objection. Probably because of the controversy surrounding Moore, he came to perceive the monument as an unconstitutional endorsement of religion

Doing his own work Van Orden sued the governor and relevant state officials for a declaration that the monument on the capitol grounds violated the Establishment Clause and an order to remove it. His pro se arguments failed at the district court and then again at the Fifth Circuit.[58] Wanting to go to the Supreme Court, he asked Douglas Laycock to represent him, but Laycock feared political retaliation against the law school and recommended that Van Orden call Erwin Chemerinsky, a well-known First Amendment scholar then at Duke. Chemerinsky agreed to write the cert petition and if granted he would argue the case. Because the Sixth Circuit had a Ten Commandments case involving Kentucky courthouses and had ruled against government officials, there was a conflict among the circuits—the prime reason the Court agrees to hear cases. The Court granted cert in each of the cases. Texas, too, got new counsel. Solicitor General Ted Cruz had prevailed at the Fifth Circuit, but Attorney General Greg Abbott chose to argue the case himself.

Membership on the Court had been unchanged since Breyer arrived in 1994. The justices knew each other well, and as *Santa Fe v. Doe* showed, there were deep divisions on how to treat the Establishment Clause, ranging from Stevens's hostility to religion to Rehnquist, Scalia, and Thomas wishing to authorize government favoritism to religion (by which they meant Christianity). If there were a wild card it would be O'Connor trying to ascertain whether a reasonable observer would think the state was endorsing religion. Such an inquiry would be easy in the Sixth Circuit case. Why else would governments put the Ten Commandments into courthouses?

Indeed O'Connor was the fifth vote to find the Ten Commandments in courthouses unconstitutional because religious liberty is threatened "when government takes the mantle of religion upon itself."[59] The majority, as had *Stone v. Graham*, found the asserted secular purpose for the choice to be a sham; "openly available data supported a common-sense conclusion that a religious objective permeated the government's action."[60]

The Texas case was much harder but only one justice—Breyer—said so. After all, the Eagles talked juvenile delinquency and the monument had rested for forty years without objection.

The four dissenters in the courthouse case were obviously going to allow the Ten Commandments on the capitol grounds. Rehnquist's opinion for them emphasized the role that religion had played in American history. He distinguished *Stone* in two ways, first as a school case and then by the fact that the monument was more passive than the same message on school walls. Furthermore the monument was but one among many on the capitol grounds. The array of monuments "represent[ed] the several strands in the State's political and legal history. The inclusion of the Ten Commandments monument in this group has a dual significance, partaking of both religion and government."[61] That dual significance was enough to preclude an Establishment Clause violation.

On the other side, Stevens saw endorsement of the message that there is "one, and only one, God."[62] David Souter thought that each monument on the capitol grounds had to be taken separately; there being "no common denominator," the Ten Commandments monument was a full-throated endorsement of religion.[63] "Texas is telling everyone who sees the monument to live up to a moral code because God requires it, with both code and conception of God being rightly understood as the inheritances specifically of Jews and Christians."[64]

Eight justices thought the issue in the Kentucky and Texas cases was the same. Breyer didn't. He found all Establishment Clause tests irrelevant because "no exact formula can dictate a resolution of such fact-intensive cases."[65] He twice referred to the case before him as "borderline."[66] One monument among many on twenty-two acres "suggests little or nothing of the sacred [and t]he setting does not readily lend itself to meditation or any other religious activity."[67]

The initial forty years of tranquility counted for something. There had been no challenges and "I am not aware of any evidence suggesting this was due to a climate of intimidation. Hence, those 40 years suggest more strongly than any set of formulaic tests that few individuals, whatever their system of beliefs, are likely to have understood the monument as amounting in any significantly detrimental way, to a government effort to favor a particular religious sect [or] to promote religion over nonreligion."[68]

The consequences of a different holding "might well encourage disputes concerning the removal of longstanding depictions of the Ten Commandments from public buildings across the Nation. And it could thereby create the very kind of religiously based divisiveness that the Establishment Clause seeks to avoid."[69] Here, in a nice irony, Breyer relied on the prospect of political reaction that had caused Laycock not to take the case.

Putting everything in perspective the Court must "distinguish between real threat and mere shadow."[70] This is shadow, not threat. But if the monument had been recently erected the result would likely be different. "In today's world, in a Nation of so many different religious and comparable nonreligious fundamental beliefs, a more contemporary state effort to focus attention upon a religious text is certainly likely to prove divisive in a way that this longstanding, preexisting monument has not."[71]

It was constitutional adverse possession.[72] But it made sense on the facts. The monument remains where it has been for almost half a century, but like its first forty years on the grounds, it rests there passively causing no problems.

Governor Rick Perry proclaimed the result a victory for all Texans. Abbott saw Texas as offering "a model for how governmental bodies across the country can constitutionally display religious symbols."[73] Laycock grudgingly concurred: "If politicians can keep their mouths shut about their religious purposes, pretend it's all secular, maybe put some secular stuff with it, they got [*sic*] a pretty good chance" of winning.[74] The Texas Department of Transportation heeded Laycock's advice. It authorizes crosses near highway fatalities not for religious reasons but because a cross is a "nonsectarian symbol of death."[75]

As everyone knows and this book reflects, Abbott became governor of Texas in 2014. Chemerinsky, who had been at the University of Southern California before going to Duke, returned to Southern California as the first dean of the University of California, Irvine Law School, subsequently becoming dean at Berkeley in the fall of 2017. Van Orden, who was able to bring the case because he had nothing left to lose (although he did keep secret where he slept at night), died at age sixty-six in Temple. In reacting to his loss, he said, "You sleep under a bush and the Supreme Court quotes you. But the practical aspects of doing it under the circumstances—no money, alone—it's difficult. You don't look back at that with any fondness."[76]

TEN

Abortion

It is the totally unreasoned judicial opinion.
—Professor Mark Tushnet on *Roe v. Wade* (1973)

There have been three major decisions on abortion laws in the United States; Texas figured in two. The first decision, *Roe v. Wade*,[1] struck down the typical nineteenth- and twentieth-century laws. The second, *Whole Woman's Health v. Hellerstedt*,[2] held unconstitutional the twenty-first-century restrictions designed as an end run around *Roe*.

I

As the nineteenth century progressed, states, at the urging of physicians including the newly formed American Medical Association, criminalized abortion. Most, but not all, statutes had a provision for therapeutic abortions to protect the life of the mother but rarely said what that entailed, a problem that became more salient in the twentieth century.

Although it was difficult to enforce prohibitions on abortions except when the procedure went wrong, there was some rigor to enforcement prior to the Great Depression, but then the American birthrate dropped to its lowest ever, with a relaxed attitude toward abortions a factor. With the end of World War II, the laxity ended and a crackdown on illegal abortions coincided with the idea that women had a patriotic duty to marry and have children.

The demand for abortions, however, remained. Although there have never been accurate statistics on illegal abortions, there are statistics on deaths, and abortions constituted an increasing percentage of maternal death from the Great Depression into the 1960s. Urban hospitals had a "Monday morning abortion line-up" of women who used their Friday paycheck to pay for a so-called "back-alley abortion" and by Monday would be lined up stretcher-to-stretcher waiting for the operating room.[3]

While laws did authorize therapeutic abortions for the life of the mother, hospitals created abortion committees to force the woman and the doctor to justify an abortion, and in the unsettled atmosphere hospitals were necessarily cautious. For those women who did obtain an abortion, the time before the committee was often demeaning. And committees often had unwritten quotas. At the top of the list, "as long as you were the banker's daughter, the doctor's daughter, the golf buddy's daughter, it was always taken care of,"[4] observed one hospital resident in the 1960s. But for the poor, it was the back alley. As a lawyer and doctor wrote in the *American Bar Association Journal*, the laws "drove large numbers of desperate women into the hands of the very person from whom the law seeks to shield them, the unskilled criminal abortionist."[5]

In the late 1950s the American Law Institute, an organization of elite lawyers, judges, and academics that was engaged in law reform proposals through Restatements and model statutes, turned to abortion as part of its Model Penal Code. Louis B. Schwartz, a law professor at the University of Pennsylvania, was the draftsman of the proposal that abortion be available if two doctors certified that the woman's physical or mental health was at stake, if the child was likely to be deformed, or if the pregnancy was the result of rape or incest. Schwartz would have liked to go farther and authorize abortion in cases of individual hardship, but that was too much for the ALI. The proposal was not about a woman's right because the decision was to be made by doctors. The ALI executive director, Herbert Wechsler, justified the liberalization on the ground that doctors of otherwise high reputations were already flouting the law when they deemed an abortion was appropriate. In 1962 the ALI added the liberalized abortion provision to its Model Penal Code (which states were free to adopt in whole or in part or not adopt at all). In 1965 the American Medical Association endorsed the ALI provision. Three years later the American College of Obstetricians and Gynecologists went farther and, echoing Schwartz, asserted that social and economic factors should also count as reasons for abortion.

II

With doctors in the lead, the late 1960s represented the high point of legislative action to reform abortion laws. Reform measures based on the ALI proposal were introduced in thirty state legislatures, including Texas, in 1967, and in California, Colorado, and North Carolina the bills passed. In the next two years seven states adopted the ALI-like proposals. Whether a state changed its laws typically depended on how organized the Catholic Church was in the state because the church was adamantly opposed to any liberalization.

In Texas the bill to reform the state's 1857 law had little chance, but when the Texas Medical Association narrowly voted that mental health should not be a factor, the bill was dead. In 1969 the ALI-like bill had the full approval of the TMA, but Archbishop Robert E. Lucey of San Antonio declared that anyone voting for it was a murderer, and the bill died in committee. Two years later a repeal bill could not get the necessary votes to be considered in the senate.

An unanticipated consequence of liberalization was that it did not have the effects supporters and opponents anticipated. Hospitals in California, Colorado, and Georgia, all states that had passed new laws, retained their quotas on the number of allowable abortions and some hospital committees became even more reluctant to authorize abortions. Thus despite liberalization, the number of abortions had but a slight uptick.

By the end of the 1960s the energy on abortion reform had passed from doctors to women in the new and energized feminist movement. These women believed that sexual freedom and reproductive control were issues for women to be decided by women. From this perspective reform was an illusion because what was necessary was repeal. Furthermore, at this time abortion was an issue widely discussed in journals from *Reader's Digest* to *Redbook* to *Time*. A Harris poll reported in *Time* stated 64 percent of Americans, including 60 percent of Catholics, believed abortion should be a question decided between the woman and her doctor.[6]

Repeal had its first success in Hawaii in 1970, supported by both labor and the chamber of commerce. The Catholic Church pressured the governor who was a Catholic to veto the bill, but saying it was a decision about the health of all state citizens, he allowed the bill to become law without his signature. Alaska and Washington followed with the latter being approved in a referendum. Not surprisingly the most publicized battle over repeal was in New York where the Catholic Church was strong. Repeal fell one vote short in the assembly, but then George Michaels, a Catholic, changed his no to an aye. The bill passed the senate the next day and was signed into law by Governor Nelson Rockefeller. It legalized all abortions in the first twenty-four weeks of pregnancy, had no residency requirement, nor one that abortions be performed in hospitals. The Catholic Church mounted a fierce attack on the law and obtained its repeal in the next legislative session only to see Rockefeller veto it.

The Catholic Church was successful elsewhere and the repeal effort stalled out at just four states. Furthermore, reform, which hadn't done that much, was also stalled. The movement for legislative change had run its course as the Catholic Church had gained allies. If further change were to occur it was likely to be from the judiciary, not additional state legislatures.

III

The same year the AMA backed abortion liberalization, abortions were first mentioned at the Supreme Court. The case wasn't about abortions;

it was about the right of married couples to obtain contraceptives, which an 1879 Connecticut law severely restricted, and the Catholic Church had successfully blocked its repeal. *Griswold v. Connecticut*[7] was the third attempt at the Court to kill the Connecticut law. In 1943 in the wake of the New Deal revolution the Court rejected a challenge by doctors to the law for lack of standing, that is, no actual injury.[8] Eventually Yale law professor Fowler Harper was able to solve the standing problem by bringing suit in the name of a doctor and woman patient who had given birth to three babies who all died shortly thereafter. Justice Felix Frankfurter convinced his Brethren that criminal laws should not be subject to challenge if no real threat of enforcement existed.[9] Justice Tom Clark, the sole Texan to sit on the Court, was so happy with this solution that he wrote to Frankfurter "Good riddance! Join me up."[10] Planned Parenthood then opened a clinic and was swiftly prosecuted. Harper had his case. But by the time it was at the Court Harper was terminally ill and the case passed to his equally liberal colleague, Thomas I. Emerson.

Emerson argued *Griswold* as a right to privacy case. Since privacy is never mentioned in the Constitution Emerson had to suggest something and he offered the kitchen sink—the First Amendment's freedom of association, the Fourth Amendment's right against unreasonable search and seizures, the Fifth Amendment's privilege against self-incrimination, the Fourteenth Amendment's Due Process Clause, and even the heretofore unused Ninth Amendment: "The enumeration in the Constitution, of certain rights, shall not be construed to deny or disparage others retained by the people." As his rebuttal argument was drawing to a close, Justice Hugo Black asked him, "Would your argument ... relating to privacy, invalidate all laws that punish people for bringing about abortions?"[11] Emerson said no because "that conduct does not occur in the privacy of the home."[12] That did not satisfy Justice Byron White: "I take it abortion involves killing a life in being, doesn't it? Isn't that a rather different problem from contraception?"[13] Emerson did what any good advocate would do and readily agreed lest the introduction of abortion derail his argument against limits on contraception. Black was not finished and asked if all abortions were killings or murder. Emerson wisely ducked: "Well, I don't know whether you could indeed characterize it that way, but it involves taking what has begun to be a life."[14]

None of the opinions in *Griswold* mention abortion. Justice William O. Douglas's majority echoed Emerson, finding the right of privacy somewhere among the penumbras and emanations of five constitutional amendments. Justice Arthur Goldberg concurred and blessed the Ninth Amendment. White and John Marshall Harlan both relied on due process, albeit for different reasons. That summer Emerson wrote a law review article entitled "Nine Justices in Search of a Doctrine" where, with victory established, he suggested *Griswold* might apply to abortion laws.[15] But one case about contraceptives in marriage was a pretty thin basis for an attack on abortion.

One of the readers of Emerson's article was Roy Lucas, a second-year law student at New York University. That year he and his girlfriend took a "vacation" in Puerto Rico so she could obtain an abortion. Lucas wrote a third-year paper on how to challenge abortion restrictions. Not surprisingly, he grabbed on to the same set of constitutional amendments that Emerson had. His thesis was then published in the *North Carolina Law Review.* He concluded: "It is an anomaly that a woman has absolute control over her personal reproductive capacities so long as she can successfully utilize contraceptives but that she forfeits this right when contraception fails."[16]

IV

Lucas called for litigation and helpfully prepared a model legal brief. Sarah Weddington, then a recent UT law grad, came across Lucas's work when, at the urging of friends in an underground abortion referral service, she was asked for advice about whether they could be convicted as accomplices. At the same time there were challenges to abortion laws in well over a dozen states. Those with doctors as the plaintiff, emphasizing the right to practice medicine without undo interference, were filed by male lawyers. Those featuring women as plaintiffs, emphasizing the woman's rights more than a doctor's, were filed by women lawyers. Lucas was assisting as many lawyers as possible in hopes and anticipation that he would get the eventual argument at the Supreme Court.

Being urged to sue, Weddington enlisted the aid of classmate Linda Coffee, who had clerked Sarah Hughes, a federal district judge in Dallas best known as the judge who swore in Lyndon Johnson as president. All Coffee and Weddington lacked was a plaintiff. Coffee went trolling, as had the NAACP, in coming up with Heman Sweatt to challenge segregation at UT. Marsha King volunteered. She had had a painful abortion in Mexico City and her doctor advised avoiding a new pregnancy; because of a medical condition she was also advised to avoid birth control pills. Her husband joined her as John and Mary Doe, although they could have a standing problem because she was not pregnant and thus any injury was speculative. Norma McCorvey, however, was pregnant, and asked an attorney about adoption. He sent her to Coffee and Weddington and she became Jane Roe. The pleadings stated she lacked the resources to travel out of state to procure a legal abortion. She would (falsely) claim to be pregnant because of rape, but the two lawyers never mentioned that in any court papers. While the suit was pending she gave birth and immediately gave the boy up to adoption. James Hallford, a licensed physician who had been arrested previously and who had two pending prosecutions, successfully petitioned to intervene as a plaintiff.

The lawyers got lucky and drew a court of Hughes, William Taylor, and Fifth Circuit judge Irving Goldberg. At oral argument it was obvious that the panel wanted to rule that the Texas law was unconstitutional under the Ninth Amendment. Less than a month later they did in a nine-page opinion.

The jurisdictional statement to the Supreme Court was written by Lucas, as Coffee had too much work at her firm and Weddington and her husband were preparing to move to Fort Worth. With the Court's agreement to hear the case, though, the Weddingtons left their jobs to write the merits brief. Lucas, nevertheless, wrote the Clerk of the Court that he would be presenting the oral argument. He sent a letter to Weddington touting his greater knowledge and experience and then dumping on Margie Hames, a Georgia lawyer who would be arguing in a companion case. Marsha King, Coffee, and women's groups felt that a woman should do the argument because women's rights were at stake. Thus Weddington got the argument and the fame that Lucas had assumed was his.

While clerking I had written the first memo on the case to William O. Douglas, and I did not mention the merits of a constitutional attack on abortion laws. The Court had just issued six decisions on the relation of federal courts to state courts and criminal prosecutions,[17] and I saw the Texas case as one dealing with those issues and likely to be disposed of without reaching the merits.[18] Between the decision to hear the case and oral argument, both Hugo Black and John Marshall Harlan died and Richard Nixon had yet to replace them. Chief Justice Warren Burger asked Potter Stewart to screen cases, suggesting which ones should be held for the full Court. Stewart thought *Roe* could be decided by the seven-man Court because, like me, he thought the case would turn on the jurisdictional issues.[19]

At the oral argument my instincts about the case seemed correct when almost all of Weddington's argument dealt with jurisdictional questions asked from the Bench. Despite the oral argument, Black and Harlan were the two justices most interested in limiting federal court interference with state criminal laws (prior to a trial). With the two gone, the Court went to the merits, with Byron White dissenting and some justices thinking Chief Justice Warren Burger did too. Hames's companion case, *Doe v. Bolton*,[20] involved an ALI-like reform law, and the vote in Conference was inconclusive. Burger nevertheless assigned both to Harry Blackmun even though Burger was not in the majority as he claimed to be. (It was such actions that led to Stewart subsequently going to Bob Woodward and setting in motion *The Brethren*, the first real-time expose of the inner workings of the Court.)

Burger and Blackmun were longtime friends, and the latter was spared from being the weakest link on the Court by the presence of the former, who was a pompous dullard (albeit he looked like a chief justice should look). There might have been several reasons for the assignment. Blackmun had been general counsel of the Mayo Clinic before President Eisenhower appointed him to the Eighth Circuit. If *Roe* was a medical case, he was the most knowledgeable. But Blackmun was also a notoriously slow writer, and Burger may have hoped he could not produce the opinions before the end of the Term; thus the cases would have to be reargued the next Term before a full court with maybe a different outcome. In June Blackmun joined Burger in supporting reargument before a Court that now included Lewis Powell and William Rehnquist. Douglas was outraged. He wrote an unheard-of dissent to the order of reargument, claiming a conspiracy by Burger to control the result. Eventually Brennan convinced Douglas not to air the Court's dirty linen in public.

Once again Lucas wrote Weddington hoping to argue the case. "His letter alternated between claiming that he could do a better job, and self-pitying whining that he was the one that had convinced the Court to hear the case, and had devoted four years of his life to the issue only to be thanklessly shoved aside. Weddington did not dignify his missive with a response."[21]

For a week of the summer recess Blackmun had gone to the library of the Mayo Clinic to learn as much as he could about the history of the medical practice of abortions. There being few legal tools to work with, he did not go to a law library. Blackmun wanted to write an opinion that would impress doctors and that meant an opinion that would stress their competence to decide. With that decision, Douglas's concerns about Blackmun changing his vote and joining with all the Nixon appointees and White to reject the constitutional challenge came to naught.

V

By far the longest part of *Roe v. Wade* is a history of abortion from ancient times to the present where Blackmun relied on his work at the Mayo Clinic and the parties' briefs. He built on this history with a following five-page section surveying the relevant state interests. Protecting the health of the woman and protecting prenatal life were both deemed legitimate.

The guts of the opinion consisted of finding that the right of privacy applied to the woman's decision to terminate her pregnancy, but that the right was not absolute. The key passage in the four-and-a-half-page discussion follows: "The right of privacy, whether it be found in the Fourteenth Amendment's concept of personal liberty and restrictions upon state action, as we feel it is, or, as the District Court determined, in the Ninth Amendment's reservation of rights to the people, is broad enough to encompass a woman's decision whether or not to terminate her pregnancy."[22]

The woman's right would nevertheless be trumped if the fetus were a person under the Fourteenth Amendment whose life could not be taken without due process of law. In the lengthiest legal discussion of the opinion, the Court rejected the possibility. No prior case had held a fetus was a person under the Fourteenth Amendment. "We need not resolve the difficult question of when life begins. When those trained in the respective disciplines of medicine, philosophy, and theology are unable to arrive at any consensus, the judiciary, at this point in the development of man's knowledge, is not in a position to speculate as to the answer."[23] Apparently if the judiciary can't, then neither can any legislature.

With the opinion nearing its end, Blackmun introduced trimesters as representing the correct balance between the woman's right and the state interests. In the first trimester of pregnancy "the attending physician, in consultation with his patient, is free to determine, without regulation by the State, that, in his medical judgment, the patient's pregnancy should be terminated."[24] In the second trimester the state may require appropriate facilities be used in order to protect the health of the woman. And finally in the third trimester the protection of pre-natal life becomes paramount.

Although I have referred to the woman's right to choose, that is too loose. As the quote about the first trimester illustrates, the right is that of the doctor, a point Blackmun reiterated: "the abortion decision and its effectuation must be left to the medical judgment of the pregnant woman's attending physician."[25]

The companion case with its ALI-like modern reform law continued with emphasis on the medical judgment of the pregnant woman's doc-tor. The Georgia law required that an abortion be performed in a nationally accredited hospital, that it be approved by a committee, and that the performing physician's decision to terminate the pregnancy be confirmed by two other doctors. The accrediting provision was uncon-stitutional because it imposed conditions unrelated to the safety of abortions and other surgeries could be performed in hospitals without that specific accreditation. The attending physician will use "his best medical judgment" and he is "perhaps more than anyone else, knowl-edgeable in this area of patient care."[26] Thus "the good physician ... will have empathy and understanding for the pregnant patient that probably are not exceed by those who participate in other areas of pro-fessional counseling."[27] Under these circumstances there is no need for the hospital committee nor the concurrence of two other doctors. The Court also noted no other surgical procedure had those requirements.

There were two dissenters, White and Rehnquist. Both emphasized that the Framers of the Fourteenth Amendment surely did not intend to outlaw abortions. As Rehnquist put it "to reach its result, the Court necessarily has had to find within the scope of the Fourteenth Amend-ment a right that was apparently completely unknown to the drafters of the Amendment."[28] Neither dissent was passionate in the least, although White, the first former law clerk (to Chief Justice Fred Vinson) to be appointed to the Court, wrote a two-pager stating the result could only flow from an exercise of "raw judicial power."[29] The fact that the dissents were mild illustrates that no one on the Court saw the firestorm coming over abortion. Just three weeks before *Roe* came down, Burger was on the phone with Richard Nixon. The two talked about a bussing case from Denver and the pending obscenity cases, but Burger did not find *Roe* significant enough to mention.

Without debating the result, the problem with *Roe* was simple: it was an opinion devoid of legal reasoning. The key passage already quoted was "the right of privacy ... is broad enough to encompass a woman's decision whether or not to terminate her pregnancy." But the sentence reads just as intelligibly with "the right is privacy ... is not broad enough ..." Since there was no reasoning backing up Blackmun's conclusion, there need be no more backing up my rewrite. Mark Tushnet, who was clerking for Thurgood Marshall when *Roe* came down, has summed it up perfectly. "We might think of Justice Blackmun's opinion in *Roe* as an innovation akin to Joyce's [in *Finnegans Wake*] or Mailer's [in *The Executioner's Song*]. It is the totally unreasoned judicial opinion. To say that it does not look like Justice Powell's decision in some other case is like saying that a Cubist 'portrait' does not look like its subject as a member of the Academy would paint it."[30] *Roe* was simply the initial example of Cubist judging. While those who opposed abortion naturally thought *Roe* was a bad decision, pro-abortion individuals like Tushnet were taken aback by how bad Blackmun's opinion was. It was impossible to think of another major case with such an unpersuasive and unprofessional opinion. John Hart Ely, then a young constitutional law professor at Yale,[31] crystalized liberals' initial concerns immediately in "The Wages of Crying Wolf," a seminal article in the *Yale Law Journal*.[32] In terms of the controversy generated *Roe* ranks with *Brown* as the twin major decisions of the second half of the twentieth century. But as *Brown* was eventually accepted by the South, *Roe* never gained acceptance by its opposition.

The unceasing criticism of *Roe* moved Blackmun from a reliable conservative to aligning himself with William J. Brennan and Thurgood

Marshall. Lewis Powell's biographer, John Jeffries, explains the transition. "The root of Blackmun's metamorphosis lay in the natural concern of a parent for a child. The parent was Harry Blackmun and the child was *Roe v. Wade*. [Hostile] remarks could not fail to wound, and they proved especially hurtful to Justice Blackmun.... *Roe* brought him ridicule, not respect. The wound was deep and was soon surrounded by defensive scar tissue.... For Blackmun the attack on *Roe* was personal. Those who kept the faith [like Brennan and Marshall] won his trust and support."[33]

VI

Sarah Weddington was running for the state legislature when *Roe* was reargued; a month later she was elected for the first of her three terms (with Ann Richards, who had yet to run for office, as her campaign manager). She championed women's rights and helped put an Equal Rights Amendment in the state constitution, and *Texas Monthly* rated her one of the ten best legislators. In her final term, however, she avoided key votes and then took a junket to China, missing the last weeks of the session. She was a special assistant to the president for women' issues during the Carter administration (where her bio noted she had won a Supreme Court case, but didn't say which one). Afterwards she gave speeches and was an adjunct professor in UT's Government Department. Essentially she more or less faded from view.

Linda Coffee stayed with her law firm and practiced bankruptcy law. Marsha King and her husband both became lawyers. When her health improved she gave birth to two healthy children. Roy Lucas periodically surfaced, offering to help lawyers in abortion cases by presenting himself as the only one who really understood the issues. He suffered from cancer and died of a heart attack in 2003.

Roe and Doe, Norma McCorvey (who died at age sixty-nine in 2017) and Sandra Bensing, both became "born-again" Christians. Both expressed regret for their participation in the litigations, and both joined militantly anti-abortion groups. In 2007 in *Gonzales v. Carhart*[34] the Court upheld the federal ban on partial birth abortions. Justice Anthony Kennedy claimed, without evidence, that many women who have abortions subsequently regret their decisions. Perhaps he was thinking of these two former plaintiffs.

VII

Roe was modified by ditching the trimesters, but nevertheless reaffirmed in the 1992 case of *Planned Parenthood v. Casey.*[35] A year later Bryon White retired and was replaced by Ruth Bader Ginsburg, often called the Thurgood Marshall of the women's movement. This made abortion impregnable at the Court.

In the 2010 elections Republicans under the "Tea Party" label filled state and congressional legislatures. Although they professed to be running against overreaching governments, by their actions at the state level they were at least as concerned about abortion as cutting government. Claiming the fetus feels pain, Republicans favored reducing the period from conception when abortions are legal. Furthermore Anthony Kennedy's fifth vote in *Gonzales v. Carhart* suggested that he might be susceptible to new restrictions on abortion. After all, he had only once found a provision regulating abortion to be an undue burden and that provision was the requirement of advance notification of the father—virtually an invitation to domestic violence.

Texas entered the fray in 2011 with a mandatory sonogram bill declared by Governor Rick Perry to be emergency legislation. It passed with overwhelming Republican support and Democratic opposition. The bill mandated that a woman seeking an abortion have a sonogram not more than seventy-two hours or less than twenty-four hours before the abortion, with Republicans expressing hope that hearing a heartbeat or seeing the fetus would dissuade women from going forward or perhaps the sonogram would help drive up the overall costs of an abortion to an unacceptable level for some women.

The sonogram mandate was just the warmup. In the next legislative session Republicans strived to put as many abortion providers out of business as possible both by driving up their cost of doing business and by added requirements on the doctors performing abortions. HB 2 contained three significant provisions. First, a physician performing an abortion must have admitting privileges at a hospital located within thirty miles of the abortion facility. Prior law had required providers to have a "working arrangement" with a doctor who had admitting privileges. When the admitting privileges provision went into effect the number of abortion facilities was halved from forty to twenty. Second, abortion facilities must meet the minimum standards for ambulatory surgical centers (ASC) under Texas law. This would impose costs between $1.5 and $3 million per clinic and would result in only seven or eight clinics remaining open—three in the Metroplex, two in Houston, one in Austin, and one or two in San Antonio. Third, the law criminalized abortions after twenty weeks of pregnancy, but with exceptions for the life or physical impairment of the mother and if there is a severe fetal abnormality.

HB 2 had been before the legislature in a special session, but Democratic state senator Wendy Davis of Fort Worth gained fame for filibustering it at the end of the session. Governor Rick Perry immediately called the legislature for a second special session and in this session HB 2 passed unamended even though there were twenty-six proposed amendments in the house and twenty in the senate. Republicans were going to have their bill the way they introduced it. It passed the house 96–49 with five Democrats in support and two Republicans negative. The senate vote was 19–11 with only a single Democrat breaking party ranks. The house sponsor, Jodie Laubenberg of Parker, explained, "It really was the hand of God."[36]

Whole Woman's Health operated clinics that HB 2 would put out of business, and it sued claiming the law created an undue burden on a woman's right to choose to terminate her pregnancy, the *Casey* test. The federal district court made a number of findings. There are approximately 5.4

million women of reproductive age in the state and somewhere between 60,000 and 72,000 legal abortions occur annually. The number of women of reproductive age living more than 50 miles from a clinic would double, the number living more than 100 miles would go up by 150%, 150 miles by 350%, and those living more than 200 miles by a whopping 2,800% (from 10,000 to 290,000). If the ASC provision were to go into effect those numbers would jump again. Finally abortions are safer than many common medical procedures, have low rates of serious complications, and virtually no deaths. With those findings the district court enjoined enforcement of the two provisions.[37]

The Fifth Circuit stayed the injunction.[38] Two weeks later the Supreme Court vacated the stay.[39] Eight months later the Fifth Circuit reversed the district court on the merits.[40] It found HB 2 did not have the purpose or effect of placing a substantial obstacle to a woman's choice and that it furthers a legitimate state interest in the health and safety of women. The court—consisting of three appointees of George W. Bush—chastised the district judge for substituting his judgment for that of the legislature on the issue of medical benefits of the law. The Supreme Court then granted certiorari.

Before oral argument, Antonin Scalia suddenly died. Assuming the other justices held to their likely position this meant the case would either be decided 5–3 to strike down the law (with Kennedy joining the Democrats) or 4–4 with the result being to affirm the Fifth Circuit. That oral argument pitted Stephanie Toti, an NYU law grad, heading the lawyers for the Center for Reproductive Rights, in her first Supreme Court argument, assisted by U.S. solicitor general Donald B. Verrilli, Jr., against the Texas solicitor general Scott Keller, a UT law grad who had clerked for Kennedy. It showed that Chief Justice John Roberts and Justice Samuel Alito were intent on affirming the Fifth Circuit. Undoubtedly they would be joined by the always silent and still embittered (from his confirmation hearings) Justice Clarence Thomas.[41] The four Democrats were highly skeptical of the Texas claims that the law was intended to improve women's health. Kennedy appeared noncommittal.

Alito was intent on debunking the idea that clinics were closing because of the law. "We're not talking about a huge number of facilities."[42] In an exchange with Toti, Justice Elena Kagan, who as dean of the Harvard Law School had rare impact and as a young justice seems destined for greatness, turned his argument into a laugher. "And is it right that in the two-week period that the ASC requirement was in effect, that over a dozen facilities shut their doors, and then when that was stayed, when that was lifted, they reopened immediately; is that right?" It was. "It's almost like the perfect controlled experiment as to the effect of the law, isn't it? It's like you put the law into effect, 12 clinics closed. You take the law out of effect, they reopen."[43]

Alito also wanted to claim eight facilities were enough to service 70,000 abortions annually because the claim that eight were not sufficient was "not based on any hard, hard statistic."[44] Verrilli responded, "Well it is. It's common sense."[45]

Justice Ruth Bader Ginsburg was curious about women in El Paso. Keller had stated they could go to the Santa Teresa facility in New Mexico. "That's—that's odd that you point to the New Mexico facility. New Mexico doesn't have any surgical—ASC requirement, and it doesn't have any admitting requirement. So if your argument is right, then New Mexico is not an available way out for Texas because Texas says that to protect our women we need these things. But send them off to Mexico—New Mexico—New Mexico where they don't get it either, no admitting privileges, no ASC. And that's perfectly all right. Well, if it's all right for the—the women in the El Paso area, why isn't it all right for the rest of the women in Texas?"[46]

Breyer wondered about the admitting privileges versus the old law that demanded a working arrangement. "Where in the record will I find evidence of women who had complications, who could not get to a hospital, even though there was a working arrangement for admission, but now they could get to a hospital because the doctor himself has to have admitting privileges?"[47] Keller noted it was not in the record; he didn't have to say because no such women exist.

For Keller the dispositive question was whether Texas had a legitimate purpose for the law. If it did—and he claimed, like the Fifth Circuit, that it did—then the law did not constitute an undue burden on women.

Toti closed her rebuttal on the strongest note. "Texas law expressly authorizes other surgical procedures, including those performed under general anesthesia—which early abortion is not—to be performed in the physician's office. And even other physicians that operate at an ASC aren't required to have admitting privileges. The facility is merely required to have a transfer agreement. So these regulations target one of the safest procedures that a patient can have in an outpatient setting for the most onerous regulations."[48]

Kennedy was persuaded and as the senior justice in the majority assigned the opinion. It might have been unwise politically for one of the women to write it and Kennedy, as a Catholic, didn't want it, so by default the 5–3 opinion fell to Breyer.

The admitting privileges provision had, as Kagan showed in oral argument, resulted in closing half the clinics in the state, some before the law took effect, some immediately thereafter. And, as Breyer's question to Keller showed, its supposed health benefits to women were nonexistent. "There was no significant health-related problem that the new law helped to cure."[49] If complications from an abortion were to occur, most would be later when the woman was not at the clinic. Furthermore, "hospitals often condition admitting privileges on reaching a certain number of admits per year."[50] That created a catch-22 "because the fact that abortions are so safe meant that providers were unlikely to have any patients to admit."[51]

The ASC requirement, when placed on top of the admitting privilege already cutting providers to twenty would further reduce them to seven or eight by driving up costs, again without benefit or need. The ASC regulates size of nursing staff, building dimensions, internal room requirements like specified width of corridors, and advanced heating and air conditioning systems. There were no similar requirements for other procedures. Childbirth is fourteen times more likely to result in death, but it can be done in the home. Colonoscopies have a mortality rate ten times that of abortions, but those facilities need not meet ASC requirements. By the ASC "Texas seeks to force women to travel long distances to get abortions in cramped to capacity superfacilities. Patients seeking these services are less likely to get the individualized attention" previously offered.[52]

As a final justification, Texas pointed to the Kermit Gosnell scandal in Philadelphia. He was an abortion provider who was convicted of murder for killing babies who had been born alive during abortions by severing their spinal cords. He chose to plead guilty to avoid a possible death sentence. His facility had not been inspected for fifteen years. Preexisting Texas law already contained numerous detailed regulations covering abortion facilities, including a requirement that they be inspected at least annually.

There were two dissents. To no one's surprise, one was by Thomas. Completing his twenty-fifth year on the Court, he was reliably conservative but often refreshing in his originality. He has been clear that he feels affirmative action stigmatized him and his autobiography portrays him as a bitter man deeply scarred by his contentious confirmation hearing. He had dissented in *Planned Parenthood v. Casey* his first Term and nothing had changed. "I remain fundamentally opposed to the Court's abortion jurisprudence."[53] He also objected to the "majority's free-floating balancing test" that considered benefits in addition to burdens.[54]

The principal dissent was by Alito, joined by Roberts and Thomas. Alito continued to fight the empirical battle he had started (and lost) during oral argument. He didn't think all the clinics closed because of HB 2 and he thought the few remaining could handle all the abortions in the state. He also bought the Gosnell argument. "If Pennsylvania had had such a [ASC] requirement in force, the Gosnell facility may have been shut down before his crimes. And if there were any similarly unsafe facilities in Texas, HB 2 was clearly intended to put them out of business."[55] The key word in the last sentence is "if." Alito did not explain how annual inspections were failing Texas women.

Texas Republican leaders were outraged by *Hellerstedt* and continued to claim HB 2 was about women's health. Senator John Cornyn claimed the decision "sets a dangerous precedent for states like Texas ... [as] today's decision is a step back in protecting the mothers across our state."[56] Senator Ted Cruz referenced women's health, but his main point was that "we know every life is a gift from God, and without life there is no liberty."[57] Governor Greg Abbott asserted that the decision "erodes States' lawmaking to safeguard the health and safety of women and subject more innocent life to being lost."[58] Lt. Governor Dan Patrick, author of the sonogram bill and one of the co-writers of HB 2, lamented the "devastating blow to the protection of the health and safety of women in Texas ... [because] now abortion clinics are free to ignore these basic safety standards and continue practicing under substandard conditions."[59] State senator Donna Campbell of New Braunfels found the decision "more than a devastating blow, it borders on evil."[60]

On the other side state senator Sylvia Garcia, chair of the Senate Hispanic Caucus, was enthusiastic. "For years, the Republican leadership has placed countless barriers on women seeking to exercise their constitutional right to abortion access. These barriers are medically unnecessary, purely aimed at preventing women from making their own healthcare decisions, and thankfully now illegal."[61] The CEO of Whole Woman's Health summed it up nicely: "This is the end of Wendy's filibuster."[62]

Garcia was right, and gender mattered. The men on the Court had split evenly in *Casey* and voted 3–2 against the right to choose in *Hellerstedt*, while the women unanimously supported the right to choose. The defeat of the Republicans was total. Yet that victory may prove transitory. Ginsburg, Kennedy, and Breyer are the three oldest members of the Court, and with Neil Gorsuch filling Scalia's seat, if any of the three leave the Court the Republican goal of wiping *Roe v. Wade* from the books may be achievable.

Just before the legislative session the state implemented a new rule that requires that fetal remains be either buried or cremated by hospitals and abortion clinics. The stated rationale is literally to give the fetus a decent burial. The rule does not apply to miscarriages or abortions that occur in the home. In late January 2017 Judge Sam Sparks, a UT alumnus and UT law grad appointed by President George H. W. Bush, issued a preliminary injunction against the rule. Nevertheless, the 2017 legislature passed an identical law. More significantly, SB 8 bans dilution and evacuation abortions—the most common and safest second trimester procedure.

Looking back at the short lifespan of HB 2, if its true intent was to reduce the number of abortions, it succeeded. Women from the Valley and West Texas had 50 percent fewer abortions in 2014 than in 2013, 2,279 compared with 4,589 the previous year.[63] In April 2017 Whole Woman's Health reopened its Austin clinic, but noted that former clinics in Corpus Christi, Midland, Lubbock, and College Station were likely to stay shuttered.

PART IV

Distinctly Texas

Texas is an unmatched distinctive state, a state of mind as well as a state in the union. From the Alamo to Edna Ferber's *Giant* to J.R. Ewing's "Dallas," everyone has an image of Texas. With vast expanses of land and ranches that could be measured against the size of Rhode Island, Texas is different. No other state can match Texas in the number of flagpoles flying the American flag and the state flag. And frequently there is a second flagpole so that a Lone Star flag can enjoy the breezes alone.

Texas is the only state that was a country at the time it joined the Union, and until displaced by OPEC in the early 1970s, the Texas Railroad Commission set the world price of oil. For better or worse Texans are enormously proud of Texas and their being Texans, points brought home by mandatory courses on Texas history. Simply put, Texas is outsized.

While gay marriage was a cultural war issue, prosecution of consensual adult sex was not. At the end of the century only Texas would prosecute such behavior conducted in private. To be sure, other states have the death penalty and execute those condemned. But Texas does it on a scale of its own. In this respect it is a nation like Iran or China. And no other state has a court like the Court of Criminal Appeals, so immune to issues of justice, so determined to see that every convicted capital defendant is executed. No state in the twentieth or twenty-first century has ever voluntarily changed congressional districts in mid-decade until Texas did so in 2003. It is remarkable that a state known for its fierce independence could be rolled by a single congressman—but Texas was (perhaps with an assist from state Democrats).

ELEVEN

Prosecuting Consensual Adult Sex

We were arrested for being gay.
—John Lawrence on his arrest
for homosexual sex

In a 1963 revision of the Texas Penal Code the legislature liberalized the prohibitions on so-called deviant sexual behavior. Sodomy was decriminalized for heterosexual couples. Bestiality was also decriminalized. Thus in an only-in-Texas, a human could legally have sex with an animal but not with another human of the same sex.

In the ensuing years there were halfhearted efforts to repeal and all failed. When the law was enforced it was because a minor, a quasi-public space, or nonconsensual sex was involved. There were no reported cases of the sodomy law being using against consensual sex in private.

I

On the evening of September 17, 1998, John Lawrence, Tyron Garner, and Robert Eubanks were in Lawrence's apartment in a working-class neighborhood of Houston. Garner was African American; the other two were white. All were gay and Garner and Eubanks were a couple. Lawrence had been drinking and Eubanks was drinking heavily. At some point Eubanks went to a pay phone and called the police. The police dispatcher alerted area patrol cars that there was a report of "a black male going crazy with a gun."[1] When the police loudly entered Lawrence's apartment they found no one with a gun, but did find Lawrence and Garner in the bedroom engaging in anal sex.

After the two were separated, Lawrence was uncooperative and mouthed off. The cops arrested the pair for Homosexual Conduct. Joe Quinn was the lead cop, and the office manager of the justice of the peace who arraigned the men stated: "I just do not think there is another police officer here in this county that would have done it."[2] Others would have just left the scene or at worst issued a citation. But Quinn and his cohorts took the pair to jail.

Word of the arrest caused lawyers to want to represent Lawrence and Garner. Michael Kaline, a local gay attorney, was the choice even though he was not a criminal defense lawyer. Ray Hill, who had prevailed in *Houston v. Hill*,[3] told him, "I wouldn't hire you to represent me in a traffic case. But, son, if you let this slip through your fingers, when you die they won't remember your name thirty minutes after you're dead. But if you take this case and see that it's done the right way, they'll carve your name in marble."[4] The right way meant contacting Lambda Legal, a national gay legal advocacy group, and Kaline did. He understood that national gay lawyers had to lead: "The case isn't just about the law. This case is about sociology, feelings of people in our country, religious issues, political issues, family issues. And it needs to be handled by a person or an organization that can appreciate all the ramifications."[5]

Lambda had been trying without success to find a state that would prosecute private homosexual conduct in order to seek the overruling of *Bowers v. Hardwick* that upheld such action in 1986.[6] Now it had one. (It bears noting that after Hardwick's arrest the Georgia prosecutor did not even take the case to a grand jury.)

There was disagreement in the Harris County prosecutor's office because some lawyers thought the Texas statute was absurd and that the office had no business defending it when consensual private conduct was involved. Tommy Holmes, the district attorney whose vote mattered, gave the go-ahead, believing that "the best way to bet rid of a bad law is to enforce it."[7]

Lambda's task was navigating the Texas courts while losing all the way. There was no way to tell how a jury might react, and a not guilty verdict would kill the case. So the defendants, with little at stake and facing no prospect of jail time, agreed to plead no contest. After the justice of the peace court, the case went to a county court-at-law where the necessary challenge to the constitutionality of the Texas law was placed in the record with a short brief. The DA's office, which "hate[s] to write" briefs, decided not to do one based on the well-founded notion that a county court-at-law judge would not hold a statute unconstitutional.[8] In fact the prosecutor had little to do with the case because once again the defendants pleaded no contest.

In the Fourteenth Court of Appeals Lambda expanded its attack on the law, especially the likely Texas defense of the law based on public morality. Lambda asserted that "'public morality,' when offered to justify a law's different treatment of people who engage in the same acts, reflects an improper effort to give legal effect to societal biases or dislikes."[9] It then questioned how public morality could be applicable to the "very *private* conduct" at issue.[10] The first point was a home run. The second avoided discussing how over time private conduct of individuals can affect public morality. Beyond questioning of the state's public morality argument, Lambda took on *Bowers* by claiming that the constitutional right to privacy protected Lawrence and Garner. Lambda made a tactical error in also challenging the law as sex discrimination under the Texas Equal Rights Amendment because if it prevailed on that issue, the case would go away and Lambda would be back at the status quo ante waiting for another state to prosecute private conduct (which might never occur).

Defending the law went from prosecutors to Bill Delmore, head of the Harris County DA's appellate division. Delmore knew the case was headed for the Supreme Court and made an important and appropriate decision. He would "take the high road. We were not going to descend to the level of name-calling. We were not going to write anything that [would offend] people in the gay community, including the legal community that happens to be gay."[11] He wrote his brief in two weeks, relying on public morality and an undefined protecting family values as justifying the Texas prohibition.

The three-judge panel for the litigation consisted of Republicans—they had, after all, swept the judiciary in Harris County in 1998—including Paul C. Murphy, who had been instrumental in getting the Republican Party in southeast Texas off the ground in the early 1970s. In the ninety minutes of oral argument the judges were more courteous and informed than the Lambda lawyers had anticipated. Delmore gave what was at best a workmanlike performance, and dealing with Lambda's animus argument, he claimed that the law did not single out gays because it equally prohibited bisexuals and heterosexuals from engaging in homosexual acts. This allowed Ruth Harlow, the Lambda attorney, to compare it to upholding a law against going to Roman Catholic mass because it applies equally to non-Catholics.

The panel agreed that John Anderson should draft an opinion. Surprisingly Anderson agreed with Lambda's argument that the law was sex discrimination in violation of the state Equal Rights Amendment. J. Harvey Hudson quickly disagreed; he did not believe the state's voters in banning sex discrimination had intended to legalize homosexual conduct. (As someone who testified in favor of the ERA at the legislature and as a voter, that had never crossed my mind.) This was in line with Delmore's reaction to the argument as "complete bullshit."[12]

As Murphy thought about the situation he could not explain why the state had decriminalized bestiality, heterosexual sodomy, and adultery but left homosexual sodomy standing. "Why did they leave this one in? ... And nobody could explain to me why."[13] Murphy joined Anderson's opinion. "Thus the distinction between legal and illegal conduct was not the act, but rather the sex of one of the participants. The defendants were treated differently solely on the basis of their sex."[14] Hudson bitterly dissented. Dale Carpenter captures it perfectly when he writes,

"Hudson's opinion was essentially a sermon, placing homosexual sinners in the hands of an angry legislature."[15] It was the opinion Harlow had expected from all three of the judges.

The handing down of the opinion closely coincided with the biennial state convention of the Texas Republican Party. The GOP responded with a platform that declared, "The Party believed that the practice of sodomy tears at the fabric of society, contributes to the breakdown of the family unit, and leads to the spread of dangerous communicable diseases. Homosexual behavior is contrary to the fundamental, unchanging truths that have been ordained by God, recognized by our country's founders, and shared by the majority of Texans."[16] The GOP went further: "We publicly rebuke judges Chief Justice Murphy and John Anderson, who ruled that the 100-year-old Texas sodomy law is unconstitutional, and ask all members of the Republican Party of Texas oppose their re-election."[17] The Harris County GOP chairman and an attorney drafted a letter to Anderson, calling on him to either reverse himself or resign. They hoped the chairs of the other thirteen counties covered by the court would sign, but some balked and the letter was never sent. Someone, however, faxed a copy to Anderson.

The Harris County DA's office asked all nine of the judges on the court to reconsider the case. Yet the judges were in a terrible position. If they reversed they were caving to political pressure, but if they affirmed (or didn't touch the case) they might be reaching a result they thought was in error. The GOP didn't care; they wanted judges who would toe the party line.

In response to the request to reconsider, the Fourteenth Court of Appeals announced it would do so without hearing oral argument—unusual to put it mildly. There was some hesitation on the court, but over a half year after agreeing to reconsider the case, a 7–2 opinion by Hudson reversed the original panel, leaving Murphy and Anderson to dissent. In one sense this was a benefit to Lambda; the case was once again viable for the Supreme Court. A month later, Lambda petitioned the Texas Court of Criminal Appeals, the highest court in the state that can hear criminal cases. Because of its specialized jurisdiction the Court of Criminal Appeals is a backwater, little noticed and little respected. The court waited a year, did not ask for briefs, and then issued an order refusing to hear the case. The path was cleared for the petition for certiorari to the United States Supreme Court, where a typical petition for certiorari has a one percent chance of being granted.

II

In leaving the Texas courts for the Supreme Court Lambda wanted to add experienced talent and selected Jenner and Block, which had an active Supreme Court practice in the business law area. In going with Jenner, Lambda was adding Paul Smith, who was gay, an experienced advocate, and former law clerk to Justice Lewis Powell. The posture of the cert petition (and subsequent briefs) was that the United States had moved well beyond the antigay animus represented by Texas law and that it was time for the Court to catch up with the country by overruling *Bowers*. The position stuck to the basics. There was no rational basis for treating homosexual sodomy differently than heterosexual sodomy. The Texas law violated the right of privacy by invading an "intimate realm of personal autonomy, family, and relationships."[18] *Bowers* was out of step with a changed country. When it was decided, twenty-four states had sodomy laws; now only thirteen did.

Back in Texas, Attorney General John Cornyn, who was running for the United States Senate, wanted no part of the case so once again it fell to Delmore. He made the decision, just as he had with the Court of Criminal Appeals, not to underscore the issues by writing an opposition to the cert petition. It didn't work. The Court requested Texas respond to the cert petition, not an ironclad guarantee of a future grant but an unmistakable showing of interest. Delmore tackled the privacy argument and an assistant dealt with equal protection. The new DA, Chuck Rosenthal, did not even read what was filed under his office's name.

When the Court granted cert, briefing began, but it followed what had already been framed in the cert petition. What was interesting were the words that got repeated again and again in the Lambda brief: "private" or "privacy" 70 times, "intimate" or "intimacy" 60 times, "relationship" 35 times, "families" or "family" 15 times. The ambiance of the brief was that this was not a case about sex—much less anal sex—but instead about traditional American family values.

Numerous organizations wished to file amicus briefs supporting Lawrence. Lambda's job was to discourage most of them. For example the New York City Bar Association. Saying it opposed the Texas law was like saying the sun sets in the west. On the other hand a brief from the American Bar Association was welcomed. The Episcopal Church, the United Church of Christ, and several liberal Baptist organizations filed a brief. Right of center think-tanks like the Cato Institute filed an amicus brief as did two Republican organizations. These amicus briefs were prepared by leading law professors and leading law firms. They were of quality and showed the broad range of support for the Lambda position in the case.

Delmore and his assistant wrote the Texas brief without outside assistance. There were parts of the brief that seemed of as much aid to the other side as they were to sustaining the law. At one point the brief characterized Lawrence's claim as "asking the Court to recognize a fundamental right of an adult to engage in private, non-commercial, consensual sex with an unrelated, unmarried adult."[19] At another point it stated that *Bowers* "stands alone as the only modern case in which the Court has approved moral tradition as a submitted rational basis for legislation."[20] Ouch—standing alone is a pretty thin justification. And finally the brief acknowledged that "the statute is unlikely to deter many individuals with an exclusively homosexual orientation."[21] But it might dissuade heterosexuals and bisexuals from same-sex experimentation. This was probably better than Chief Judge Murphy's conclusion that there was no rational basis for the law, but it came pretty close to it. Nevertheless, the brief did get off a good response to Lambda's claim about changed American attitudes: "The petitioners mistake new growth for deep roots."[22]

Unlike Lambda, the Harris County DA's office did not coordinate or do anything else with amicus groups. Unlike Lambda, no major law firms would touch the Texas side of the case. The two most prominent supporters of Texas were Jay Alan Sekulow of the American Center for Law and Justice and Robert P. George, a Princeton philosophy professor well known for his Catholic and natural law positions. The rest of the amicus filers were either conservative or religious (or both) and unknown except in their own circles. Their briefs reflected incredible animus against gays and unintentionally reinforced Lambda's position that the Texas law was intentionally discriminatory.

Alabama, South Carolina, and Utah referred to the "severe physical, emotional, psychological, and spiritual consequences" of homosexuality.[23] The Pro-Family Law Center along with the Traditional Values Coalition saw gays as absorbed in "Dionysian self-interest."[24] They further claimed that gays infiltrated various organizations to seize control: "The organization would thus appear to reflect the percentage of homosexuals in the general public, yet be entirely in the political control of 'gay' activists."[25] Shades of the Communist Party in the 1930s and '40s. Sekulow called sodomy "an abusive act."[26] George, for the Family Research Council, asserted that it was "impossible for them [two people of the same sex] to enter into bodily communion."[27] No wonder Lambda was cheering for more amicus briefs on the other side.

With the briefing done, it was time to prepare oral arguments. On both sides there was initial doubt about who would present the case. Harvard's Laurence Tribe, author of the leading treatise on constitutional law and the losing counsel in *Bowers,* approached the Jenner-Lambda team to argue the case, but there was wonder if he was the right person and as soon as the decision was made that counsel had to be gay, he was out. Two other lawyers, one of whom was Harlow who had argued the case in Texas, took themselves out of contention because neither had previously argued at the Court. Paul Smith had, eight times (for commercial clients), and he was the choice.

As a former Powell clerk, Smith was aware that when *Bowers* was argued, Powell told one of his clerks that he did not understand homosexuality and that he had never met a homosexual. The clerk, Cabell Chinnis, was gay, but did not tell Powell. Nor, obviously, had Smith who clerked some years before. Powell, in fact, had had more gay clerks than any other justice but obviously did not know that. The pressure of undoing Powell's fifth vote may have weighed more heavily on Smith than if the case had gone to someone else, and Smith spent three weeks prior to the oral argument preparing—perhaps overpreparing—for it.

In Houston there was a quick discussion about who should take the case, one that included the possibility that it might be Rosenthal. A day later, in the midst of a phone discussion of another case, Rosenthal told Delmore that he had decided to do it himself. Rosenthal was not an appellate advocate and not surprisingly had never argued before the Court. Rosenthal did five moot courts—two in the DA's office, two at South Texas School of Law, and one in D.C. at the Heritage Foundation. He fared poorly in all of them. Whether Texas could have acquired an experienced Supreme Court advocate is problematical, but the DA's office should have tried (if they cared about increasing the chances of winning). The subsequent creation of the position of solicitor general in the attorney general's office and staffing it with young able lawyers like Greg Coleman and Ted Cruz solved the problem for the future. But for the present the lawyering was a throwback to the earlier era where the state was consistently outgunned by better counsel.

III

Among the groups outside the Court the day of argument was the then-unknown Westboro Baptist Church of Topeka, Kansas, with their signs "God Hates Fags" and "AIDS Is God's Revenge."[28] A group of about fifteen African American girls in uniforms who happened to be walking by recited the Pledge of Allegiance to drown out an anti-American song. Inside the Court there was decorum, as always.

Smith went first and within seconds had asserted there was a fundamental right to be free from state intrusion into personal decisions
about sexual expression. Chief Justice William Rehnquist, a sure vote
against him, challenged the historical basis for the fundamental right
Smith was asserting. This conduct "has been banned for a long time."[29]
But the long time was a ban on all sodomy and did not focus on same-
sex couples, Smith replied. Accurately.

Smith kept with his brief and fielded 35 questions in 26 minutes.
Twenty-three of those came from Antonin Scalia and all were hostile
to an argument everyone knew Scalia would reject. Smith tried to keep
the focus on the fact that Texas did not prohibit the act, just who could
commit it; that the laws on the books were unenforced; and that America had changed (and therefore so should the Court). Harlow, sitting at
counsel's table, passed him a note simply stating, "Good job!"[30]

No one would pass a similar note to Rosenthal, an advocate sorely
out of his depth. He could not understand that Scalia was trying to help
him. He could not answer questions about Texas law, like whether
same-sex couples could adopt. They could. Eventually the justices
ignored him except to use him as a conduit to argue with one another.
Linda Greenhouse, the Supreme Court correspondent for the *New York
Times*, wrote the next day that this was "a mismatch of advocates to a
degree rarely seen at the court."[31]

IV

With Rehnquist dissenting, John Paul Stevens became the senior jus-
tice in the majority and he assigned the opinion to Anthony Kennedy, a
Californian who went to Stanford and then Harvard law before return-
ing home to practice. He was appointed by Gerald R. Ford to the Ninth
Circuit and became the beneficiary of the Senate's rejection of Robert
Bork and the subsequent withdrawal of Douglas Ginsburg. The Justice
Department looked for a noncontroversial judge and Kennedy fit that
quality perfectly. After a brief period on the Court he joined Sandra

Day O'Connor in the center and when she retired he became the swing vote on a Court otherwise split 4–4.

The opinion assignment made perfect sense. Four votes—Stevens, David Souter, Ruth Bader Ginsburg, and Stephen Breyer—were solid. Having Kennedy write would mean the opinion would fit his views and solidify his vote. In all probability Kennedy wanted the assignment because he had written the majority in *Romer v. Evans,*[32] the only gay rights opinion since *Bowers.* In *Romer* the Court invalidated Colorado's Amendment Two that had prohibited adding gays to local antidiscrimination laws.

The principal thrust of Kennedy's majority[33] in *Lawrence* is a takedown of *Bowers,* which the opinion says "was not correct the day it was decided, and it is not correct today."[34] Kennedy began his demolition of *Bowers* by stating the Court had asked the wrong question, referencing "the court's own failure to appreciate the extent of the liberty at stake. To say that the issue in *Bowers* was simply the right to engage in certain sexual conduct demeans the claim the individual put forward."[35] Kennedy continued to assert "as a general rule [states and courts should not] define the meaning of the relationship or to set its boundaries absent injury to a person or abuse of an institution the law protects."[36] That mention of "relationship" was just one of eleven in the opinion.

Then Kennedy turned to *Bowers*'s history of sodomy and found it wanting. Thus "there is no longstanding history in this country of laws directed at homosexual conduct as a distinct matter.... Thus early American sodomy laws were not directed at homosexuals as such but instead sought to prohibit non-procreative sexual activity more generally."[37]

Having taken *Bowers* apart, the Court noted that Europe had moved away from the criminalization of same-sex acts and that of the twenty-four states that had criminalized same-sex sodomy when *Bowers* was decided only thirteen still had the laws on the books. Apparently only four made an attempt to enforce them. The Court concluded by flatly rejecting Texas's "morality" rationale: "the Texas statute furthers no legitimate state interest which can justify its intrusion into the person and private life of the individual."[38] Instead "the petitioners are entitled to respect for their private lives. The State cannot demean their existence or control their destiny by making their private sexual conduct a crime."[39]

Did any of this suggest laws limiting marriage to a man and a woman were invalid? No; this was not at issue. The case "does not involve whether the government must give formal recognition to any relationship that homosexual persons seek to enter."[40]

An outraged Scalia, for Rehnquist and Thomas, took the rare step of reading his entire dissent from the bench as a way of showing his disapproval of the majority. Scalia is always a pleasure to read when he was angry and his dissent did not disappoint. In rejecting constitutional protection for Lawrence's conduct Scalia wrote that "an 'emerging awareness' is by definition not 'deeply rooted in the Nation's history and tradition[s]' as we have said 'fundament right' status requires. Constitutional entitlements do not spring into existence because some States choose to lessen or eliminate criminal sanctions on certain behavior. Much less do they spring into existence, as the Court seems to believe, because *foreign nations* decriminalize conduct."[41]

Scalia complained that *Lawrence* signaled the end of morals legislation. "The Texas statute undeniably seeks to further the belief that certain forms of behavior are 'immoral and unacceptable.... the same interest furthered by criminal laws against fornication, bigamy, adultery, adult incest, bestiality, and obscenity.... If, as the Court asserts, the promotion of majoritarian sexual morality is not even a *legitimate* state interest, none of the above-mentioned laws can survive rational-basis review."[42]

Then he attacked elites. "Today's decision is the product of a Court, which is the product of a law-profession culture, that has signed on to the so-called homosexual agenda, by which I mean the agenda promoted by some homosexual activists directed at eliminating the moral opprobrium that has traditionally attached to homosexual conduct."[43] Guess where Scalia stood on that tradition of moral opprobrium.

Scalia noted that neither citizens nor legislatures had to be consistent; they "unlike judges need not carry things to their logical conclusion.... The Court today pretends that it possesses a similar freedom of action."[44] But that just wasn't true, he asserted. "Today's opinion dismantles the structure of constitutional law that has permitted a distinction to be made between heterosexual and homosexual unions, insofar as formal recognition of marriage is concerned.... This case 'does not involve' the issues of homosexual marriage only if one entertains the belief that principle and logic have nothing to do with the decisions of this Court."[45] At the time of *Bowers* Chief Justice Warren Burger sent Powell an over-the-top memo that the case "presents for me the most far reaching issue of those 30 years [that he had spent on the bench]."[46] Perhaps he was seeing the same future that Scalia was predicting.

Reaction of activists in Texas split on predictable lines. There was a gay rights rally at Houston's City Hall and numerous gays and lesbians applauded the decision. Lawrence was more low-key: "The ruling lets us get on with our lives, and it opens the door for gay people all across the country to be treated equally."[47] The president of the conservative Texas Eagle Forum claimed she was "heartbroken for the families of Texas" and chided the Court for being unable to "discern the difference between right and wrong."[48] Governor Rick Perry stated the obvious: "Texas will abide by the decision."[49] Rosenthal, who knew his performance at oral argument did not go well, simply expressed disappointment as good losers typically do.

V

As President Bush's invasion of Iraq went from "Mission Accomplished" to quagmire thereby diminishing his chances for reelection, his so-called "brain," Karl Rove, decided to rally Republicans with the fear of the coming of same-sex marriage. Bush himself proposed amending the Constitution to enshrine marriage as between a man and a woman. But it is all but impossible to amend the Constitution no matter how popular the idea and Bush's proposal was successfully filibustered in the Senate and failed the two-thirds requirement in the House. Still a national survey in the spring of 2004 showed same-sex marriage out-polled both guns and abortion as an important issue to voters.

Rove also encouraged Republicans to put local same-sex marriage prohibitions on the ballot, and thirteen states adopted them. Texas was a year behind, voting on a constitutional amendment in November 2005. With 17 percent of the electorate turning out—actually high for an odd-year election—it passed with 3–1 support, carrying 253 of the 254 counties. Only Travis voted no—at a 60 percent rate. A state representative claimed, "That's where it was won, from the pulpits of the state of Texas."[50] Kelly Shackelford of Texans for Marriage stated, "Texans know marriage is between a man and a woman, and children deserve both a mom and a dad. They don't need a Ph.D. or a degree in anything to teach them that."[51]

The swift adoption of those state constitutional amendments was an illustration of the backlash thesis popularized by political scientist Gerald Rosenberg[52] and law professor Michael Klarman.[53] Relying principally on desegregation and abortion, the thesis holds that when the Court gets too far ahead of the country there will be a backlash that halts progress unless and until the country catches up. What stunned observers was how quickly (rather than whether) the country changed on gay marriage so that when, a decade later, the Supreme Court, following the logic Scalia knew it would, declared gay marriage a constitutional right in an opinion by Anthony Kennedy the decision was accepted in all but a handful of areas.[54]

VI

The actual facts of that night in September 1998 may not have been as the courts had thought. In his masterful book about the case, Dale Carpenter suggests that it was unlikely that Lawrence and Garner were having sex at all. They were not a couple and had initially stated they were not guilty. But the key point is that Joe Quinn's story about the arrest is not credible with the exception that the cops entered the apartment loudly. If that is true, typically people would have immediately ceased having sex. But Quinn claimed to have caught them in the act. Indeed Quinn claimed both were naked with Lawrence on the bed on all fours receiving anal sex from Garner, which they continued after being ordered to stop by Quinn. Continuing with cops in the room ordering a halt?

The other cop could not be sure whether they were having anal sex or oral sex (in 2005 he was coming down on the side of oral). Given Quinn's graphic description there should not have been any ambiguity. The other cop said Lawrence was naked but Garner was not. Arresting officers in a bedroom in an apartment should be able to tell if someone is naked or not and should be able to distinguish anal sex from oral sex. Lawrence claimed right from the start that "we were arrested for being gay."[55] The flagrant conduct in the title of Carpenter's book was not that of Lawrence and Garner but rather that of the Houston police who arrested them.

What this means is that for the case to succeed the way it ultimately did, it could not go to trial. There was a lot of good lawyering to keep the case clean with the no contest pleas. Michael Kaline may not have his name carved in marble as Ray Hill predicted, but his call to Lambda was truly prescient.

By the time the Court legalized same-sex marriage Lawrence, Garner, and Eubanks were dead. The latter was assaulted by an unknown person or persons and died a couple of days later in 2000. His family kept Garner from the funeral. The reason has never been explained; it could have been that they did not approve of gays or because Garner was black, or they thought he was the murderer (he was a suspect, but a grand jury refused to indict). Garner was next. Ill for many months, he died in 2006. He was cremated by the county for no cost, but his family could not even afford a modest urn for his ashes. Lawrence, the oldest of the three, lived until 2011, dying in Houston in the care of his longtime partner, Jose Garcia.

Chief Judge Paul Murphy retired when his term was up. Judge John Anderson had already won the Republican primary and thus was unopposed in 2000. With *Lawrence* in the past, he served until retirement in 2012. With the exception of Chuck Rosenthal the attorneys all seemed to be doing fine. Rosenthal was reelected in 2004, but resigned in disgrace three years later amid a series of scandals. He "blamed prescription drugs for impairing his judgment" while in office.[56]

TWELVE

Capital Punishment

The State of Texas has a very thoughtful, a very clear process.

> —Governor Rick Perry on capital punishment
> in Texas

Texas leads the nation in executions. There is no close second. In just four years between 1997 and 2000 Texas executed 132 people—that is significantly more than any other state has executed since executions resumed after 1976. In this century alone Texas has executed well over 300 people. Over the entire time period half the capital cases came from Harris County where aggressive district attorneys, especially Johnny Holmes, have sought the death penalty.

The day the Supreme Court agreed to hear a challenge to Kentucky's lethal injection protocol,[1] attorneys for Michael Richard, who was scheduled to be executed that night under Texas's protocol that was identical to Kentucky's, called Presiding Judge Sharon Keller of the Court of Criminal Appeals at 4:45 p.m. They said they were having computer problems in preparing a motion to stay the execution (based on the grant in the Kentucky case) and asked for the clerk's office to remain open until 5:15 or 5:30. Keller, who had been in the Dallas district attorney's office before the CCA and had earned the nickname "Sharon Killer," refused, explaining "we close at five."[2] Richard, who had an IQ of 64, was executed three hours later.

Two days later lawyers for Carlton Turner, the next inmate scheduled for lethal injection, filed a motion for a stay and the CCA denied it by a 5–4 vote. The CCA acts as if its purpose is to facilitate executions. Indicating how it might have handled Richard's case (if it had gotten there) the Supreme Court granted Turner's stay.[3]

I

Thanks to a brilliant litigation strategy by University of Pennsylvania law professor Anthony Amsterdam, a former Felix Frankfurter clerk, for the NAACP Legal Defense Fund, the Court started chipping away at capital punishment in the late 1960s. One result was the ending of so-called "death qualified" juries that excluded anyone with qualms about the death penalty. Coming at a time when support for the death penalty was at an all-time low and declining, the Wichita Falls district attorney expressed a common lament among prosecutors: "I'm so mad, I'm speechless. We don't know what to do."[4] The Georgia attorney general stated it would end the death penalty in his state. A second result was a decade-long moratorium on executions. An LDF lawyer explained, "The politics of abolition boiled down to this: for each year the United States went without executions, the more hollow would ring claims that the American people could not do without them.... The longer death-row inmates waited, the greater their numbers, the more difficult it would be for the courts to permit the first execution."[5]

In the 1970 Term the Court set two issues of Amsterdam's strategy for argument. One was standardless sentencing where state laws left jurors (and prosecutors) absolutely free to decide who the few among the large number of offenders would be sentenced to death. The LDF argued that states should inform the jurors to consider explicit aggravating and mitigating factors in their decision on whether or not to impose death. The other issue was bifurcated juries where guilt and punishment were split. By splitting them a defendant who chose not to testify could talk to the jury in the sentencing phase. It would also allow the defense to enter evidence about the defendant that was not relevant to guilt or innocence. In an irony, that Term was the one Term where Amsterdam did not argue a capital case; the Court rejected his request to join the arguments as amicus.

The Court ruled against the defendants in each case by 6–3 votes with William O. Douglas, William J. Brennan, and Thurgood Marshall being the dissenters.[6] In rejecting the standardless sentencing claim, Justice John Marshall Harlan expressed doubts that sentencing would be improved by additional jury instructions. But the Court had a more fundamental problem—identifying the appropriate characteristics would be impossible. "To identify before the fact those characteristics of criminal homicides and their perpetrators which call for the death penalty, and to express these characteristics in language which can fairly be understood and applied by the sentencing authority, appear to be tasks which are beyond present human ability."[7] Checkmate. Seven hundred death-row inmates were now eligible for execution, including the 200 whose petitions for certiorari were about to be denied.

II

Justice Hugo Black was a strong proponent of the constitutionality of the death penalty. He was a textualist and the text of the Constitution in both the Fifth and Fourteenth Amendments authorized depriving a person of life if done consistently with due process of law; furthermore there could be no claim that the Framers believed the death penalty unconstitutional. Black now saw a chance to put the issue to rest. Instead of denying certiorari in all the pending death penalty cases, grant cert on the Eighth Amendment cruel and unusual punishment issue and collect the seven or eight votes (depending on whether Marshall joined Brennan) and "once and for all make it clear to the nation that the death penalty in all its aspects pass[es] constitutional muster."[8] After the justices agreed to hear an Eighth Amendment claim—which internally they had already rejected—Chief Justice Warren E. Burger asked Brennan and Byron R. White to find four "clean" cases where no extraneous issues could prevent the justices from reaching the ultimate issue.

Brennan and White selected one case where the LDF was representing the defendant to ensure this time that Amsterdam would argue the case. They wanted an equivalent argument on the other side and so selected *Branch v. Texas.* Charles Alan Wright had represented Texas in the eighteen-year-old vote case and the justices were under the mistaken impression that he would represent the state in any case coming before the Court. When word got to Attorney General Crawford Martin that Burger wanted Wright to argue *Branch,* Martin quickly arranged for that to happen.

Before oral argument both Black and Harlan retired and died, to be replaced by Lewis Powell and William Rehnquist. President Nixon filled four vacancies with a year to go in his first term. Furthermore, for the first time in decades there was a Republican majority on the Court—Potter Stewart joining the four Nixon appointees. Yet in an amazing and wholly unanticipated twist in *Furman v. Georgia* the five Warren Court holdovers outvoted the four Nixon appointees to hold capital punishment, as practiced, unconstitutional.[9] One reason may have been Amsterdam, who was dazzling in oral argument; White called it the best he had ever heard.

The five in the majority each wrote a separate opinion and none of them joined the opinion of another. Thus there were five different reasons why capital punishment was unconstitutional, although the dominant theme of the opinions was that the discretion within the system created inconsistent and discriminatory outcomes. Brennan believed the death penalty was always unconstitutional because it was an affront to human dignity. Over the summer Marshall had changed his mind on capital punishment and concluded that the average American, if informed of the facts surrounding it, would "find it shocking to his conscience and sense of justice" as Marshall now did.[10] In this evolution Americans had achieved "a major milestone in the long road from barbarism."[11] Douglas saw capital punishment as limited to the poor and to minorities. If the law had so limited to the poor and minorities, everyone would find it unconstitutional; for Douglas it was sufficient that the law in fact operated in this fashion.

The wild cards were Stewart and White. The former was morally opposed to the death penalty; the latter was definitely not. Stewart worried that too many death-row inmates would be executed if the Court gave a go-ahead. In predicting his vote, Brennan told his clerks, "Potter will not pull the switch on 600 people."[12] White believed too few people were being executed, thus undermining any claim that the penalty served no purpose whatsoever.

In the standardless sentencing case the previous Term, Harlan had said that offering the jurors statutory guidance was impossible. The best reading of *Furman*'s five opinions was that states must do the impossible. Thus it was no wonder that the *New York Times* ran a six-column headline proclaiming the end of the death penalty. Everyone agreed capital punishment was dead. Except the people and their elected representatives. Just as there had been with the Court's embrace of bussing for desegregation and would be with constitutionalizing abortion, there was a large and immediate backlash to *Furman*.

III

Thirty-five states and the federal government passed new legislation reinstating the death penalty. With the exception of Texas (and Oregon) the statutes were of one of two kinds. A handful of states made capital punishment mandatory for certain homicides. A majority of states attempted to do what Harlan had declared impossible and offer a list of aggravating and mitigating considerations for juries. The Texas statute asked the jury three questions: Did the defendant act deliberately? If the victim had provoked the defendant did the defendant nevertheless act unreasonably? And finally—and most importantly— "whether there is a probability that the defendant would commit criminal acts of violence that would constitute a continuing threat to society?"[13] There was not much discretion in the Texas statute. If the defendant acted deliberately and was a future danger, then death was the punishment.

For the 1975 Term the Court agreed to hear cases from Florida, Georgia, Louisiana, North Carolina, and Texas that offered a complete look at the newly enacted death penalty statutes. Amsterdam was counsel in three of the cases, including *Jurek v. Texas*. As a result he had three different statutory regimes affecting his clients. Nevertheless he adopted a single approach for all three cases; the statutes authorized excessive discretion, which meant that inconsistent results would exist just as they had in the pre-*Furman* world. The strategy had the positive benefit that it would not have the mandatory death cases claiming guided discretion was the way to go or the guided discretion cases pointing to mandatory statutes as the proper route. The drawback of the argument was that it appeared to claim no system of capital punishment could be found that would be constitutional, and with thirty-six jurisdictions authorizing death that was a tall order. This was underscored when Amsterdam refused to concede that any procedural framework could satisfy constitutional standards. As Carol and Jordan Steiker note, the justices were "openly incredulous" with Amsterdam's argument.[14] He had Brennan and Marshall going in, and that was all he had going out.

While counsel from the state attorneys general's office were overmatched, Yale law professor and U.S. solicitor general Robert Bork argued as amicus in favor of the states. He took Amsterdam's argument head-on and noted that there was discretion in every facet of the criminal justice system, not just in death cases. "There is not a single argument petitioners put forward that could not equally be made in regard, for example, to the penalty of life imprisonment for first-degree murder."[15] That was accurate and could only be countered by accepting Amsterdam's argument that death is different because of its finality and so capital punishment could be a law unto itself. The Court accepted that argument in striking down the mandatory death statutes[16] but in *Gregg v. Georgia* it sustained those offering guided discretion.[17]

Six justices wanted the worst of the worst to face execution with consistency across results and for capital defendants to receive individualized consideration of their circumstances. The justices could have either one of the two or neither, but they could not have both because the two are fundamentally inconsistent. This would create a major problem in the Court's jurisprudence. Brennan and Marshall had a consistent solution; the death penalty no matter how structured was unconstitutional. Rehnquist, too, had a consistent solution—get the Court out of the business.

IV

Amsterdam's argument of excessive discretion slighted the Texas statute, which in fact limited jury discretion by constraining the consideration of mitigating evidence. Both Rehnquist and White, who voted to sustain all the statutes, stated that the Texas statute "more closely approximates" the mandatory statutes.[18] Jordan Steiker observes that "for more than a decade following *Jurek,* Texas capital defendants were virtually alone nationwide in being subject to the death penalty without having a sentencer determine that they deserved to die."[19]

That was but one of a number of problems Texas capital defendants faced. A major one was that for appellate purposes Texas split civil and criminal litigation. Criminal cases went to the Court of Criminal Appeals, where the judges run statewide with party labels. It had discretionary jurisdiction in most cases, but mandatory jurisdiction in capital cases. Unlike the Texas Supreme Court, the CCA has no supervisory powers over lawyers, and since it lacks a civil side, the CCA never sees high-powered lawyers arguing major cases. A true backwater, its own standards are shockingly lax. Counsel in death cases often waived their right to oral argument, something that would never happen on the civil side. Lawyers sleeping through parts of a capital case do not merit a rebuke, much less a finding of inadequate representation. Trial lawyers, with little or no appellate experience, take cases on appeal because the little money provided for representation of indigent defendants at trial is augmented on the appeal. Furthermore, it took years and years before lawyers in capital cases came to understand that the sentencing hearing was likely to be the one place open to protect their clients. If there were a capital defense bar that would have been understood sooner.

The CCA resolved cases quickly, indicating it may not have afforded them the consideration that would be their due. As an elected criminal court its reversal rate was low compared to state supreme courts. Its capital reversal rate was shockingly low. At times the CCA looked like an extension of the prosecutor's office. Thus it has not been bothered by "brazenly discriminatory use of preemptive strikes, prosecutorial failure to disclose exculpatory evidence, and state-sponsored testimony regarding the 'dangerousness' of Hispanics."[20]

After the CCA affirms a conviction, post-conviction review begins, again within the Texas system. Many death-row inmates did not have representation, a recipe for a further loss. For those who do have a lawyer, the state offers a piddling sum for representation and investigation. If there were disputed facts, the trial court often resolved them without an evidentiary hearing, typically copying the state's briefs. The resulting loss is all but inevitable.

In 2010 Texas created an office for post-conviction representation. The result has been a more professional practice with trial courts more willing to hold a contested hearing. But this doesn't change the facts about the CCA where the post-conviction part of the case ends like the direct appeal with a judgment upholding the death penalty. Furthermore, the new office handles only new cases, not those dozens of death-row inmates who have already gone through their state post-conviction hearings.

When state post-conviction litigation ends, federal habeas corpus litigation begins with the relitigation of what occurred in the state post-conviction litigation. Texas death-row inmates had little chance before the CCA. They have little chance in the Fifth Circuit Court of Appeals, which is openly hostile to capital cases to a degree unapproached elsewhere in the nation. Until mid-2017 judges on the Fifth Circuit had successfully opposed the creation of a capital defender's office for inmates within the jurisdiction even though such offices had been established throughout the nation. If that were not enough, a 1996 federal statute forbids federal courts from reversing capital cases where the state court makes an error of federal law. The federal courts can only reverse for such errors when it concludes the state court was "unreasonably" wrong. It is no wonder Texas is one of the top two (with Virginia) in executing those sentenced to death. It wants to. As Governor Rick Perry stated in the September 2011 Republican debate, "in the state of Texas, our citizens have made that decision [to have capital punishment], and they made it clear, and they don't want you to commit those crimes against our citizens. And if you do, you will face ultimate justice."[21]

Perry had prefaced that statement with praise for the Texas system. "The State of Texas has a very thoughtful, a clear process in place which—when someone commits the most heinous of crimes against our citizens, they get a fair hearing, they go through an appellate process."[22] University of California law professor and capital punishment expert Frank Zimring offers the reality—a state "can have full and fair criminal procedures, or it can have a regularly functioning process of executing prisoners; but the evidence suggests it can't have both."[23] The Texas choice has been clear.

V

Johnny Paul Penry had a troubled childhood. His mother beat him every day, isolated him without toilet privileges, and made him drink urine. In the language of the time, he was "mentally retarded"—words the Court would use until 2014 when the current term "intellectually disabled" was substituted—with an IQ somewhere in the 50s and the comprehension level of a child of six and a half. He could not read nor write; he did not know the days of the week; he could not name the months of the year and did not know how many hours were in a day. He had been placed in the Mexia State School, a school for the mentally retarded where he did not do well and been diagnosed as psychotic.

Penry committed his first rape at age nineteen. He was sentenced to five years in jail, but paroled after two. A year later, in 1979, he decided to rape Pamela Moseley Carpenter who lived in Livingston. He had delivered appliances to her home and came back under the false pretense of seeing if the stove was working. In the ensuing fight, he slapped Carpenter several times, raped her, took a pair of scissors that she had tried to defend herself with and plunged them into her chest. She was able to call a friend and say what happened before she died several hours later in a hospital. Penry was arrested and confessed.

There was outrage about the brutality of the crime, but also about the light sentence for his first rape, and the fact of parole. Additional attention came from Carpenter being the sister of Mark Moseley, an NFL star and the only placekicker to win the league's MVP award. The small-town prosecutor would go for the death sentence.

As was common at the time, defense counsel concentrated on the guilt-innocence phase of the case, trying to have Penry's confession suppressed because he could not knowingly waive the right to counsel and putting on an insanity defense. When these failed it was on to the punishment phase with the three questions *Jurek* approved, and there was no doubt that the crime had been unprovoked and deliberate, so the only issue was Penry's future dangerousness. He didn't have a chance. "If anything, Penry's inability to learn from his mistakes—which was central to his insanity defense—virtually proved the state's case on future dangerousness."[24] With affirmative answers to the three questions the jury had decided Penry's fate without ever being asked if he deserved to die. "Worse still ... the very evidence that in most jurisdictions was treated as mitigating (such as abusive background or mental retardation) would have only *aggravating* significance in Texas, as enhancing the defendant's prospects for dangerousness."[25]

The CCA affirmed the conviction and the Supreme Court denied certiorari. Post-conviction litigation was no more successful, but after the Fifth Circuit denied Penry's claim the Court granted certiorari principally to consider the Eight Amendment claim that it is cruel and unusual punishment to execute the mentally retarded. That claim was rejected 5–4. But the Court also considered the special issues questions, this time without Amsterdam's fudging of what was involved. By a different 5–4 majority, Justice Sandra Day O'Connor being the fifth vote in each, the Court held the Texas special issues statute unconstitutional as applied because nowhere did it call for a jury to be asked if, on balance, the defendant deserved to live or die.[26]

At the punishment phase Penry's lawyer noted Penry had tried to deflect the prediction of future dangerousness. "But a boy with this mentality, with this mental affliction, even though you have found that issue against us as to insanity, I don't think that there is any question in a single one of you juror's [*sic*] minds there that is something definitely wrong, basically, with this boy. And I think there is not a single one of you that doesn't believe this boy has brain damage."[27] With that setup he asked the jurors to "see if you don't find that we're inquiring into the mental state of the defendant in each [special issues question]."[28] Seeing this for what it was, a plea for jury nullification, the prosecutor reminded the jurors that "You've all taken an oath to follow the law and you know what the law is."[29] As O'Connor summed it up, "we conclude that the jury was not provided with a vehicle for expressing 'its reasoned moral response' to that evidence in rendering the sentencing decision ... .we do not 'risk that the death penalty will be imposed in spite of factors which may call for a less severe penalty.'"[30]

Penry came down right after the 1989 legislative session had ended and so it was not until 1991 that the special issues statute was fixed. Scores upon scores of death-row inmates had been convicted without the chance to have jurors consider their mitigating evidence. Many had been executed. Many would be executed over the next two decades because the CCA, the Fifth Circuit, and a Supreme Court where

Brennan and Marshall had retired all treated the case in the narrowest possible fashion.[31]

The CCA, with agreement from the Fifth Circuit, concluded that all evidence—from drug addiction, sexual abuse, low intelligence, etc.—"could be adequately addressed via the dangerousness issue despite the fact that such evidence plainly supported rather than undermined a jury's finding of dangerousness."[32] In the fourteen years after *Penry* the Fifth Circuit granted relief in just a single *Penry*-issue case[33]—that's right, just one—at a time Texas was going on the execution spree mentioned in the introductory paragraph of this chapter.

VI

The Polk County DA wanted Penry executed. Although a retrial could cost the county more than its annual budget, the DA believed cost was no issue when justice was at stake. Over defense objections the trial was held in neighboring Walker County where the Texas Department of Corrections employs one-third of the workers and Penry was the TDC's most famous inmate. The *Huntsville Item* had reacted to *Penry* with an editorial entitled "Mitigating Circumstances—A Bunch of Junk."[34]

The retrial covered much the same ground as the first although Penry's team had been enhanced and offered more extensive evidence of his childhood abuse. The retrial occurred before the new Texas special issues law took effect and so the jury was asked the same three questions that the Court had declared constitutionally deficient. Penry's judge, like others during this period, tried to remedy the problem by giving a nullification instruction to the effect that if they believed the defendant should not die they should falsely answer "no" to one of the special issues questions, but the instruction was highly convoluted at best. (The CCA had upheld a nullification instruction as curing the *Penry* problem.) Penry was once again sentenced to death.

Penry lost on direct appeal, lost on state post-conviction, lost on federal habeas at the district court level, and lost again at the Fifth Circuit, which did not even deem his case to warrant a full appeal. An execution date was set for November 16, 2000. The Supreme Court unexpectedly entered a stay and subsequently granted certiorari in the case to consider a procedure that had been replaced a decade earlier. The nullification instruction did not cure the constitutional infirmity. Requiring jurors to answer a special issues question dishonestly in order to give effect to the evidence "made the jury charge as a whole internally contradictory, and placed law-abiding jurors in an impossible situation."[35] Quoting from her dissent in one of the earlier cases gutting *Penry*, O'Connor stated that error occurs when a jury cannot give "*full* consideration and *full* effect to mitigating evidence."[36] Rehnquist, Scalia, and Thomas dissented.

At the time of decision the Texas legislature had passed a bill precluding the execution of the mentally retarded, but two weeks later Governor Rick Perry vetoed it. In his veto message he proclaimed: "We do not execute mentally retarded murderers."[37] The statement was palpably false. Texas led the nation here too.

A year later, in *Atkins v. Virginia*, the Court overruled the conservative half of the first *Penry* decision and held that the Eighth Amendment forbids the execution of mentally retarded murderers.[38] The decision came down during Penry's new sentencing trial and the defense immediately moved for a mistrial, claiming the evidence clearly established Penry's mental retardation.

The trial judge denied the motion and made her own finding that Penry was not mentally retarded. She could not put that question directly to the jury so instead she issued her own nullification instruction to the jury. The sentence was once again death. Running for reelection, the judge emphasized her treatment of Penry. "When the John Paul Penry capital murder trial came before her court in 2002, Judge Corker cleared the way for the jury to issue a death sentence."[39] Amazingly, in 2005 the CCA reversed the sentence.

VII

A new majority had formed in the second *Penry* decision when Kennedy changed his position, and the result was that in a highly reduced Supreme Court docket, Texas death penalty cases were getting a disproportionate share of unwanted attention. I wrote "amazingly" because otherwise the CCA and the Fifth Circuit seemed fixated on continuing to affirm all death penalty convictions and the reversal of Penry's sentence was very much out of step (although the CCA may have understood that the Supreme Court was not impressed with nullification instructions). Between 2004 and 2007 the Court issued five opinions reversing Texas death penalty convictions, sending an incredible and deserved rebuke to the death-happy CCA and Fifth Circuit.

Robert Tennard had an IQ of 67 and was sentenced under the pre-*Penry* special issues. His problem was identical to Penry's; evidence of a low IQ helped on culpability (which the jury could not consider) but hurt on future dangerousness. Again, the jury could sentence Tennard to death because of his intellectual disability, but could not withhold the death penalty on that ground. The CCA rejected his claim because he did not prove he had full-blown mental retardation. The Fifth Circuit didn't find his IQ deficiency to be severe enough nor that Tennard had proven the murder was attributable to a low IQ. O'Connor's opinion reversed because of *Penry II*. This was federal habeas; thus, the reversal meant that the CCA opinion was not just wrong but rather unreasonably wrong.[40]

Smith v. Texas[41] was another low IQ case under the pre-1991 special issues where a nullification instruction had been given. The CCA concluded that evidence of low IQ was not constitutionally relevant and the nullification instruction cured any errors because it was clearer than the instruction given to Penry's jury. Two judges decided to take *Penry II* head-on. "[H]aving decided that no federal constitutional error occurred in this case, we may disagree with the United States Supreme Court that Texas jurors are incapable of remembering, understanding and giving effect to the straightforward and manageable 'nullification' instruction such as the one in this case."[42] The opinion was by Judge Barbara Hervey, who has won two subsequent elections.

It is never wise for a lower court to take a direct slap at an appellate court with the power to reverse. The Supreme Court summarily reversed the CCA without bothering for briefs on the merits.[43] And it blasted the CCA over the nullification instruction. "*Penry II* identified a broad and intractable problem—a problem that the state court ignored here—inherent in any requirement that the jury nullify special issues contained within a verdict form."[44] *Penry II* along with *Smith* "identified a broad and intractable problem" and so held that the nullification instruction could not "cure" the constitutional defect *Penry I* outlined.[45]

The CCA was having none of it. The judges liked the nullification instruction so much that they nullified the Supreme Court. On remand they found the *Penry II* error was harmless because the nullification instruction was so clear that the jurors likely gave effect to Smith's mitigating evidence.[46] Hervey, a St. Mary's Law School grad who had chided the Court for underestimating Texas jurors, took another shot at the Court by repeating the language she had used previously. "[W]e are not bound by the view expressed in *Penry II* that Texas jurors are incapable of remembering, understanding and giving effect to the straightforward and manageable 'nullification' instruction such as the one in this case."[47]

I'll also repeat myself: it is never wise for a lower court to take a direct slap at an appellate court with the power to reverse (even if the composition of the Court had changed with the retirement of O'Connor and the death of Rehnquist). It was an argument of heavyweights, Texas solicitor general Ted Cruz for the state against UT law professor Jordan Steiker, a former Thurgood Marshall clerk and co-director of UT's Capital Punishment Clinic, for Smith. Steiker won because the CCA judges could not bring themselves to realize that the pre-1991 special issues instructions created a constitutional problem that could not be cured—period. In two companion Fifth Circuit cases the Court reversed (over dissents by Chief Justice John Roberts, Scalia, Thomas, and Samuel Alito), hoping to bring the recalcitrant circuit into line with the rest of the federal judiciary.[48] This was almost twenty years from *Penry I* and the remaining number of inmates was low. The "intractable" *Penry* problem was over.[49]

VIII

Jose Ernesto Medellin and Humberto Leal Garcia were both Mexican nationals who raped and then killed young girls. At a time when the guilt of death-row inmates nationwide was under question, there was no doubt that Medellin and Leal Garcia were guilty. After conviction of capital murder each raised an issue under the Vienna Convention on Consular Rights, which requires states to inform foreign consulates upon arrest of one of their citizens. In neither case had Texas done that and the International Court of Justice found it binding on the signators. President George W. Bush issued a memorandum to that effect, asking the Texas courts to determine whether failure to comply with the treaty caused prejudice to the inmates. In Medellin's case the Supreme Court held by a 6–3 vote that the ICJ decision was not binding absent an implementing statute by Congress.[50] Notwithstanding requests by Bush and from Mexico and despite the violation of the treaty, Medellin was executed.

Leal Garcia's case was identical but for one added fact. Senator Patrick Leahy had introduced implementing legislation in Congress (which never passed). A 5–4 Court refused to stay his execution because it thought there was no real distinction between his case and Medellin's. Texas then executed him.[51] As the *Penry* saga illustrated, Texas had enough difficulties recognizing judgments of the Court; it certainly wasn't going to recognize the judgment of foreigners on the ICJ.

During this period there were also a handful of cases raising lesser issues, from the standards to determine if a death-row inmate is no longer competent to be executed, to issues that can be raised on habeas, to which statutes can be used to force DNA testing. They shared one common feature: the CCA and Fifth Circuit, denying relief at every turn, were always wrong.[52] The Court did not have Governor Perry's nor the CCA's nor the Fifth Circuit's faith in the Texas system.

IX

In 2017 the Court decided two Texas death penalty cases adversely to the CCA and Fifth Circuit. One demanded a fundamental change in the Texas system. The other will have no effect on the administration of capital punishment but did justice for the individual involved.

The Court returned to issues of intellectual disability in Bobby J. Moore's case where his IQ tests had been as low as 59 and as high as 78, averaging a shade above 70. The prosecution's psychologist testified that he was borderline in his intellectual function. On state post-conviction review, the trial judge, using current medical standards on intellectual disability, recommended that Moore receive relief under *Atkins*. The CCA rejected that recommendation. Since 2004 the CCA had used the "Lennie standard" based on the dim-witted fictional character in John Steinbeck's novel *Of Mice and Men* who loves soft animals but kills them because he is unaware of his own strength and he did the same with a woman he met. The "Lennie standard" offered seven different considerations bearing on intellectual disability such as whether the person can plan or lie in self-interest, factors which reinforce older stereotypes. Moore could play pool and mow lawns and so he exceeded the Lennie Standard. As the CCA saw its duty, it was to "define that level and degree of mental retardation at which a consensus of Texas citizens would agree that a person should be exempted from the death penalty."[53]

In *Moore* the CCA did not find that the trial court misapplied current medical standards; it flatly prohibited using them. No other state has done that. At the Court, Texas solicitor general Scott Keller did not mention Lennie in the state's brief, but defended the Texas considerations by asserting that judges and juries, not medical professionals, should decide who should be spared the death penalty. He was echoing a dissent in *Hall v. Florida* by Alito for Roberts, Scalia, and Thomas from the majority's objecting to the rigidity of Florida setting an IQ of 70 or lower as its mental disability baseline.[54] (The Fifth Circuit does not believe *Hall* affected the Texas standard because "the word 'Texas' nowhere appears in the opinion [about Florida law]."[55])

Oral argument suggested the future 5–3 victory for Moore. Keller asserted that is was not Texas's goal "to screen out individuals and deny them relief." It sure looked that way and Kennedy, the author of the *Hall* majority, said so. Breyer opined that the Court would be unable to lay down clear standards but nevertheless he made clear his unhappiness with the consensus of Texans setting the constitutional standard. On the other side Alito questioned why the Constitution—and therefore the states—should follow the views of medical societies in deciding who to execute.

Ginsburg's majority opinion triply faulted the CCA, first for ignoring the latest medical guidance, second for overemphasizing positive adaptive behaviors while slighting negative ones, and finally for rejecting the seven lay factors that went into the CCA's decisions on mental disability.[56] Roberts's dissent agreed with the latter point but found Moore's IQ to be sufficient to justify his execution for a murder he committed thirty-seven years previously. Neither opinion mentioned Lennie.

Duane Buck was represented by incompetent counsel (one of his lawyers has managed to lose twenty capital cases). At the punishment phase they called as a witness Dr. Walter Quijano, and he testified, as he had in other capital cases, that Buck was more likely to commit violent crimes in the future *because he was black.* Counsel asked him to recount the factors going into future dangerousness and he responded that "race" was among the "statistical factors" for future dangerousness because "[i]t's a sad commentary that minorities, Hispanics and black people, are overrepresented in the criminal justice system."[57] The prosecution capitalized on counsel's error in underscoring Buck's supposed future dangerousness based on his race: "You heard from Dr. Quijano, who has a lot of experience in the Texas Department of Corrections, who told you there was a probability that [Mr. Buck] would commit future acts of violence."[58] During two days of sentencing deliberation the jury asked for and received Quijano's notes to the same effect.

In his initial state post-conviction habeas Buck's lawyers did not raise either the ineffectiveness of counsel or the racial bias of Quijano's statement. While that was pending, Attorney General John Cornyn confessed error in another case involving Quijano's testimony and promised to do so in the six pending cases—including Buck's—where similar statements had been made by Quijano because the introduction of racial bias undermines confidence in the criminal justice system, The state kept its word in all cases except Buck's, apparently believing that because Buck's lawyers had called Quijano, the state was not to blame (even though two other cases where the state confessed errors also had defense counsel using Quijano). Buck filed a second petition for state habeas thereafter. The CCA denied the first petition and then dismissed the second petition as an abuse of the writ.

Buck next turned to federal habeas, but the district court rejected his claim as procedurally defaulted for failure to raise it earlier and also that he failed to establish prejudice he needed to show to excuse the default. The Fifth Circuit agreed and the Court denied certiorari. Since then Buck had bounced back and forth between the Texas and federal courts but never gained a hearing on his demand for the resentencing that all his similarly situated defendants received. As Buck's lawyers argued: "Mr. Buck's case is the only one in which Texas has broken its promise to waive procedural defenses and concede error, leaving Mr. Buck as the only individual in Texas facing execution without having been afforded a fair and unbiased sentencing hearing."[59] The state responded that Buck had not made a substantial showing that the state made a binding promise and that he has not been prejudiced because the jury would have sentenced him to death anyway (even if his counsel gave "at least [a] debatably deficient performance").[60]

For a man unconstitutionally sentenced to die because his incompetent lawyers brought race into the sentencing decision, Buck's case is the most procedurally convoluted and protracted of them all. As the Court described it, Buck's case had "entered a labyrinth of state and federal collateral review, where it has wandered for the better part of two decades."[61] Credit goes to the CCA and the Fifth Circuit and the vindictiveness of the state attorney general's office which could have done justice at every single hearing by confessing error (as it initially promised).

At oral argument Christina Swarns, the litigation director of the NAACP Legal Defense Fund, kept stressing two points. First, that an appeal to racial bias undermines the faith in the criminal justice system. Second, and this was repeated again and again, that Buck's situation is "unique," by which counsel meant that the Court could do justice in the individual case without setting a dangerous precedent.

Based on the questions asked, both Keller and the Fifth Circuit took a beating. Everyone understood that Buck's trial lawyer was incompetent and everyone knew the Fifth Circuit was an absolute outlier among the federal circuits in capital cases. And everyone knew, in Alito's words, that "what occurred at the penalty phase of this trial was indefensible."[62] Keller's best deflection was that the prosecution didn't do it, but as Kagan kept pointing out to him, that showed how incompetent defense counsel was and how the jury could more easily believe future dangerousness because it came from a defense expert. His other deflection was that Buck's crime was heinous, but Roberts retorted that was undoubtedly true of the others who benefited from the state's confession of error. At the end of oral argument Swarns could be confident of victory, perhaps a unanimous one. And poor Scott Keller—once again before the Court arguing that an outrageous decision by Texas was nevertheless appropriate under the circumstances because finality is an important value in the legal system—was about to add yet another loss to his record at the Court.

The opinion reversing the Fifth Circuit was written by Chief Justice John Roberts and it agreed with Swarns about the "extraordinary nature of the case" where the incompetence of counsel was so obvious everyone could agree on it (and that reaching the merits would not really affect future decisions).[63] Quitano's testimony was prejudicial because it "appealed to the racial stereotype that black men are prone to violence."[64] Buck's race was an "immutable characteristic [and he] would always be black."[65] That must be constitutionally irrelevant because we "punish people for what they do, not who they are."[66] (The strong stand against racial discrimination resulted in justice for one man; contrast that with the gutting of the Voting Rights Act in *Shelby County v. Holder*[67] which affected millions of African Americans.)

Despite his observation during oral argument of the "indefensible" actions of counsel, Alito joined Clarence Thomas in a dissent that described Buck's murders in detail (as if the horrendous nature of any murder justified the death penalty). The two asserted that the Court should not reach the merits but rather allow the claim (and Buck) to die in the procedural labyrinth. But in claiming the decision has "few ramifications," the dissent was saying that doing justice to the individual and the system (where Buck's incompetent lawyer has been allowed to "defend" (unsuccessfully) men charged with capital murder) wasn't worth the time.[68]

X

Penry never faced a fourth sentencing jury. Instead a new DA allowed him to plead to a life sentence—on one condition. He had to acknowledge that he was not mentally retarded. That was easy since it meant living over another bout with the death penalty. So after two nullification instructions, Penry was allowed to nullify the truth in order to live. It was a good deal.

With capital cases costing a county upward of $750,000 more than a comparable life in prison, Texas DAs, contra the Polk County DA who was fixated on executing Penry, are forced to take costs into account. When a Panhandle prosecutor in 2009 decided to seek death for a person already serving life in another state, he didn't win, but spent 10 percent of the county budget so that taxes had to go up and employees didn't get raises. Because costs are now being taken into account there has been a serious decline in death verdicts from forty-eight in 1998 to nine a decade later to just two death sentences in 2015. Similarly, the number of executions has gone down in the second decade of the century from about fifteen a year during 2010–14 to thirteen in 2015, and just nine in 2016. Most notably Harris County, the death sentence capital of the United States with 126 executions in the modern era, registered no death sentences in both 2015 and 2016, and in 2016 elected a district attorney who promised to exhibit restraint on seeking the death penalty.

For those who didn't get a good deal, the Court's reversals of Texas death penalties early in this century show that the former Texas statute with its special issues features was more like a mandatory death sentence, which had been held unconstitutional in 1976. Jordan Steiker, who has worked tirelessly to explain all features of capital punishment, offers his judgment: "a large proportion of the inmates executed in America's most active executing state were condemned unconstitutionally— without a genuine assessment of whether they deserved to die."[69] Thanks to the superb lawyering efforts of the Capital Punishment Clinic, men not deserving to be executed spent the rest of their lives in prison. But as Steiker observed to me, the CCA deserves a big assist for the Clinic's undefeated record at the Court.

THIRTEEN

Tom DeLay's Redistricting

> We must stress that a map that returns [Martin] Frost, [Chet]
> Edwards, and [Lloyd] Doggett is unacceptable and not worth
> all the time invested in this project.
> —Tom DeLay aide Jim Ellis, who supervised
>   Texas's mid-decade redistricting

After the 2002 election, the Texas congressional delegation consisted of 17 Democrats and 15 Republicans. After the 2004 election, the delegation was 21 Republicans and 11 Democrats. The dramatic change was the result of the 2003 redistricting effort demanded and orchestrated by United States House majority leader Tom ("The Hammer") DeLay of Sugar Land. It completed the process of turning Texas into a Republican state.

The mid-decade redistricting was unique in two respects. First, no states redistrict in mid-decade unless forced to by a court order. Texas did so voluntarily. Or not so voluntarily; the legislature really didn't want to do it, but DeLay demanded action and successfully rolled the Republicans into following.

I

In the 1960s the Supreme Court required decennial redistricting to equal population districts based on the latest census. In 1971 there were 3 Republicans in the Texas congressional delegation along with 20 Democrats. The Republican proportion of the delegation was well below the percentage of votes cast for Republicans statewide, a pattern that would hold through the 2002 elections. The 1971 plan had two special features. First, like all plans for the next thirty years, it protected incumbents. Second, it resulted in the election of the first African American since Reconstruction—Barbara Jordan of Houston.

In 1978 Texas elected Bill Clements, the first Republican governor since Reconstruction. For the 1981 redistricting, he demanded a minority-majority district in Dallas. A year later a federal court dismantled that district and spread the minority voters among several districts. The congressional delegation had 23 Democrats and 6 Republicans.

As this shows, Texas was gaining additional representation in the House because of population growth. The influx included Republicans, causing Lt. Governor Bill Hobby to quip that new Texans "come from states where they don't know it is socially unacceptable to be a Republican. We hope to educate them to our mores and customs."[1] Our mores and customs were changing as conservative Democrats were migrating to the GOP, and the tale of Texas politics in the latter part of the century is that of the decline and eventual eclipse of the once-dominant Democratic Party.

In *The Almanac of American Politics* Michael Barone gave the 1991 Texas redistricting "the Phil Burton award for the decade—for creatively drawn lines in unlikely places ... for the partisan effrontery which enabled the Democrats to protect all but one of their incumbents and capture the state's three new seats as well."[2] Over the course of the decade, three majority-minority districts were modified after a Supreme Court decision,[3] and several seats turned Republican, and Democrats ceased to win statewide races. Nowhere was this clearer than when incumbent governor Ann Richards lost to George W. Bush in 1994.

II

After the 2000 elections Texas Republicans held the governorship and the state senate. The legislature intentionally failed to redistrict the state in 2001. The reason was simple. A failure to redistrict the state house and senate sent the issue to the Legislative Redistricting Board consisting of the governor, the lieutenant governor (actually in this case the acting lieutenant governor), the comptroller, the land commissioner, and the House speaker. The first four were Republicans, the latter a Democrat. The four Republicans could redistrict as they pleased, and they did, creating new districts that heavily favored Republicans. Democrats were not interested in a legislative solution to congressional redistricting. They felt, correctly, that districts drawn by a court would be more favorable than anything they could get through the legislature that the governor would sign. Thus congressional redistricting fell to a federal court, which essentially copied the 1991 plan while adding two new seats. Incumbent protection was the order of the day although with the state trending Republican, some Democrats would be losers.

From Washington, DeLay criticized the map as "incumbent protection." He noted both a failure to create new minority districts as well as not giving Republicans their due. As Steve Bickerstaff wryly noted, "four years later another three-judge court (with two of the same judges on the panel in 2001) concluded that by making only a minimum of changes, the court in 2001 had unintentionally 'perpetuated much of the 1991 Democratic Party gerrymander.'"[4]

The result of the LRB plan was a Republican takeover of the state house after a 130-year drought. DeLay stated he wanted a new congressional plan, one that could be endorsed by the entire Texas delegation—as if that were possible. Few Republicans in the legislature saw redistricting as a priority, but none were opposed. Governor Rick Perry was supportive although he also pledged he would not call a special session for redistricting.

Republicans could make a good case for a new plan. Republicans were winning statewide, but that was not reflected in the composition of the congressional delegation. Political fairness mandated for the undoing of the prior Democratic gerrymander. Then, as a makeweight, they also claimed it was the duty of the legislature to replace a court-devised plan.

III

Redistricting is always divisive, and so legislators were more cautious than DeLay wished. Any redistricting would adversely affect rural Texas with its Democratic incumbents. While their ticket-splitting constituents were voting Republican in statewide offices, they also enjoyed the perks of seniority. To defeat these rural Democrats the legislature would have to create unwieldy districts that attached large rural areas to the suburbs where Republicans dominated.

DeLay's push for new districts lasted through the regular session and three special sessions. Democrats, who would be losers, had some good reasons for opposing action. They refused to compromise or offer alternatives because they did not wish to determine which congressmen would be sacrificed. They worried that Republicans would cheat and substitute a more partisan map at the end of any process. They were right; Republicans did just that. Congresswoman Sheila Jackson Lee of Houston expressed a view that would come to dominate minority members of the legislature: the Republicans "want to pretend to be friends of minorities as a ruse to send more Republicans to Washington to vote against everything minorities care about."[5] Minority legislators grew angry over Anglo Republicans telling them what was best for their constituents. But as African American state senator Rodney Ellis noted, the Republicans intended to marginalize Democrats as the party of blacks and Hispanics by defeating all Anglo Democratic congressmen. That was true; the objective was to increase Republican representation in Congress; the means were to make the Democratic Party the party of minorities.

Finally, the Democrats' lawyers told them they would prevail in the courts. This was interesting advice since the Republicans had always challenged the Democratic gerrymanders in court and had always lost.

The 140-day regular session opened in mid-January with a host of issues to be dealt with, the most important of which was a real budget shortfall. That was one reason all the major newspapers in the state (and the medium sized as well) opposed wasting any time on redistricting. To get the ball rolling, in February Representative Joe Crabb of the House Redistricting Committee wrote the attorney general asking what the responsibilities of the legislature were with respect the congressional districting. On April 23 the attorney general responded, "This federal-court drawn map, however, is only effective unless and until the Texas Legislature redraws it—that is, unless and until lawmakers 'renew and continue efforts to fulfill their constitutional duties.'"[6]

While waiting for the opinion, Crabb had introduced a redistricting bill. On May 7 the bill cleared committee. If passed it would likely defeat five Democrats. Its "goal," expressed by DeLay staffer Jim Ellis (who would spend half of 2003 in Austin), "is to elect more Republicans."[7] In fact DeLay's goal was to defeat all Anglo Democrats in the delegation.

The bill was sure to pass and so the Democrats weighed their options under the house rules. One rule prevented the house from taking up its own bill after the 123rd day of the 140-day session (so that the senate would have time to consider any house action). The 123rd day was May 15. In secret, Democrats decided to deny the house a quorum by leaving the state, and on Sunday May 11, fifty-one house Democrats left for Ardmore, Oklahoma, returning on May 16. While there, both sides battled to win the public relations war. For Republicans the outcome was at best a draw. For Democrats it looked like a victory. They drew national attention to the issue and were able to portray an already divisive DeLay as the villain. But the denial of a quorum angered Republicans and united them in a determination to adopt a new map. Moderate Republican Jeff Wentworth stated, "We Republicans felt we were mistreated by the Democrat majority in redistricting in 1971, 1981, and 1991, but 'run and hide' was not, in our judgment, a legitimate response to our being outvoted by the majority party at the time."[8] Perry's pledge of no special session for redistricting was out the window.

IV

On June 16 the governor, lieutenant governor, speaker of the house, attorney general, and DeLay plus their chief staffers met at the governor's residence. Two days later Perry issued a call for a special session for redistricting to commence June 30. Passing a bill had become a Republican litmus test; blocking it was a Democratic litmus test. It took the house only a week to pass its bill.

In the senate things were trickier. Republicans had a 19–12 majority, but through the operation of several senate rules, the senate would consider a bill only if it first had the support of two-thirds of the senators. Thus eleven Democrats would be sufficient to block the house bill and that was it.

Perry had stated he would call another special session and Lt. Governor David Dewhurst announced that he would no longer require two-thirds support before consideration of a bill. It had not been required in previous special sessions dealing with redistricting. Thus the redistricting plan would pass in the next special session. Except it didn't. Eleven Democratic senators fled to Albuquerque, New Mexico, and stayed out of Texas for forty days to much national publicity. The Democrats started emphasizing the racial aspects of Republican redistricting. But this was a two-edged sword. It painted the Democrats as the party of minorities and the Republicans as the party of Anglos, just as DeLay wished.

Being away from home had both emotional and monetary costs. Public opinion, in the one poll taken, was decisively against the boycott. The Democrats needed an endgame and the only option looked to be the federal courts. Democrats claimed that abandoning the two-thirds rule violated the Voting Rights Act. Happily forum shopping, they filed suit in Laredo before a friendly Democratic-appointed judge, Keith P.

Ellison. But he recused himself and the case went before another Democratic appointee, George Kazan. He quickly ruled against the Democrats by noting that those without majority votes will lose in the legislative process.

The senators returned home and faced a third special session, one in which Kazan's observation would hold. They would lose. The process was truly ugly. The house passed its bill. Then the senate passed a different bill and it went to a conference committee of five senators and five house members. The committee was not bound to accept the outlines of either bill; it could do anything it wanted. But it never met. Instead the house and senate sponsors with constant input from DeLay aide Ellis drew their own bill, moving 9.8 million people among Texas districts. Ellis stated, "we must stress that a map that returns [Martin] Frost, [Chet] Edwards, and [Lloyd] Doggett is unacceptable and not worth all the time invested in this project."[9] DeLay wanted them gerrymandered out of Congress at any cost. Thus Ellis asserted the map must reflect the priorities of the congressional delegation (by which he meant Tom DeLay), not the legislature. It targeted all ten Anglo Democrats. Some would face Republican incumbents; all would have many voters who they had never previously represented, and none had an attractive alternative district in which to run.

Travis County, to use but one example, went from a compact district to three districts. One stretched from Austin to the Houston suburbs. Another went from southeast Travis 350 miles to the Rio Grande Valley; it was 63 percent Hispanic, and 60 percent of its population lived outside of Travis. The third put the University of Texas in San Antonio congressman Lamar Smith's district.

V

Now it was the lawyer's turn. The best hope was the preclearance requirement by the Justice Department under the Voting Rights Act. The career lawyers thought the plan clearly violated the VRA and recommended that it be rejected. But political appointees overruled them and cleared the map. (Two years later the career lawyers were forbidden to make recommendations.) The next step was a three-judge district court, but that proved unavailing too.[10] Federal courts simply do not strike down legislative maps because they are deemed too partisan. There was an unbroken stream of cases to that effect.

Once the three-judge district court rendered its negative decision the challengers took a direct appeal to the Supreme Court. There was already a gerrymandering case before the Court, *Vieth v. Jubelier*,[11] and when decided, four Republican justices asserted gerrymandering was nonjusticiable because of a lack of judicially manageable standards. The fifth vote was Anthony Kennedy, who did not rule out justiciability if someone could show him a manageable standard. With *Vieth* as the law, the Court remanded DeLay's redistricting for reconsideration in light of the decision.[12] During the rebriefing period, Steve Bickerstaff wrote an amicus brief. He was a former assistant attorney general who then went into private practice representing governments and officials, from both political parties in election matters, especially redistricting. At the time he wrote the amicus brief he was an adjunct professor at UT's law school, a friend and colleague of mine. He sought about a dozen professors to join him on the brief and I was one of them.

The brief was a model of simplicity. Congressional districts had to be of equal population. States could use the decennial census as the best evidence of population right after the census and when ordered to redistrict by a court. By if a state replaced a valid existing plan, it could not rely on the "legal fiction" that the census was still accurate.[13] The state had the burden of proving that the new districts were in fact of equal population.

As oral argument approached, the court sua sponte—on its own motion—ordered the seven challengers' attorneys to cede some of their time to counsel for the university professors to argue. The court clearly wanted to hear from Bickerstaff. Shortly thereafter the attorney general's office informed Bickerstaff that he had a conflict of interest and could not argue the case. He disagreed, but nevertheless yielded. As the most experienced of the signers, it fell to me to argue his theory before the three-judge district court.

I was allotted more time to argue than any of the other challengers because all ceded some of their time and one ceded all of his; and the court let me keep arguing after my time expired. Adding to Bickerstaff's legal argument, I made the policy point that if the state's theory were adopted, then Texas (and other states) could do a gerrymandering redistricting in 2009 in preparation to gerrymander in the required redistricting in 2011. That, I claimed, was bad for our democracy. I felt that was my best point.

The state was represented by its solicitor general, Ted Cruz, a former law clerk to Chief Justice William Rehnquist. He did an excellent job for the state. One of the judges asked him my hypothetical about the state's theory justifying redistricting in 2009. Cruz agreed that it did, but then asserted that of course the state would not do that.

Several months later the court once again gave its okay to the gerrymander, noting that the Texas congressional seats had been gerrymandered for at least four and a half decades and that there was no constitutional rule preventing it. Absent a way to measure the substantive fairness of the decision, there was nothing a court could do. "For example, it is not clear that acting to undo a perceived disadvantage imposed previously by an opposing party is irrational."[14] Bickerstaff's novel claim about mid-decade voluntary redistricting was very politely rejected.

"[A]ll recognize that the 2001 plan is no more a reflection of today's actual population distribution that the 2003 legislative plan; both are based on 2000 census numbers. Neither plan would produce equipopulous districts for elections held in 2006."[15] Bickerstaff's proposed rule "would require us to apply an established doctrine in a novel way, with uncertain basis and effect."[16] That, plus a wonder whether this issue was outside the mandate of the remand, was enough.[17]

VI

It was back to the Supreme Court, where the challengers' case was argued by Paul Smith of the Washington office of Jenner and Block, the winning counsel in *Lawrence v. Texas*.[18] Smith had, however, been losing counsel in *Vieth v. Jubelier*. In the two years since *Vieth*, John Roberts and Samuel Alito had joined the Court; so Kennedy still held the deciding vote on gerrymandering. What Smith needed was to offer Kennedy something new; instead, he reargued *Vieth* and not surprisingly lost again.

The only issue that had a chance was Bickerstaff's equal population / mid-decade claim rejected below. Indeed, Texas attorney general Greg Abbott had privately stated it was the only issue the state feared. Smith devoted less than sixty seconds to it at the end of his rebuttal. His argument was absolutely inexplicable, and left Texas Democrats with a devastating loss from which they have not recovered.

Six opinions covering 130 pages produced little light.[19] The justices still disagreed on the justiciability of partisan gerrymandering, but Texas won on the facts. Seven justices rejected the mid-decade / equal population argument that Smith never tried to make. On one issue the Court reversed. It held that Republican Henry Bonilla's District 23 west of San Antonio violated the Voting Rights Act because the Republican plan had moved Hispanics out of the district and Anglos in in order to protect their Hispanic incumbent.

Patrick Higginbotham's decision for the court below was correct in that there seemed no way to measure political fairness. There are no inherent legislative districts; all districting is gerrymandering of some sort. Thus the *Austin American-Statesman* editorial title "Partisanship Is Big Winner in Court's Redistricting Ruling" is spot-on.[20] The value of the Bickerstaff rule is that it prevents rolling gerrymandering through a decade. Bickerstaff and I subsequently wrote a critique of the prevailing Kennedy opinion where we opined that one day mid-decade gerrymandering should be prohibited, but that day depends on the future composition of the Court.[21] We also believe the Court should place substantive limits on gerrymandering because of its threat to democracy.

VII

It is probably time to pick winners and losers from this tale. The biggest winner is the Republican Party. It continues to dominate the Texas delegation with 25 members to just 11 Democrats. The *Houston Chronicle*'s conclusion that the Court had handed the Republicans a Pyrrhic victory was wrong the day it was written and continues to be wrong to this day.[22] What it might have said was that the redistricting accelerated the future by eight years.

Governor Perry, Lt. Governor Dewhurst, and Attorney General Abbott were all reelected in 2006 and 2010. Austin congressman and progressive Democrat Lloyd Doggett was an unexpected winner. His congressional district was dismantled and the only one of the three new districts encompassing Austin (now there are six splitting Travis County) that could elect a Democrat was the one stretching hundreds of miles south with a Hispanic majority. But Doggett bested a Hispanic in the Democratic primary and continued in Congress. Republicans tried again to eliminate Doggett with the 2011 redistricting placing him in a district with heavy San Antonio representation, but he continued to win and remains in Congress.

Two other targeted Democrats survived. Gene Green from East Houston still serves and Ralph Hall of Rockwell switched parties to win. When he retired in 2015 he was the oldest member of Congress at age ninety-one. Chet Edwards of Waco was also victorious in 2004, but was defeated in 2010.

On the losing side, Jim Turner of Crockett retired rather than going down to defeat with Max Sandlin of Marshall (to Louie Gohmert of all people), Nick Lampson of Beaumont, Charles Stenholm of Abilene, and most importantly for DeLay, Martin Frost of Dallas. Chris Bell was placed in an African American district and lost in the Democratic primary.

There were Republican losers, too, although that took a while. Henry Bonilla won in 2004, but the Court had ordered his district redrawn to add Hispanics. He lost a special election in December 2006. With Perry, Dewhurst, and Abbott staying in place, ambitious Republicans (including the latter two) could not move up the electoral food chain. Then when Kay Bailey Hutchison retired, Dewhurst went for her Senate seat, but litigation postponed the Republican primary long enough for Ted Cruz to establish name recognition and win.

Ironically, the biggest loser was Tom DeLay. The fall of 2005, the Public Integrity Unit of the Travis County district attorney's office indicted DeLay (along with Jim Ellis and others) on money laundering and conspiracy to violate election law charges. In January 2006, under pressure, he resigned as House majority leader and soon thereafter from Congress. *Washington Post* columnist David Broder saw DeLay's fall as "a classic case of pride going before a fall, a hard-edged, arrogant political operative tripped up by his own tactics."[23] (That might explain the *Houston Chronicle*'s Pyrrhic victory claim, but how could the paper be that clairvoyant to know an indictment lay in the future?)

DeLay was represented by an excellent legal team led by Dick DeGuerin, one of the state's most respected criminal defense lawyers, and containing Richard Keeton, son of the legendary UT law school dean Page Keeton. After much legal skirmishing and time, DeLay was convicted in 2011. His conviction was overturned in 2013 and that was affirmed on appeal a year later. Congressional politics has become much uglier since DeLay left, but no one thinks his absence is the cause.

Conclusion

Let me repeat what I wrote in the Introduction: Texas has generated more national constitutional law than any other state. The entire basic law school course in Constitutional Law could be taught using nothing but Texas cases. Following the outline of a Constitutional Law course also nicely illustrates the structure and text of the Constitution itself. That, however, understates the richness of the history and politics of Texas that contributed to the cases. Beyond representing all doctrinal areas of constitutional law, Texas cases deal with the major issues of the nation, from race to wealth and poverty to civil liberties to the relationship of the states and the federal government to war. The cases reflect the changing Courts of the past seven decades, and by votes sort the justices into the familiar pattern of liberals, conservatives, and centrists.

I

Most Constitutional Law courses begin with judicial review and the iconic *Marbury v. Madison*.[1] No one can match that, but *Marbury* is cited in *City of Boerne v. Flores*,[2] which was an exercise in judicial review striking down the Religious Freedom Restoration Act as it applied to states. *Flores*, like *Marbury*, was an example of the Court protecting itself from what it saw, non-self-critically, as legislative overreaching to intrude into the judicial prerogative. *Flores* adopts the modern reading of *Marbury* to emphatically stand for the proposition that it is the Court's function to settle constitutional meaning. If Congress could alter the Constitution's meaning (as determined by the Court) "no longer would the Constitution be 'superior paramount law, unchangeable by ordinary means.'"[3] The echoes of *Marbury* here are loud and clear.

After judicial review, Constitutional Law casebooks usually turn to National Powers. As the battle over the annexation of Texas showed, when a ruling majority wants badly to do something, it will find the authority to do so implied in the Constitution. Still, witnessing Jacksonian Democrats relying on an implied power and the Whigs distancing themselves was a shocker—at least until one realizes that the true issue was slavery and the issue trumped everything (as the reaction to the Kansas-Nebraska Act would prove).

In the twentieth century the Commerce Clause came to prominence because most national legislation is based on—or seeks to be justified by—the power to regulate interstate commerce. And as we saw in the chapter on Railroads, the power extends as well to those intrastate actions that affect interstate commerce.[4] Following the New Deal revolution, whereby President Franklin D. Roosevelt appointed eight justices between 1937 and 1943, it was possible to believe that federal power could reach anything and everything. Decades later, spurred by William Rehnquist, the Court tried, with minimal success, to place some limits on federal power.

In 1974 Congress extended the wages and hours provisions of the Fair Labor Standards Act to employees of state and local governments. Two years later in *National League of Cities v. Usery*,[5] an opinion by Rehnquist, joined by the other three Nixon appointees and Potter Stewart, held the extension unconstitutional even though they agreed that it affected interstate commerce. The Court created a new affirmative limitation on acknowledged federal powers. Congress could not regulate the "states qua states"; essential functions of state and local governments were beyond the purview of federal powers even if the Constitution was silent on the point. *National League of Cities* proved unstable, and when the wages and hours provisions were applied to the San Antonio [Texas] Municipal Transit Authority, a 5–4 Court, with Harry Blackmun changing his mind, overruled it as unworkable.[6]

Taking a different tack, Rehnquist tried again when the Court struck down the Gun-Free School Zone Act in *United States v. Lopez*.[7] A senior brought a gun to his San Antonio high school, and based on a tip he was arrested and charged under Texas law. A day later the federal prosecutor filed charges under the Gun-Free School Zone Act, and Texas, having been big-footed, dropped the state charges. The federal statute makes no mention of interstate commerce; it reads like a standard criminal statute. Three Texans on the Fifth Circuit held the law exceeded federal power under the Commerce Clause, thereby forcing the Court to grant review.[8] At the Court, Solicitor General Drew Days, otherwise a Yale constitutional law professor, was asked if there were any limits on federal power. He would not, perhaps because he could not, offer any. A 5–4 Court then did offer a limit—a statute justified under the commerce power must have some relation to interstate commerce.

As we saw in the chapter on Oil, cases from Texas established that federal power over federal property is plenary. States and individuals—like Sandra Day O'Connor's family[9]—may not like it, but that's the way it is. The same can be said for the federal power to control the border. Southwestern states may be unhappy with what the federal government does or does not do, but the power to act is not theirs. Thus in the challenge to President Obama's no deportation orders in Deferred Action for Parents of Americans (DAPA) initiated by Texas, no one suggested that immigration policy could be controlled by the states although the states were affected by the costs DAPA supposedly imposed on them and that was sufficient to grant standing.

The Court has stated that "the Constitution divides authority between federal and state governments for the protection of individuals."[10] That is nonsense, as decades of slavery and then segregation attest. Federalism instead presupposes some areas where the states have the ability to choose for themselves. Indeed that is its core: the ability of a state to order its affairs as its citizens—not those of the nation—choose. Nowhere is the tension between the boundaries of state and federal power better illustrated than Texas's love affair with capital punishment, where Texas predominates on the Court's docket. *San Antonio Independent School District v. Rodriguez*[11] left choices of educational funding entirely to the states. *Northwest Austin Municipal Utility District v. Holder*[12] flagged the federalism concerns of Congress invading state prerogatives in the Voting Rights Act that became the "equal sovereignty" of states in *Shelby County v. Holder*.[13] Attorneys General Greg Abbott and Ken Paxton made a fetish of their willingness to sue the federal government in the hopes of maintaining an autonomy of action for Texas, and they enjoyed some success.

Texas put the nature of a federal union to the extreme test when it seceded from the United States in 1861 and then fought to remain outside the former Union. During Reconstruction *Texas v. White*[14] answered Texas's claims of a right to secede with a resounding no (even if Governor Rick Perry, before he joined the federal government, opined that it might be necessary to secede in the twenty-first century). Texas was a fellow traveler with the rest of the South in trying to nullify *Brown v. Board of Education*. And in this century with respect to both voter ID and especially abortion, Texas has attempted to nullify constitutional rights by what opponents claim are pretextual justifications.

At this point our casebooks turn to separation of powers. That concern was apparent in *Flores* where the Court lectured Congress about knowing its place in our constitutional system (a place fully subordinate to the Court on constitutional interpretation). The injunction against implementation of DAPA is another example, this time of a president invading the province of Congress. If excessive delegation of legislative powers to the executive is dormant rather than dead, the *Panama Oil and Refining v. Ryan*[15] might have applicability.

While federal power is constrained by federalism and separation of powers, all governmental authority is limited by the Constitution's demarcation of individual rights and liberties. Today's Constitutional Law casebooks are full of such cases and Texas has provided the stimulus for many of them. The speech cases in chapter 8 illustrate major First Amendment themes. Probably none is more important than the realization that speech cannot be suppressed even if it offends us to our core—that was the message of *Texas v. Johnson*,[16] the flag burning case. When it comes to problems speech is supposed to cause, governments typically overreact as Texas did with the CIO speech in *Thomas v. Collins*[17] as well as the action under the Suppression Act in *Stanford v. Texas*.[18] Low-level law enforcement too often goes unnoticed. *Acker v. Texas*[19] and *Houston v. Hill*[20] thus both stand for a larger point that even the most insignificant encounters with law enforcement should be held to constitutional standards. Justice William O. Douglas lectured me one day—in a case involving Texas oilman Sid Richardson's estate[21]— that rich people have constitutional rights, too. Billie Sol Estes's victory on cameras in the courtroom proves him right.[22]

Speech by government is immune from constitutional standards (religion excepted) and thus Texas could pick and choose among messages allowed on its license plates, preferring Indian-hunting Buffalo Soldiers to those who were fighting for the right to own slaves.[23] The Court's action to declare certain actions of the Texas Rangers unconstitutional was too late to help the striking farmworkers, but it did recognize that official repression is wrong, and thus it heralded a diminished future for the Rangers.[24]

With respect to religion, Texas cases illustrate well the entire range of applicable rules. *Flores* reaffirmed the free exercise principle that laws of general applicability trump religious rights. *Santa Fe v. Doe*[25] is a reminder of how seriously the Court takes attempts to insert official prayer into the schools. *Van Orden*[26] was a win for an expressly religious monument, but it was surrounded by others that had no religious meaning. Finally, *Texas Monthly v. Bullock*[27] offers the necessary reminder that taxation should neither favor nor disfavor religious organizations.

Over a decade after *Lopez* the Court recognized an individual Second Amendment right to possess firearms. But before one assumed that a future *Lopez* would also be litigated as a Second Amendment case, one must note that the Court's seminal Second Amendment decision stated that "nothing in our opinion should be taken to cast doubt on long-standing prohibitions ... forbidding the carrying of firearms in sensitive places such as schools."[28]

Fourteenth Amendment litigation is split between the Due Process Clause and the Equal Protection Clause, with the former being more important in the first half of the twentieth century and the latter more important thereafter. *Reagan v. Farmers' Loan and Trust*,[29] holding the initial Railroad Commission rates unreasonably low, represents the Due Process Clause prior to the New Deal revolution. After that revolution economic or social legislation became immune to challenges, although one can read *Rodriguez* to suggest that a complete denial of education would transgress a constitutional line.

Roe v. Wade[30] represents a modern view of due process. Its modification in *Planned Parenthood v. Casey*[31] and *Whole Woman's Health v. Hellerstedt*[32] allows for a burden to be placed on a woman's right to choose so long as that burden is not undue. *Lawrence v. Texas*[33] found that criminalization of homosexual sodomy violates due process because it serves no legitimate state interest. When the Court subsequently legalized gay marriage it was combining due process and equal protection, as had *Loving v. Virginia* in 1967.[34] *Loving* involved interracial marriage, triggering equal protection while marriage itself was protected by the Due Process Clause.

Texas cases also teach where and how laws will be held to survive due process and equal protection challenges. *Rodriguez* is a classic example of the Court's rational basis test in both due process and equal protection. Unless the law is crazy it withstands constitutional scrutiny. That stands in stark contrast with strict scrutiny, which is applied in the race cases like *Fisher v. University of Texas*.[35] There the Court demands a compelling state interest and that the law be narrowly tailored to serve that interest. In between the two rigid, almost result-determinative, tests is *Plyler v. Doe*,[36] where the Court applied some form of intermediate scrutiny to prevent Texas from excluding undocumented children from a public education.

Smith v. Allwright[37] invalidating the all-white primary is the classic Fifteenth Amendment case. But remedial power under the Reconstruction Amendments is more limited than that of national powers under Article I, as the suggested problems with the Voting Rights Act flagged in *Northwest Austin MUD* came to pass in *Shelby County v. Holder.*

II

Texas cases do more than fill out a Constitutional Law casebook. What Texas, through all its litigious permutations, has done is offer a window on the relation of constitutional litigation to ordinary politics at the Supreme Court. Here it offers the stuff of political science courses. All of the great national divides over the policies reflected in the Constitution have been present.

First there is race and Texas's treatment of African Americans. It begins with the all-white primary and continues through desegregating the University of Texas and the controversies over affirmative action at UT. But it also includes battles over voting, Pullman "abstention" on the Railroad Commission order to have Pullman conductors on all sleeping cars,[38] and is an underlying text of capital punishment (underlying because the Court studiously avoids mentioning it) and Tom DeLay's effort to make the Democratic Party the party of minorities.

While Hispanics have been nowhere near as prevalent in constitutional adjudication, they were the key factor in school finance litigation and traditionally the major issue in immigration. They, too, are important parts of capital punishment and DeLay's redistricting.

Money talks and often loudly enough to prevail. More affluent school districts have been reluctant to share their wealth with the less well-off. Commercial constitutional litigation is invariably about money and the railroad and oil cases would not have existed were they not about money.

On the other side, many of the cases involve those with less money like the residents of the Edgewood Independent School District or the undocumented immigrants in chapter 7 who have come to the United States in search of a better life. *Hellerstedt* was in no small part based on a plan to drive up the cost of abortions so that there would be fewer of them. The poll tax was intended to cause the less affluent to cede their right to vote. And everyone who follows capital punishment knows it is reserved for the poor. (To use a non-Texas case, those who prosecuted O.J. Simpson for that horrific double murder knew that no jury would give him the death penalty so they didn't even bother to ask for it.)

After Independence Texas even created foreign policy issues between the United States and Mexico (and potentially Great Britain). These created constitutional issues. First, should the United States recognize the newly independent nation on its border? Second, could the United States add a foreign country as a state by the Treaty Power? Third, was a simple Joint Resolution of Congress sufficient to annex Texas (with the latter's consent)? In the background were issues of the War Powers (where Article I of the Constitution gives Congress the power to declare war) because Mexico had indicated that war was likely if Texas became part of the United States. When President James K. Polk ordered troops to the disputed border of the Rio Grande, hostilities were initiated (apparently by Mexico). Some Whigs, including one-term Illinois congressman Abraham Lincoln, thought the ensuing war was unconstitutional because of Polk's actions in sending the troops south of the Nueces River. The Democratic majority in Congress cleansed Polk's action with a formal declaration of war. But this sequence of events foreshadowed issues of the twentieth and twenty-first centuries over how much authority the president has to commit the country to war without congressional action.

Rights are often contentious issues because one person's rights may be an invasion of another person's rights. Several Texas cases illustrate this point. Johnson's right to express himself by burning the flag was offensive to most Americans, but only one side can prevail. The same holds true in the religion cases where the rights of the majority to pray in school and at football games were trumped by the rights of a minority to have the state stay out of religious matters. Finally, a woman's right to choose whether or not to terminate her pregnancy, as well as a gay couple's right to marry, conflicts with many Americans' felt right to live in what they would call a decent society.

For non-Texans cases involving the Texas Rangers may not matter, but the times the Rangers and the National Guard have appeared in the foregoing pages they have always been acting illegally. First, they were used by Governor Sterling to impose production quotas on the East Texas oil fields; then Governor Shivers used the Rangers to block school desegregation in Mansfield; and finally the Rangers helped break the farmworkers' strike in the Rio Grande Valley.

That was Texas until the last quarter of the twentieth century— virulently anti-labor. That may have eased, but the pro-business views of the state have not (including business support for affirmative action). Cases on religion, abortion, gays, and the death penalty illuminate a morally conservative and culturally Protestant state. Perhaps the popular caricature of Anglo Texas is a mirror.

III

Constitutional Law is not an abstract academic exercise. The Constitution governs conflicts that matter deeply. In Texas some cases mattered a lot; others less so. The race cases top the list of cases that mattered. With *Smith v. Allwright* ending the all-white primary the number of blacks voting in Texas significantly increased. Thurgood Marshall could look back on his victory and call it "the greatest ... it changed the whole complexion in the South."[39] *Sweatt v. Painter*[40] ordered UT desegregated and signaled that it was time for the litigation that produced *Brown*. *Fisher II* preserved affirmative action thereby guaranteeing schools like UT would serve the entire population of Texas rather than just being an Anglo enclave.

The *Tidelands Cases* were of importance both economically—Texas got oil royalties—and politically.[41] Harry Truman had whopped Thomas Dewey in Texas by 41 ½ points in the 1948 elections. After Truman authorized the suit against Texas and then vetoed a quitclaim of the tidelands to the state, Dwight Eisenhower beat Adlai Stevenson by 6 ½ points in the 1952 elections as Texas separated itself from the Democratic solid South. When Ike fulfilled his promise to sign the tidelands quitclaim, he got 55 percent of the Texas vote in 1956 and bested Stevenson by 11 points.

Roe and *Hellerstedt* created and then protected a woman's right to choose an abortion. *Santa Fe v. Doe* ended official prayers at public school functions. *Jurek*[42] and *Penry*[43] authorized Texas to lead the nation in executions, and *Medellín* allowed the state to thumb its nose at both the federal government and the International Court of Justice.[44] Finally, in affirming Tom DeLay's mid-decade redistricting, Texas turned fully Republican and assisted that party in controlling the House of Representatives.[45]

On the other side, the railroad cases and the overproduction of oil are problems from the first third of the last century. *Lawrence* was important as a doctrinal stepping-stone to same-sex marriage, but its actual issue of prosecution for sodomy was hardly an issue—just that one cop in Houston cared (along with the delegates of the 2000 Texas Republican Convention and the members of the Westboro Baptist Church).[46] *Stanford* stopped the seizure of Communist literature at a time when concerns about Communism in America were vanishing. *Texas v. Johnson* is an important First Amendment case, but until Donald Trump was elected only Middle East residents burned American flags. *Flores* had no practical importance because states were not infringing on religious freedom. (In those states where contraception is now an issue, legislatures are likely to enact little RFRAs.)

Possibly the biggest case of little importance is *Rodriguez*. A decade after the Court rejected the funding claim, the Texas Supreme Court stepped in. There seems little doubt that the Texas legislature responded better—more mildly—to a command from its own courts than it would have to one from the federal courts.

One surprising feature of the survey of Texas cases at the Court is the paucity of cases decided by the Warren Court. There is *Hernandez*[47] on discrimination against Hispanics, *Stanford* on search warrants for books, *Estes* on cameras in the courtroom, and two *Tidelands Cases,* the first sustaining the federal law ceding them to the states and the second interpreting that law to give Texas three leagues rather than three miles.[48] Not surprisingly no one today looks to these tidelands cases for anything.

There were three other cases, one involving criminal law, the other two involving criminal procedure. One of the latter was *Aguilar v. Texas,*[49] where the Court tightened significantly the standards for obtaining a search warrant through information from an unidentified confidential informant. (Nineteen years later *Aguilar* was overruled, a casualty of the war on drugs.[50]) The other, *Pointer v. Texas,*[51] held that the Confrontation Clause of the Sixth Amendment applied to the states through the Due Process Clause. A major Warren Court project was making the criminal procedure provisions of the Bill of Rights fully applicable to the states and *Pointer* fit right in.

Texas lost in *Hernandez, Stanford, Estes, Aguilar,* and *Pointer;* indeed in three of the five there was not a dissenting vote. Texas prevailed, however, in *Powell v. Texas,*[52] a case about public intoxication. Leroy Powell was a peaceful alcoholic who had a propensity to pass out in public places. At his trial his lawyer introduced evidence, via a single doctor, that Powell was a chronic alcoholic who had no choice but to drink. Therefore, the lawyer claimed Powell was not morally culpable and thus any punishment was cruel and unusual in violation of the Eighth Amendment. This was yet another case where the fine was so low that there was no appellate review in the Texas courts; so *Powell* went directly to the Supreme Court.

Powell relied on *Robinson v. California*[53] where the Court had invalidated a statute making it a crime "to be addicted to the use of narcotics." This was not an apt analogy because Texas didn't care if Powell got wasted; the state cared only if he did it in public places. The Court split 5–4 rejecting Powell's claim. *Powell* represents the only time in the Court's history where there were three liberals on each side of a case. Warren, Hugo Black, and Thurgood Marshall (with Harlan and White) voted to affirm the conviction. Douglas, William J. Brennan, and Abe Fortas (with Stewart) dissented. Had the dissenters prevailed, logic would dictate that an alcoholic could not be punished for drunk driving!

Like the Warren era, the Burger Court had more Texas losses, but also saw some big Texas victories. *Rodriguez* left school financing intact, and *Jurek* not only sustained the new capital punishment statute but opened the way for the incredible spree of executions in Texas at the end of the century. *Roe v. Wade* was clearly a loss for the state if not for its residents, as were lesser cases like being forced to educate undocumented children and limiting the strikebreaking of the Texas Rangers.[54]

The Rehnquist Court handed Texas some big losses—flag burning as protected speech, *Lawrence* and sodomy, *Flores* (where of all things Texas supported the federal statute against a Texas city), prayer at Friday Night Lights. Despite being allowed to execute the intellectually disabled for a while, Texas lost three capital cases. These were not offset by the victories in keeping the Ten Commandments Monument at the capitol and *Penry I*'s initially allowing executions of the intellectually disabled.

The Roberts Court has been by far the most friendly to the state. To be sure Texas continued to lose capital cases, but the only other loss to date was in *Hellerstedt*. Balanced against these have been a strong string of victories. *Northwest Austin MUD* set in motion the demise of preclearance under the Voting Rights Act, which in turn allowed Texas to implement voter ID. Even though the district court and the Fifth Circuit found voter ID violated the Voting Rights Act, the Court stayed their decisions for the 2016 elections. Tom DeLay's gerrymander was sustained because four justices believed the underlying issue was nonjusticiable and Anthony Kennedy voted with them. DAPA was invalidated by the Fifth Circuit and that was affirmed by an equally divided Court. The state did not have to celebrate Confederate veterans on its license plates and affirmative action at the University of Texas was allowed to continue. It allowed for Medellin's and Leal Garcia's executions even though the International Court of Justice found their rights under the Vienna Convention had been violated.[55]

Texas's losses at the Court represented victories for the Court's liberals. Texas's victories mostly favored the Court's conservatives, but as the *Tidelands Cases, Powell,* and *Fisher II* illustrate, that was not always the case. In any event, when a state loses before the Court—in cases such as *Roe* or *Johnson*—it is open to question just who wins and who loses. Perhaps in those cases the Texas government lost while some of the governed won.

IV

If we look at the votes of individual justices we can see some who were centrists, some who invariably sided with Texas, and some who did just the opposite. The liberal justices consistently voted against Texas with William O. Douglas the leader, never once favoring the state even when Texas clearly was in the right in the *Tidelands Cases.* Thurgood Marshall only voted with Texas once, wisely in *Powell.* William J. Brennan cast two votes for the state, once in the three leagues *Tidelands Case,* the other time to affirm Estes's conviction. These three were joined by the final acknowledged liberals John Paul Stevens at three and Ruth Bader Ginsburg at four.

The opposite side begins with William Rehnquist, who only once voted against Texas, and that was in *Flores* where Attorney General Dan Morales filed an amicus brief supporting the constitutionality of RFRA. Clarence Thomas came in next followed by Warren E. Burger, John Roberts, and Samuel Alito. Antonin Scalia fills out the group and had he lived four months longer to have votes counted in *Fisher II, Hellerstedt,* and *DAPA* his record would be a little mixed because of his contempt for affirmative action. The Roberts Court was more friendly to

Texas precisely because it was populated by the most conservative justices in almost a century.

In the middle are the centrists. Texan Tom Clark had as many votes for the state as he did against it. The same holds for Byron R. White (who was on the Court because his patron John F. Kennedy carried Texas because of Lyndon B. Johnson). The group would have also included Anthony Kennedy but for his votes in 2017 to overturn capital sentences. Those same two votes by Breyer place him at even between supporting and opposing the state. And, of course, Sandra Day O'Connor and Lewis Powell, the centrists of their eras, avoided the extremes in Texas cases, with the former being the fifth vote on both sides of the *Penry I* decision and the latter matching *Rodriguez* with *Plyler.* Harry Blackmun is an example of an unusual centrist but in a different way. He began as a conservative, but ended as a liberal with his votes during the two periods balancing each other out.

V

Constitutional cases litigated by and in Texas hit all the doctrinal areas of modern constitutional law. They capture the major themes of the relation of law and politics in the country. They split the justices into liberals, conservatives, and centrists. No other state could make such claims. Texas is a vast land, a state of mind, and a window into the story of the Court and the Constitution.

Yet for Texans the multifaceted nature of Texas and its constitutional litigation has been both a blessing and a curse. The blessing is that Texas has constantly been at the forefront of working out, on many dimensions, the relative rights and responsibilities of the Union and its constituent parts. The curse is, from the day Texans voted to accept annexation, they surrendered a sovereignty that many Texans believe, rightly or wrongly, they ought to enjoy. For Texans who have been consistently on the wrong side of electoral majorities, however, that curse is instead a further blessing.

NOTES

INTRODUCTION

1. Harlow Giles Unger, *John Quincy Adams* (Boston: Da Capo, 2012), 280–81.

2. Clyde A. Milner II, "National Initiatives," in *The Oxford History of the American West*, ed. Clyde A. Milner II, Carol A. O'Connor, and Martha A. Sandweiss (New York: Oxford University Press, 1994), 163.

3. Joel H. Silbey, *Storm over Texas: The Annexation Controversy and the Road to Civil War* (New York: Oxford University Press, 2005), 8.

4. Id. at 7. Jackson's statement parallels that of Publius (John Jay) in Federalist Number 2: "this one connected country, to one united people, a people descended from the same ancestors, speaking the same language, professing the same religion, attached to the same principles of government, very similar in their manners and customs." Alexander Hamilton, James Madison, and John Jay, *The Federalist*, ed. J.R. Pole (Indianapolis: Hackett, 2005), 6. For a modern take on *The Federalist*, see Sanford Levinson, *An Argument Open to All: Reading* The Federalist *in the 21st Century* (New Haven, CT, and London: Yale University Press, 2016).

5. Id. at 26.

6. Edward Everett and William Everett, eds., *Writings and Speeches of Daniel Webster*, vol. 2 (Boston: Little, Brown, 1903), 205.

7. Sibley, *Storm over Texas*, at 41.

8. Id. at 45.

9. James D. Richardson, ed., *Messages and Papers of the Presidents*, vol. 4 (Washington, DC: Bureau of National Literature, 1899), 323.

10. Sibley, *Storm over Texas,* at 69–70.

11. Richardson, *Messages and Papers,* vol. 4, at 344.

12. 26 U.S. (1 Pet.) 511, 542 (1828).

13. Richardson, *Messages and Papers,* vol. 4, at 442.

14. 60 U.S. (19 How.) 393 (1857).

15. 74 U.S. (7 Wall.) 700 (1869).

16. Id. at 725.

17. Id. at 731.

18. Id.

19. Michael Les Benedict, email to author, May 10, 2016.

20. Id.

21. Sanford Levinson, "Introduction," in *Nullification and Secession in Modern Constitutional Thought,* ed. Sanford Levinson (Lawrence: University Press of Kansas, 2016), 6.

1. THE ALL-WHITE PRIMARY

1. "The people of Texas are informed that in accordance with a proclamation from the Executive of the United States 'all slaves are free.'" *Galveston Civilian and Gazette,* July 11, 1865.

2. Carl Moneyhon, *Republicanism in Reconstruction Texas* (Austin: University of Texas Press, 1980), 79–80.

3. Id. at 211.

4. Eric Foner, *Reconstruction: America's Unfinished Revolution, 1863–1877* (New York: HarperCollins, 1988), 354.

5. Charles L. Zelden, *The Battle for the Black Ballot:* Smith v. Allwright *and the Defeat of the All-White Primary* (Lawrence: University Press of Kansas, 2004), 23; Darlene Clark Hine, ed., *Black Victory: The Rise and Fall of the White Primary in Texas* (Columbia: University of Missouri Press, 2003), 71.

6. Moneyhon, *Republicanism in Reconstruction Texas,* at 191.

7. H. W. Brands, *The Man Who Saved the Union: Ulysses S. Grant in War and Peace* (New York: Doubleday, 2012), 528–30.

8. Moneyhon, *Republicanism in Reconstruction Texas,* at 193.

9. C. Vann Woodward, *Origins of the New South* (Baton Rouge: Louisiana State University Press, 1951), 25.

10. Zelden, *Battle for the Black Ballot,* at 32–33.

11. Hine, *Black Victory,* at 80.

12. Zelden, *Battle for the Black Ballot,* at 18.

13. Id. at 37, quoting Forest Wood.

14. Hine, *Black Victory*, at 89–91.

15. General Laws of Texas, 38th Legislative Journal, 2d Called Session 74 (1923).

16. Civil Rights Cases, 109 U.S. 3 (1883). One can read United States v. Cruikshank, 92 U.S. 542 (1876) to make the same point.

17. Love v. Griffith, 266 U.S. 32, 33 (1924).

18. Id.

19. Giles v. Harris, 189 U.S. 475, 489 (1905).

20. Zelden, *Battle for the Black Ballot*, at 54.

21. Id. at 56 erroneously states the case was reargued after the NAACP filed a response to the state's brief.

22. Nixon v. Herndon, 273 U.S. 536, 541 (1927)

23. Nixon v. Condon, 286 U.S. 73 (1932).

24. Id. at 84.

25. Id.

26. Grovey v. Townsend, 295 U.S. 45, 47 (1935).

27. 372 U.S. 335 (1963).

28. 5 U.S. (1 Cranch) 137 (1803).

29. 295 U.S. 45 (1935).

30. Gary M. Lavengue, *Before Brown: Heman Marion Sweatt, Thurgood Marshall, and the Long Road to Justice* (Austin: University of Texas Press, 2010), 52.

31. L.A. Powe, Jr., "Two Great Leaders," *New York Law School Law Review* 57 (2013): 465, 477; the label was bestowed by T.R. Powell.

32. For instance in Burton v. Wilmington Parking Authority, 365 U.S. 715 (1961), a private concessionaire in a public garage was deemed a state actor because, in part, the garage flew both the Delaware and American flags.

33. Michael Klarman, "The White Primary Rulings: A Case Study in the Consequences of Supreme Court Decisionmaking," *Florida State University Law Review* 29, no. 1 (2001): 55, 61.

34. Lucas A. Powe, Jr., *The Supreme Court and the American Elite, 1789–2008* (Cambridge, MA: Harvard University Press, 2009), 215; L.A. Powe, Jr., "From the New Deal to the Reagan Revolution," in *The Oxford Handbook on the U.S. Constitution*, ed. Mark Graber, Sanford Levinson, and Mark Tushnet (New York: Oxford University Press, 2015), 91, 93–94.

35. 313 U.S. 299 (1941).

36. Id. at 314.

37. The dissenters agreed with the majority on the constitutional issues but disagreed on statutory construction. They thought the statute "lacks the requisite specificity" as written and noted that Congress was traditionally unwilling to extend federal law to primary elections. Id. at 340 (dissent).

38. Quoted in Zelden, *Battle for the Black Ballot*, at 83.

39. 376 U.S. 254 (1964) (constitutionalizing the law of libel).

40. 321 U.S. 649 (1944).

41. Id. at 664.

42. Id. at 666 (dissent).

43. Id. at 669.

44. Zelden, *Battle for the Black Ballot*, at 110.

45. Michael J. Klarman, *From Jim Crow to Civil Rights: The Supreme Court and the Struggle for Racial Equality* (New York: Oxford University Press, 2004), 453–54, 459.

46. Klarman, "White Primary Rulings," at 69.

47. Zelden, *Battle for the Black Ballot*, at 130.

48. Mark V. Tushnet, ed., *Thurgood Marshall: His Speeches, Writings, Arguments, Opinions, and Reminiscences* (Chicago: Chicago Review Press, 2001), 512.

49. Klarman, "White Primary Rulings," at 70.

50. Terry v. Adams. 345 U.S. 461 (1953).

51. Quoted in Klarman, *From Jim Crow to Civil Rights*, at 203.

52. The Voting Rights Act directed the attorney general to challenge poll taxes for state office (left unaffected by the Twenty-Fourth Amendment) and the government did so successfully. Harper v. Virginia Board of Elections, 383 U.S. 663 (1966).

2. AFTER THE VOTING RIGHTS ACT

1. Oregon v. Mitchell, 400 U.S. 112, 125 (1970).

2. Steve Bickerstaff, *Lines in the Sand: Congressional Redistricting in Texas and the Downfall of Tom Delay* (Austin: University of Texas Press, 2007), 418.

3. 517 U.S. 952 (1996).

4. Section 4 covered Alabama, Georgia, Louisiana, Mississippi, South Carolina, and Virginia, plus thirty-nine counties in North Carolina and one in Arizona.

5. Several counties in California, New Hampshire, and New York were added to Section 4.

6. Alaska, Arizona, and Texas plus counties in California, Florida, Michigan, New York, North Carolina, and South Dakota were added to section 4.

7. Michael Waldman, *The Fight to Vote* (New York: Simon & Schuster, 2016), 230.

8. *Texas Tribune*, February 23, 2012.

9. Charles L. Bullock III, Ronald Keith Gaddie, and Justin T. Wert, *The Rise and Fall of the Voting Rights Act* (Norman: University of Oklahoma Press, 2016), 152.

10. 557 U.S. 193 (2009).

11. Id. at 202.

12. Id.

13. Id. at 203.

14. Id. at 204.

15. *Austin American-Statesman*, November 8, 2006.

16. Waldman, *Fight to Vote,* at 232.

17. Id.

18. Shelby County v. Holder, 133 S. Ct. 2612, 2622, 2623, 2624 (2013).

19. Id. at 2618–19.

20. Id. at 2624.

21. Id. at 2631.

22. Id. at 2650 (dissent).

23. Evenwel v. Abbott, 136 S. Ct. 1120, 1128 (2016).

24. Id.

25. Id. at 1132.

26. Texas brief at 48–49.

27. Purcell v. Gonzales, 549 U.S. 1, 2 (2006).

28. Crawford v. Marion County, 553 U.S. 181 (2008).

29. Waldman, *Fight to Vote*, 190.

30. Id. at 190.

31. *New York Times*, September 20, 2016, at A16.

32. Waldman, *Fight to Vote*, at 201.

33. *New York Times*, September 20, 2016, at A16.

34. North Carolina State Conference of NAACP v. McCrory, 831 F.3d 204, 214 (4th Cir. 2016).

35. 73 F. Supp. 3d 627, 647 (S.D. Tex. 2014).

36. Texas v. Holder, 888 F. Supp. 2d 113 (D.D.C. 2012).

37. *Houston Chronicle,* June 26, 2013.

38. Waldman, *Fight to Vote*, at 235.

39. Veasey v. Perry, 71 F. Supp. 2d 627 (S.D. Tex. 2014).

40. Veasey v. Perry, 769 F.3d 890, 892 (5th Cir. 2014).

41. Veasey v. Perry, 135 S. Ct. 9, 12 (2014).

42. Veasey v. Abbott, 796 F.3d 487 (5th Cir. 2015).

43. Veasey v. Abbott, 830 F.3d 216, 305 (5th Cir. 2016) (dissent).

44. Id. at 281.

45. Abbott v. Veasey, 137 S. Ct. 612 (2017).

46. *New York Times*, February 11, 2017.

47. *New York Times*, March 21, 2017.

3. FROM DISCRIMINATION TO AFFIRMATIVE ACTION

1. 347 U.S. 483 (1954).

2. Fisher v. University of Texas, 136 S. Ct. 2198 (2016).

3. Smith v. Allwright, 321 U.S. 649 (1944).

4. Missouri ex rel. Gaines v. Canada, 305 U.S. 337 (1938).

5. Gary M. Lavergne, *Before Brown: Heman Marion Sweatt, Thurgood Marshall, and the Long Road to Justice* (Austin: University of Texas Press, 2010), 41–43.

6. Id. at 104.

7. Id. at 167.

8. Id.

9. McLaurin v. Oklahoma, 339 U.S. 637 (1950).

10. Henderson v. United States, 339 U.S. 816 (1950).

11. Attorneys General's Amicus Brief at 10.

12. Lavergne, *Before Brown*, at 242–43.

13. *Austin American-Statesman*, January 20, 1950.

14. 347 U.S. 483, 492 (1954).

15. Sweatt v. Painter, 339 U.S. 629, 631 (1950).

16. 321 U.S. 649 (1944).

17. Memorandum dated April, 1950, Tom Clark Papers, Box A2, Folder 3, Tarlton Law Library, University of Texas School of Law.

18. Quoted in Mark V. Tushnet, *Making Civil Rights Law: Thurgood Marshall and the Supreme Court, 1936–1961* (New York: Oxford University Press, 1994), 140.

19. Bernard Schwartz, *Super Chief: Earl Warren and His Supreme Court—A Judicial Biography* (New York: NYU Press, 1983), 72.

20. 339 U.S. at 633.

21. Id. at 634.

22. Id.

23. 339 U.S. 637 (1950).

24. 347 U.S. 483 (1954).

25. *Dallas Morning News,* June 5, 1950.

26. *Dallas Morning News,* June 6, 1950.

27. Robyn Duff Ladino, *Desegregating Texas Schools: Eisenhower, Shivers, and the Crisis at Mansfield High* (Austin: University of Texas Press, 1996), 83–84.

28. Jackson v. Rawdon, 235 F. 2d 93 (5th Cir. 1956).

29. Rawdon v. Jackson, 352 U. S. 925 (1956).

30. Ladino, *Desegregating Texas Schools,* at 102.

31. Id. at 111.

32. Id. at 115.

33. Cooper v. Aaron, 358 U. S. 1 (1958).

34. 402 U. S. 1 (1971).

35. Tasby v. Estes, 412 F. Supp. 1192 (N. D. Tex. 1976).

36. Tasby v. Estes, 572 F. 2d 1010 (5th Cir. 1978).

37. 402 U. S. at 26.

38. Estes v. NAACP, 444 U. S. 437 (1980).

39. Missouri v. Jenkins, 515 U. S. 70 (1995).

40. Keyes v. Denver School District, 413 U. S. 189, 217 (1973).

41. Michael J. Graetz and Linda Greenhouse, *The Burger Court and the Rise of the Judicial Right* (New York: Simon & Schuster, 2016), 89.

42. *Dallas Morning News,* January 22, 1980.

43. *Dallas Morning News,* January 24, 1980.

44. 438 U. S. 265 (1978).

45. John C. Jeffries, Jr., *Justice Lewis F. Powell, Jr.* (New York: Scribner, 1994), 469.

46. Hopwood v. Texas, 861 F. Supp. 551 (W. D. Tex. 1994).

47. Hopwood v. Texas, 78 F. 3rd 932 (5th Cir. 1996).

48. Id. at 944.

49. Id.

50. 531 U. S. 98 (2000).

51. Hopwood, Opposition to Certiorari at 3.

52. Texas v. Hopwood, 518 U. S. 1033 (1996).

53. *Austin American-Statesman,* July 4, 1996.

54. "M. Michael Sharlot: An Oral History Interview" (Austin: Jamail Center for Legal Research, University of Texas, 2009), 36.

55. 539 U. S. 306 (2003).

56. Nikole Hannah-Jones, "What Abigail Fisher's Affirmative Action Case Was Really About," *ProPublica,* June 23, 2016.

57. Fisher v. University of Texas, 645 F. Supp. 2d 587 (W. D. Tex. 2009).

58. Fisher v. University of Texas, 631 F. 2d 213 (5th Cir. 2011).

59. Fisher v. University of Texas, 133 S. Ct. 2411 (2013).

60. Adam Liptak, "Supreme Court Justices' Comments Don't Bode Well for Affirmative Action," *New York Times*, December 10, 2015 (discussing oral argument).

61. 133 S. Ct. at 2415.

62. Id. at 2419.

63. Id. at 2421.

64. *New York Times*, October 11, 2012.

65. 631 F. 3d at 266.

66. For the historical record, on November 5, 1991, Thomas's second day on the Bench (having been silent on his first day), I received his first two questions. The case was Collins v. Harker Heights, 503 U.S. 115, 130 (1992), a unanimous opinion by John Paul Stevens holding "the Due Process Clause does not impose an individual federal obligation upon municipalities to provide certain minimal levels of safety and security in the workplace and the city's alleged failure to train or warn its sanitation department employees was not arbitrary in the constitutional sense." I represented Harker Heights, a municipality created by Harley Harker to be "wet" next to Fort Hood.

67. Liptak, "Supreme Court Justices' Comments."

68. Richard H. Sander and Stuart Taylor, Jr., *Mismatch: How Affirmative Action Hurts Students It's Intended to Help, and Why Universities Won't Admit It* (New York: Basic Books, 2012).

69. 163 U.S. 537, 559 (1896) (dissent).

70. 136 S. Ct. 2198, 2209 (2016).

71. Id. at 2215.

72. *Austin American-Statesman*, June 24, 2014.

73. Id.

4. RAILROADS

1. William R. Childs, *The Texas Railroad Commission: Understanding Regulation in America to the Mid-Twentieth Century* (College Station: Texas A&M University Press, 2005), 50.

2. Id. at 61.

3. Id. at 62.

4. Id. at 70.

5. Id. at 81.

6. Dred Scott v. Sandford, 60 U.S. (19 How.) 393 (1857).

7. John Forrest Dillon, *Municipal Corporations* (Chicago: J. Cockcroft, 1872).

8. 154 U.S. at 381.

9. Id. at 382.

10. 154 U.S. 362 (1894).

11. 209 U.S. 123 (1908) (The Eleventh Amendment prohibiting lawsuits against a state does not prevent suing state enforcement officials when the claim is that the law being enforced violates the Constitution.)

12. 154 U.S. at 389.

13. Id. at 392.

14. Id. at 399, 410.

15. Id. at 413 (emphasis deleted).

16. 169 U.S. 466 (1898).

17. Federal Power Commission v. Hope Natural Gas, 320 U.S. 491 (1944).

18. Houston E. & W.T. Ry. v. United States (Shreveport Rate Cases), 234 U.S. 342 (1914).

19. Id. at 351–52.

20. Id. at 353.

21. Railroad Commission Brief at 16.

22. Record at 335.

23. William S. Osborn, "Curtains for Jim Crow: Law, Race, and the Texas Railroads," *Southwestern Historical Quarterly* 105, no. 3 (2002): 393, 407.

24. Pullman Brief at 77.

25. Id. at 86.

26. *Yale Law Journal* 69, no. 3 (1960): 421.

27. 347 U.S. 483 (1954).

28. Railroad Commission v. Pullman Company, 312 U.S. 496, 498 (1941).

29. Id.

30. Id.

31. Id. at 500.

32. Id. at 501.

33. Osborn, "Curtains for Jim Crow," at 411.

34. Ireland Graves and Kenneth McCalla to the members of the Texas Railroad Association, RG D-4, Box 188, Folder 12, Houston Metropolitan Research Center.

5. OIL

1. Art. 6014 of the Revised Statutes.

2. William R. Childs, *The Texas Railroad Commission: Understanding Regulation in America to the Mid-Twentieth Century* (College Station: Texas A&M University Press, 2005), 149.

3. Id. at 206.

4. Warner E. Mills, *Martial Law in East Texas* (Indianapolis: Bobbs-Merrill, 1960), 25.

5. Id. at 27.

6. Id. at 32.

7. Id. at 36.

8. Id.

9. Champlin v. Oklahoma Corp. Comm., 286 U.S. 210 (1932).

10. Childs, *Texas Railroad Commission*, at 215.

11. 287 U.S. 378 (1932).

12. Id. at 397.

13. Id.

14. Id. at 399.

15. Id. at 402.

16. John G. Clark, *Energy and the Federal Government: Fossil Fuel Policies, 1900–1946* (Champaign: University of Illinois Press, 1987), 221–22.

17. Childs, *Texas Railroad Commission*, at 219.

18. Id.

19. Nicholas George Malavis, *Bless the Pure and Humble: Texas Lawyers and Oil Regulation, 1919–1936* (College Station: Texas A&M University Press, 1996), 152. The title is a play on Pure Oil Company and Humble Oil and Refining.

20. Id. at 179.

21. Id. at 168.

22. Id.

23. Id. at 181.

24. Id.

25. First Inaugural Address, March 4, 1933, in *Inaugural Addresses of the Presidents of the United States*, 269 (Senate Doc. 101–10, 1989).

26. 293 U.S. 388 (1935).

27. Id. at 415.

28. Id.

29. Id.

30. Id.

31. Id. at 418.

32. Id. at 430.

33. 295 U.S. 495 (1935).

34. *Complete Presidential Press Conferences of Franklin D. Roosevelt*, vol. 5 (May 31, 1935) (New York: Da Capo, 1972), 309, 336.

35. Lindsy Escoe Pack, *The Political Aspects of the Texas Tidelands Controversy* (College Station: Texas A&M University Press, 1979), 24.

36. 332 U.S. 19 (1947).

37. Pack, *Texas Tidelands Controversy*, at 39.

38. Id. at 40.

39. Id. at 60.

40. Id. at 62.

41. Id. at 67.

42. Id. at 77.

43. 339 U.S. 707 (1950).

44. *Austin American-Statesman*, June 6, 1950.

45. Pack, *Texas Tidelands Controversy*, at 97.

46. *Austin American-Statesman*, June 6, 1950.

47. Pack, *Texas Tidelands Controversy*, at 100.

48. Id. at 114.

49. Id. at 139.

50. Id. at 158.

51. FF to Brethren, February 9, 1954, Tom C. Clark Papers, Box A27, Folder 3, Tarlton Law Library, University of Texas School of Law.

52. Alabama v. Texas, 347 U.S. 272 (1954).

53. United States v. Louisiana, 363 U.S. 1 (1960).

54. *Dallas Morning News*, June 1, 1960.

55. *Dallas Morning News*, June 2, 1960.

56. The seven were Will Wilson, James Ludhum, James Rogers, Houghton Brownless, James P. Hart, J. Chrys Dougherty, and Robert Tate Lewis.

6. SCHOOL FINANCE

1. Brief in Opposition at 4.

2. Docket Sheet, Tom C. Clark Papers, Box C70, Folder 3, Tarlton Law Library, University of Texas School of Law.

3. 347 U.S. 483 (1954).

4. Hernandez v. Texas, 347 U.S. 475 (1954).

5. Id. at 482.

6. Id at 476.

7. Id. at 482.

8. 330 F. Supp. 1377 (S.D. Tex. 1971).

9. Richard Schragger, "*San Antonio v. Rodriguez* and the Legal Geography of School Finance Reform," in *Civil Rights Stories*, ed. Miyrium E. Gilles and Risa L. Goluboff (New York: Foundation Press, 2008), 84, 92.

10. Hobson v. Hansen, 269 F. Supp. 406 (D.D.C.1967).

11. 487 P.2d 1241 (Cal. 1971).

12. Paul A. Sracic, San Antonio v. Rodriguez *and the Pursuit of Equal Education: The Debate over Discrimination and School Funding* (Lawrence: University Press of Kansas, 2006), 41.

13. Rodriguez v. San Antonio Independent School District, 337 F. Supp. 280, 282 (W.D. Tex. 1971).

14. Carolyn Dineen King, "Charles Alan Wright: Preceptor for the Federal Courts," in *A Tribute Charles Alan Wright: The Man and the Scholar* (Austin: Jamail Center for Legal Research, University of Texas, 2000), 9.

15. *Rodriquez* Brief at 11–13, 35.

16. Schragger, "Legal Geography," at 96.

17. That was the description of one of Powell's 1974 Term clerks, Penny Clark (a UT law grad). Linda Hirshman, *Sisters in Law: How Sandra Day O'Connor and Ruth Bader Ginsburg Went to the Supreme Court and Changed the World* (New York: HarperCollins, 2015), 144.

18. Schragger, "Legal Geography," at 99.

19. Michael Graetz and Linda Greenhouse, *The Burger Court and the Rise of the Legal Right* (New York: Simon & Schuster, 2016), 120.

20. Id. at 119.

21. Id. at 118.

22. Pollock v. Farmers' Loan and Trust, 157 U.S. 429, 532 (1895).

23. Id. at 583.

24. Graetz and Greenhouse, *Burger Court*, at 120.

25. Id. at 119 (Burger and Blackmun).

26. John C. Jeffries, Jr., *Justice Lewis F. Powell, Jr.* (New York: Scribner, 1994).

27. 411 U.S. at 39.

28. 383 U.S. 663 (1966).

29. Id. at 668.

30. Gideon v. Wainwright, 372 U.S. 335 (1963).

31. Griffin v. Illinois, 351 U. S. 12 (1956).

32. Williams v. Illinois, 399 U. S. 235 (1969).

33. 411 U. S. at 20.

34. Id. at 23.

35. Id. at 46.

36. Id. at 24.

37. Id. at 29.

38. 347 U. S. at 493.

39. 411 U. S. at 30.

40. Id. at 33–34.

41. Id. at 31.

42. Id. at 41.

43. Id. at 42.

44. Id. at 55.

45. L. A. Powe, Jr., "*Griswold* and Its Surroundings," *American University Law Review* 64 (2015): 1443, 1461–63.

46. 410 U. S. 113 (1973).

47. 411 U. S. at 71 (dissent).

48. Id. at 82.

49. Id. at 89.

50. Id. at 124.

51. Id. at 132.

52. *Dallas Morning News*, March 23, 1973.

53. *Dallas Morning News*, March 22, 1973.

54. Id.

55. Driver makes this observation in his magnificent book, *The Schoolhouse Gate: Public Education, the Supreme Court, and the Shaping of America's Constitutional Rights* (New York: Pantheon, 2018), 194, about the Detroit suburbs' reaction to Milliken v. Bradley, 418 U. S. 717 (1974) where the Court ruled (by the same 5–4 vote as *Rodriguez*) that they could not be judicially joined with Detroit for the purposes of racial balance.

56. West Orange-Cove Consolidated Independent School Dist. v. Alanis, 107 S. W. 3d 558, 563–64 (Tex. 2003).

57. Edgewood Independent School Dist. v. Kirby (Edgewood I), 777 S. W. 2d 391, 394 (Tex. 1989).

58. Id. at 392.

59. Edgewood Independent School Dist. v. Kirby (Edgewood II), 804 S. W. 2d 491, 496 (Tex. 1991).

60. Edgewood Independent School Dist. v. Kirby (Edgewood III), 826 S.W.2d 489, 493 (Tex. 1992).

61. Id. at 524.

62. Smith v. Travis County Education District, 791 F. Supp. 1170 (W.D. Tex. 1992).

63. 50 Stat. 738 (1937) codified as 28 U.S.C. 1341.

64. Smith v. Travis County Education District, 968 F.2d 453 (5th Cir. 1992).

65. Edgewood Independent School Dist. v. Memo (Edgewood IV), 917 S.W.2d 717, 730 (Tex. 1995).

66. Morath v. Texas Taxpayer and Student Fairness Coalition, 490 S.W.3d 826, 868 (Tex. 2016).

67. Mark Yudof, "School Finance Reform in Texas," *Harvard Journal on Legislation* 28 (1991): 499.

68. Maryland v. Wirtz, 392 U.S. 183 (1968) (federal power over minimum wage for state employees) overruled by National League of Cities v. Usery, 426 U.S. 833 (1976). Wright's Eleventh Amendment claim was deemed premature in Wirtz, but became the law in Seminole Tribe v. Florida, 517 U.S. 44 (1996) and Alden v. Maine, 527 U.S. 706 (1999). Texas v. Mitchell, 400 U.S. 112 (1970) (on the eighteen-year-old vote) was overturned by the Twenty-Sixth Amendment. Branch v. Texas 408 U.S. 238 (1972) (capital punishment) was dispatched by Gregg v. Georgia, 428 U.S. 153 (1976).

7. IMMIGRATION

1. Hernandez v. Houston Independent School District, 558 S.W.2d 121 (Tex. Civ. App. 1977).

2. Doe v. Plyler, 458 F. Supp. 569 (E.D. Tex. 1978).

3. 458 F. Supp. at 577.

4. Id.

5. Id.

6. In re Alien Children Litigation, 501 F. Supp. 544, 582 (S.D. Tex. 1980).

7. Plyler v. Doe, 628 F.2d 448 (5th Cir. 1980).

8. 411 U.S. 1 (1973).

9. Texas Brief at 5.

10. Id. at 6.

11. Id. at 32.

12. Id. at 9.

13. Id.

14. Id. at 10.

15. Reply Brief at 7.

16. 457 U.S. 202 (1982).

17. L.A. Powe, Jr., "October Term 1963: 'The Second American Constitutional Convention,'" *Journal of Supreme Court History* 38, no. 2 (2013): 194, 197.

18. 457 U.S. at 211.

19. Id. at 213.

20. Id. at 219.

21. Id. at 220.

22. Id.

23. Id. at 222.

24. Id. at 228.

25. Id. at 230.

26. Id. at 241 (concurring).

27. Id. at 254 (dissent).

28. Id. at 249.

29. Id. at 243.

30. Id. at 242.

31. 100 Stat. 3445 (1986).

32. *Dallas Morning News,* June 16, 1982.

33. *Dallas Morning News,* June 20, 1982.

34. Robert R. Bezdek and Ray Cross wrote a paper for the National Hispanic Leadership Conference in 1984, "Hispanics in South/West Texas: Demographic and School Enrollment Trends," and the information is taken from that paper.

35. *New York Times,* December 18, 2010.

36. White House Press Conference, December 22, 2010.

37. Josh Blackman, "Gridlock," *Harvard Law Review* 130 (2016): 241, 291.

38. Id.

39. www.youtube.com/watch?v = -e9lmy 8FMZ

40. Blackman, "Gridlock," at 291.

41. Id. at 298.

42. Id. at 294.

43. Texas Brief at 13.

44. Youngstown Sheet and Tube v. Sawyer, 343 U.S. 579, 647 (1952) (concurring).

45. FDA v. Brown & Williamson Tobacco Corp., 529 U.S. 120, 159 (2000).

46. United States brief at 10.

47. Texas v. United States, 86 F. Supp. 3d 591 (S.D. Tex. 2015).

48. Texas v. United States, 787 F.3d 733, 759 (5th Cir. 2015).

49. Texas v. United States, 809 F.3d 134 (5th Cir. 2015).

50. 343 U.S. 579 (1952).

51. Id. at 632, 633–34 (concurring).

52. Id. at 635 (concurring).

53. Id. at 637.

54. Id.

55. Id. at 650.

56. *New York Times,* Editorial, April 16, 2016.

57. 132 S. Ct. 2492 (2012).

58. Adam Liptak, "Blocking Part of Arizona Law," *New York Times,* June 25, 2012.

59. Id.

60. Mark V. Tushnet draws a similar conclusion from Scalia's questioning during oral argument over the Affordable Care Act (Obamacare); *In the Balance: Law and Politics on the Roberts Court* (New York: W.W. Norton, 2013), 14–15.

61. *New York Magazine,* October 6, 2013.

8. FREEDOM OF SPEECH AND THE PRESS

1. George N. Green, "Anti-Labor Politics in Texas 1941–57," in *American Labor and the Southwest: The First One Hundred Years,* ed. James C. Foster (Tucson: University of Arizona Press, 1982), 217

2. Id. at 218.

3. Acts of the Forty-Eighth Legislature, chapter 104, section 1 (1943).

4. Thomas v. Collins, 323 U.S. 516, 524 (1945).

5. Id. at 522.

6. Id. at 535.

7. Id. at 528.

8. Id. at 534.

9. Id. at 536.

10. Id. at 545 (concurring).

11. Id. at 547.

12. Id. at 548.

13. *Dallas Morning News,* January 27, 1954.

14. Stanford v. Texas, 379 U.S. 476 (1965).

15. *San Antonio Express-News,* January 19, 1965.

16. The best discussion is Mary Margaret McAllen Amberson, "'Better to Die on Our Feet Than to Live on Our Knees': United Farm Workers and Strikes in the Lower Rio Grande Valley, 1966–1967," in *Texas Labor History,* ed. Bruce A. Glasrud and James C. Maroney (College Station: Texas A&M University Press, 2013), 367.

17. 416 U.S. 802 (1974).

18. Id. at 813–14.

19. Id. at 810.

20. Id. at 814.

21. Ray Martinez to Pamela Colloff, "Law of the Land," *Texas Monthly,* April 2007.

22. Robert Draper, "The Twilight of the Texas Rangers," *Texas Monthly,* February 1994.

23. Jurisdictional Statement at 9.

24. Allison later represented Michael Morton, who was convicted of brutally murdering his wife in Williamson County. It was worse than that because District Attorney Ken Anderson, a UT law grad, presented the case as Morton beating his wife to death and then masturbating over her dead body. Anderson was especially proud of the conviction, which rested wholly on circumstantial evidence. Allison believed his client was innocent and that Anderson deliberately withheld exculpatory evidence—this being the 1980s, it was not DNA—that would convince a jury not to convict. In a two-part series in *Texas Monthly,* Allison was quoted: "I've practiced law for forty-one years. In terms of psychological toll that cases have taken on me, Michael's was the worst. I couldn't get over it. I went into a three-year tailspin." Pamela Colloff, "The Innocent Man," part 2, *Texas Monthly,* December 2012.

Fortunately Morton was not sentenced to death because twenty-six years later Allison, with the UT School of Law's Center for Actual Innocence, got the exculpatory evidence that freed Morton and led to Anderson, then a district judge, being jailed and disbarred. Anderson's successor as DA fought all the way to preclude subsequent DNA testing, claiming Morton was obviously guilty. When a court ordered the testing, it pointed elsewhere. With Morton's case reopened Allison got notes from a police interview with Morton's then very young child. The boy had seen the murder and knew the culprit was not his father, which matched Allison's initial views of the case.

25. Jurisdictional Statement at 8.

26. 403 U.S. 15 (1971).

27. Rosenfeld v. New Jersey, 408 U.S. 901 (1972); Brown v. Oklahoma, 408 U.S. 914 (1972); Papish v. Board of Curators, 410 U.S. 667 (1973); Lewis v. New Orleans, 415 U.S. 130 (1974).

28. Acker v. Texas, 430 U.S. 962 (1977).

29. Dale Carpenter, *Flagrant Conduct: The Story of* Lawrence v. Texas (New York: W.W. Norton, 2012), 122.

30. Hill v. Houston, 789 F. 2d 1103 (5th Cir. 1986).

31. 411 U.S. 1 (1973).

32. Houston v. Hill, 482 U.S. 451 (1987).

33. Id. at 457.

34. Id. at 461 quoting Terminiello v. Chicago, 337 U.S. 1, 4 (1949).

35. Id. at 462–63.

36. Id. at 472.

37. 491 U.S. 397 (1989).

38. Id. at 399.

39. Id. at 410.

40. Id. at 413.

41. Id. at 418.

42. Id. at 422 (dissent).

43. Id. at 431.

44. Id. at 432.

45. Id. at 429.

46. Id. at 436.

47. Id. at 437.

48. Id. at 439.

49. United States v. Eichman, 496 U.S. 310 (1990).

50. 135 S. Ct. 2239 (2015).

51. Id. at 2245.

52. Tex. Govt. Code section 662.003(b)(1).

53. Texas Division, Sons of Confederate Veterans v. Vandergriff, 759 F. 3d 388 (5th Cir. 2014).

54. 555 U.S. 460 (2009).

55. Walker v. Sons of Confederate Veterans, 135 S. Ct. 2239, 2246 (2015).

56. Id. at 2248.

57. Id.

58. Id.

59. Wooley v. Maynard, 430 U.S. 705 (1977).

60. 135 S. Ct. at 2249.

61. Id.

62. Id. at 2255 (dissent).

63. Id.

64. Id. at 2256.

65. Id. at 2257.

66. Id.

67. Id. at 2258.

68. *San Antonio Express-News,* June 19, 2015

69. *Houston Chronicle,* June 19, 2015.

70. *Austin American-Statesman,* June 19, 2015.

71. *New York Times,* June 28, 2015.

72. Bernard Schwartz, *Super Chief: Earl Warren and His Supreme Court—A Judicial Biography* (New York: NYU Press, 1983), 545.

73. 347 U.S. 483 (1954).

74. Draft concurring opinion, May 1965, Tom Clark Papers, Box A175, Folder 6, Tarlton Law Library, University of Texas School of Law.

9. FREEDOM OF AND FROM RELIGION

1. Texas Monthly v. Bullock, 489 U.S. 1 (1989).

2. Employment Division v. Smith, 494 U.S. 872 (1990).

3. Id. at 890.

4. 410 U.S. 113 (1973).

5. Planned Parenthood v. Casey, 505 U.S. 833 (1992).

6. "Remarks on Signing the Religion Freedom Restoration Act of 1993," *Weekly Compilation of Presidential Documents* 29, no. 46 (November 16, 1993): 2377.

7. *Federal News Service,* November 16, 1993.

8. "Congress Defends Religious Freedom," *New York Times,* October 25, 1993, at A18.

9. 521 U.S. 507 (1997).

10. Mark V. Tushnet, "The Story of City of *Boerne v. Flores,*" in *Constitutional Law Stories,* ed. Michael C. Dorf (New York: Foundation Press, 2009), 483, 485.

11. Id. at 486.

12. Church of the Lukumi Babalu Aye v. City of Hialeah, 508 U.S. 520 (1993).

13. The separate opinion of Kennedy, O'Connor, and Souter in Planned Parenthood v. Casey, 505 U.S. 833 (1992), was explicit on the point that the Court would not cave to political pressure.

14. 521 U.S. at 519.

15. 5 U.S. (1 Cranch) 137 (1803).

16. 521 U.S. at 529.

17. Id. at 534.

18. Id. at 530.

19. Id.

20. Id. at 520.

21. Id. at 532.

22. Id.

23. South Carolina v. Katzenbach, 383 U.S. 301 (1966).

24. 17 U.S. (4 Wheat.) 316 (1819).

25. 383 U.S. at 326 quoting 17 U.S. at 421.

26. Id. at 536.

27. Id. at 535–36.

28. Id. at 537.

29. Holt v. Hobbs, 135 S. Ct. 853 (2015).

30. Greece v. Galloway, 134 S. Ct. 1811 (2014).

31. Everson v. Board of Education, 330 U.S. 1, 16 (1947).

32. Engel v. Vitale, 370 U.S. 421 (1962).

33. Abington School District v. Schempp, 374 U.S. 203 (1963).

34. Paul Horowitz, "Religion and American Politics," *University of Memphis Law Review* 39 (2009): 973, 978.

35. Lee v. Weisman, 505 U.S. 577 (1992).

36. Peter Irons, *God on Trial: Dispatches from America's Religious Battlefields* (New York: Viking Adult, 2007), 139.

37. Id. at 140.

38. Paul Horowitz, "The Story of Santa Fe v. Doe," in *First Amendment Stories*, ed. Richard W. Garnett and Andrew Koppleman (New York: Foundation Press, 2012), 481, 487.

39. Peter Irons, *The Courage of Their Convictions: Sixteen Americans Who Fought Their Way to the Supreme Court* (New York: Free Press, 1988), 142.

40. Horowitz, "Story of Santa Fe v. Doe," at 488.

41. Id. at 495.

42. 530 U.S. 294 n.1.

43. Douglas Laycock, "Government-Sponsored Religious Displays," *Case Western Law Review* 61 (2010–11): 1211, 1224.

44. 530 U.S. at 315.

45. Id. at 302.

46. Id. at 305.

47. Id. at 307.

48. Id. at 310–11.

49. Van Orden v. Perry, 545 U.S. 677, 691 (2005).

50. Id. at 313.

51. Id. at 318 (dissent).

52. *Houston Chronicle*, June 20, 2000.

53. Id.

54. *San Antonio Express-News*, June 20, 2000.

55. *Houston Chronicle*, June 20, 2000.

56. 449 U.S. 39 (1980).

57. Id. at 41.

58. Van Orden v. Perry, 351 F.3d 173 (5th Cir. 2003).

59. McCreary County v. ACLU, 545 U.S. 844, 883 (2005) (concurring).

60. Id. at 863.

61. Van Orden v. Perry, 545 U.S. 667, 691–92 (2005).

62. Id. at 712 (dissent).

63. Id. at 742.

64. Id. at 739–40.

65. Id. at 700 (concurring).

66. Id. at 700, 704.

67. Id. at 702.

68. Id.

69. Id. at 704.

70. Id.

71. Id. at 703.

72. For those who have not gone to law school, adverse possession is a property law rule that says if someone stays on another's land in an open, notorious way for the requisite number of years—typically twenty-one— then the land passes from the landowner to the person occupying the land. Constitutional adverse possession, a term I coined, stands for the proposition that if you do something unconstitutional for long enough, courts will conclude that in fact it is constitutional.

73. *San Antonio Express-News,* June 28, 2005.

74. Id.

75. *Austin American-Statesman,* July 8, 2017.

76. *Houston Chronicle,* June 28, 2005.

10. ABORTION

1. 410 U.S. 113 (1973).

2. 136 S. Ct. 2292 (2016).

3. Carole Joffe, *Doctors of Conscience: The Struggle to Provide Abortion before and after* Roe v. Wade (Boston: Beacon Press, 1995), 60.

4. Id. at 64.

5. N.E.H. Hull and Peter Charles Hoffer, Roe v. Wade: *The Abortion Rights Controversy in American History* (Lawrence: University Press of Kansas, 2001), 99.

6. *Time,* June 6, 1969, at 26–27.

7. 381 U.S. 479 (1965).

8. Tileston v. Ullman, 318 U.S. 44 (1943).

9. Poe v. Ullman, 368 U.S. 497 (1961).

10. TCC to Felix [Frankfurter], June 6, 1961, Tom Clark Papers, Box A109, Folder 11, Tarlton Law Library, University of Texas School of Law.

11. Hull and Hoffer, *Abortion Rights Controversy,* at 87.

12. Id.

13. Id.

14. Id. at 87–88.

15. Thomas I. Emerson, "Nine Justices in Search of a Doctrine," *Michigan Law Review* 64 (1965): 219.

16. Roy Lucas, "Federal Constitutional Limitations on Enforcement and Administration of State Abortion Statutes," *North Carolina Law Review* 46 (1968): 730, 759.

17. The lead case was Younger v. Harris, 401 U.S. 37 (1971).

18. In fact the Does and Dr. Hallford were found to lack standing.

19. Linda Greenhouse, *Becoming Justice Blackmun: Harry Blackmun's Supreme Court Journey* (New York: Henry Holt, 2005), 80.

20. 410 U.S. 179 (1973).

21. Lucinda Finley, "The Story of *Roe v. Wade,*" in *Constitutional Law Stories,* ed. Michael C. Dorf (New York: Foundation Press, 2009), 331, 370.

22. 410 U.S. at 153.

23. Id. at 159.

24. Id. at 163.

25. Id. at 164.

26. Doe v. Bolton, 410 U.S. at 192, 196.

27. Id. at 197.

28. Id. at 174 (dissent).

29. Doe v. Bolton, 410 U.S. at 222 (dissent).

30. Mark Tushnet, "Following Rules Laid Down," *Harvard Law Review* 96 (1983): 781, 821.

31. Ely is the only professor to have completed the hat-trick of being tenured at America's three best law schools: Yale, Harvard, and Stanford. Because of his love of scuba diving, he finished his distinguished career at the University of Miami.

32. John Hart Ely, "The Wages of Crying Wolf: A Comment on *Roe v. Wade*," *Yale Law Journal* 82 (1973): 920.

33. John C. Jeffries, Jr., *Justice Lewis F. Powell, Jr.: A Biography* (New York: Scribner, 1994), 367–69.

34. 550 U.S. 124 (2007).

35. 505 U.S. 833 (1992).

36. www.statesman.com/news/state—regional-goovt—politics/perrysigns-abortion-bill-into-law/mgkgz9mqxnaıj6ygDveeEO/

37. Whole Woman's Health v. Lakey, 46 F. Supp. 3d 673 (W.D. Tex. 2014).

38. Whole Woman's Health v. Lakey, 769 F.3d 285 (5th Cir. 2014).

39. 135 S. Ct. 399 (2014).

40. Whole Woman's Health v. Cole, 790 F.3d 563, modified 790 F.3d 598 (5th Cir. 2015).

41. Clarence Thomas, *My Grandfather's Son: A Memoir* (New York: Harper-Collins, 2007), ix. He likened himself to Tom Robinson, who Atticus Finch defends in *To Kill a Mockingbird*. "It is the story of an ordinary man to which extraordinary things happened. Putting it down on paper forced me to suffer old hurts, endure old pains, and revisit old doubts. At times I was surprised by how fresh my feelings still were." Kevin Merida and Michael A. Fletcher, *Supreme Discontent: The Divided Soul of Clarence Thomas* (New York: Doubleday, 2007), 6: "He has not been the same man since [the confirmation hearings]. Some, in fact, believe the scars of that ordeal have affected his judicial judgment, making him more rigid in his deliberation of cases than he might otherwise have been."

42. Transcript of oral argument at 12.

43. Transcript of oral argument at 14.

44. Id. at 32.
45. Id.
46. Id. at 37.
47. Id. at 47.
48. Id. at 77.
49. Whole Woman's Health v. Hellerstedt, 136 S. Ct. 2292, 2311.
50. Id. at 2312, quoting amicus brief of the Society of Hospital Medicine.
51. Id.
52. Id. at 2318.
53. Id. at 2324.
54. Id.
55. Id. at 2344 (dissent).
56. *Houston Chronicle,* June 27, 2016.
57. Id.
58. Id.
59. Id.
60. Id.
61. Id.
62. *Austin American-Statesman,* June 27, 2016.
63. *Austin American-Statesman,* January 20, 2017.

II. PROSECUTING CONSENSUAL ADULT SEX

1. Dale Carpenter, *Flagrant Conduct: The Story of* Lawrence v. Texas (New York: W. W. Norton, 2012), 6.
2. Id. at 54.
3. 482 U.S. 451 (1987).
4. Carpenter, *Flagrant Conduct,* at 123.
5. Id. at 124–25.
6. 478 U.S. 186 (1986).
7. Carpenter, *Flagrant Conduct,* at 138.
8. Id. at 149.
9. Id. at 157.
10. Id.
11. Id. at 159.
12. Id.
13. Id. at 167.
14. Id. at 168.

15. Id. at 170.

16. Id. at 171.

17. Id. at 171–72.

18. Lawrence Certiorari Petition at 22.

19. Texas Reply Brief at 6.

20. Id. at 52.

21. Id. at 48 n.31.

22. Id. at 14.

23. Amicus Brief of Alabama, South Carolina, and Utah at 17.

24. Amicus Brief of Pro-Family Law Center and Traditional Values Coalition at 3.

25. Id. at 15.

26. Amicus Brief of American Center for Law and Justice at 19.

27. Amicus Brief of Family Research Council at 17.

28. In Snyder v. Phelps, 562 U.S. 443 (2011), the Court ruled that the church's protest outside a Marine's funeral was constitutionally protected.

29. Carpenter, *Flagrant Conduct*, at 223.

30. Id. at 234.

31. *New York Times*, March 27, 2003.

32. 517 U.S. 620 (1996).

33. O'Connor concurred separately on equal protection grounds that the conduct was criminal only if done by members of the same sex.

34. Lawrence v. Texas, 539 U.S. 558, 578 (2003).

35. Id. at 567.

36. Id.

37. Id. at 568.

38. Id. at 578.

39. Id.

40. Id.

41. Id. at 598.

42. Id. at 599.

43. Id. at 602.

44. Id. at 604.

45. Id. at 604–5.

46. Michael Graetz and Linda Greenhouse, *The Burger Court and the Rise of the Judicial Right* (New York: Simon & Schuster, 2016), 209.

47. *El Paso Times*, June 28, 2003.

48. *Houston Chronicle*, June 27, 2003.

49. Id.

50. Warren Chisum in the *Houston Chronicle,* November 9, 2005.

51. *Washington Post,* November 9, 2005.

52. Gerald Rosenberg, *The Hollow Hope: Can Courts Bring about Social Change?* (Chicago: University of Chicago Press, 1991).

53. Michael J. Klarman, *From the Closet to the Altar: Courts, Backlash, and the Struggle for Same-Sex Marriage* (New York: Oxford University Press, 2013).

54. Obergefell v. Holdges, 135 S. Ct. 2584 (2015).

55. Carpenter, *Flagrant Conduct,* at 109.

56. Id. at 265.

12. CAPITAL PUNISHMENT

1. Baze v. Rees, 553 U.S. 35 (2008) (sustain the protocol).

2. Michael Hall, "The Judgment of Sharon Keller," *Texas Monthly,* August 2009, at 106.

3. Turner v. Texas, 551 U.S. 1193 (2007).

4. Evan J. Mandery, *A Wild Justice: The Death and Resurrection of Capital Punishment in America* (New York: W. W. Norton, 2013), 64.

5. Carol S. Steiker and Jordan M. Steiker, *Courting Death: The Supreme Court and Capital Punishment* (Cambridge, MA: Belknap Press, 2016), 43.

6. McGautha v. California and Crampton v. Ohio, 402 U.S. 183 (1971).

7. Id. at 208.

8. Mandery, *Wild Justice,* at 115.

9. 408 U.S. 283 (1972).

10. Id. at 360.

11. Id. at 371.

12. Mandery, *Wild Justice,* at 172.

13. Texas Code of Criminal Procedure Annotated, Art. 37.071(b) (Vernon 1981).

14. Steiker and Steiker, *Courting Death,* at 65.

15. Mandery, *Wild Justice,* at 367.

16. Woodson v. North Carolina, 428 U.S. 280 (1976).

17. 428 U.S. 153 (1976).

18. Id. at 315 (Rehnquist), 359 (White).

19. Jordan Steiker, *Penry v. Lynaugh,* in *Death Penalty Stories,* ed. John H. Blume and Jordan M. Steiker (New York: Foundation Press, 2009), 277, 295.

This chapter could not have been written without this superb piece of scholarship from one of the nation's leading scholars of the death penalty and a longtime colleague and friend.

20. Id. at 310.

21. http://2012 election.procon.org/sources/Sep 7 2011 republican debate .pdf at 40.

22. Id.

23. Frank Zimring, "Postscript: The Peculiar Present of American Capital Punishment," in *Beyond Repair? America's Death Penalty*, ed. Stephen P. Garvey (Durham, NC: Duke University Press, 2003), 229.

24. Steiker, *Penry v. Lynaugh*, at 286.

25. Id. at 287.

26. Penry v. Lynaugh, 492 U.S. 302 (1989).

27. Id. at 325.

28. Id.

29. Id.

30. Id. at 328.

31. Graham v. Collins, 506 U.S. 461 (1993); Johnson v. Texas, 509 U.S. 350 (1993).

32. Steiker, *Penry v. Lynaugh*, at 301.

33. The case was Blue v. Cockrell, 298 F.3d 318 (5th Cir. 2002). An en banc Fifth Circuit decision surveyed the post-Penry decisions of the circuit. Robertson v. Cockrell, 325 F.3d 243 (5th Cir. 2003).

34. Steiker, *Penry v. Lynaugh*, at 302.

35. Penry v. Johnson, 532 U.S. 782, 799 (2001).

36. Id. at 797.

37. Quoted 536 U.S. at 315 n.17.

38. 536 U.S. 304 (2002).

39. Steiker, *Penry v. Lynaugh*, at 316.

40. Tennard v. Dretke, 542 U.S. 274 (2004).

41. 543 U.S. 37 (2004).

42. Ex parte Smith, 132 S.W.3d 407, 427 (Tex. Crim. App. 2004) (concurring).

43. 543 U.S. 37 (2004).

44. Id. at 46.

45. Smith v. Texas, 550 U.S. 297, 310, 312, 314 (2007).

46. Ex parte Smith, 185 S.W.3d 455 (Tex. Crim. App. 2006).

47. Id. at 474.

48. Abdul-Kabir v. Quarterman, 550 U.S. 233 (2007); Brewer v. Quarterman, 550 U.S. 286 (2007).

49. 550 U.S. at 310.

50. Medellin v. Texas, 552 U.S. 491 (2008).

51. Leal Garcia v. Texas, 564 U.S. 940 (2011).

52. Panetti v. Quarterman 551 U.S. 930 (2007); Trevino v. Thaler, 133 S. Ct. 1911 (2013); Jennings v. Stephens, 135 S. Ct. 793 (2015); Skinner v. Switzer, 562 U.S. 521 (2011).

53. Ex parte Briseno, 135 S.W. 3d 1, 6 (Tex. Crim. App. 2004).

54. 134 S. Ct. 1986 (2014).

55. Mays v. Stephens, 757 F. 3d 211, 218 (5th Cir. 2014).

56. Moore v. Texas, 137 S. Ct. 1039 (2017).

57. Petitioner's Brief at 7.

58. Id. at 8.

59. Id. at 20.

60. State's Brief at 1.

61. Buck v. Davis, 137 S. Ct. 759, 769 (2017).

62. Transcript of oral argument at 10.

63. 137 S. Ct. at 772.

64. Id. at 776.

65. Id.

66. Id. at 778.

67. 133 S. Ct. 2612 (2013).

68. 137 S. Ct. at 781 (dissent).

69. Steiker, *Penry v. Lynaugh*, at 309.

13. TOM DELAY'S REDISTRICTING

1. Steve Bickerstaff, *Lines in the Sand: Congressional Redistricting and the Downfall of Tom DeLay* (Austin: University of Texas Press, 2007), 22.

2. Michael Barone and Grant Ujifusa, *The Almanac of American Politics* (New York: Crown, 1994), 1209.

3. Bush v. Vera, 517 U.S. 952 (1996).

4. Bickerstaff, *Lines in the Sand*, at 31; Henderson v. Perry, 399 F. Supp. 2d 756, 764 (E.D. Tex. 2005).

5. Id. at 127.

6. Id. at 128.

7. Id. at 132.

8. Id. at 158–59.

9. Id. at 245.

10. Sessions v. Perry, 298 F. Supp. 2d 451 (E. D. Tex. 2004).

11. 541 U. S. 267 (2004).

12. 543 U. S. 941 (2004).

13. The district court summarized it: "Rather, the strength lies with the power of the proposed rule itself. It asks why a state legislative body under no legal requirement to redistrict should face anything less than the full reach of the constitutional strictures of one person, one vote, that is, why should it benefit from a fiction born of necessity." 399 F. Supp. 2d at 775.

14. Henderson v. Perry, 399 F. Supp. 2d 756, 767 (E. D. Tex. 2005).

15. Id. at 776.

16. Id. at 777. Some years later, one of the judges reiterated to me that our claim was too novel for a lower court to adopt. Interestingly, the opinion refers to me as Scot Powe—my nickname that everyone who knows me uses—even though on all court papers I use my real name under which I am a member of the Texas Bar. Id. at 774.

17. A third judge concurred, agreeing with the Bickerstaff rule, but finding it outside the scope of the remand.

18. 539 U. S. 558 (2003).

19. League of United Latin American Citizens v. Perry, 548 U. S. 399 (2006).

20. *Austin American-Statesman,* June 29, 2006.

21. Scot Powe and Steve Bickerstaff, "Anthony Kennedy's Blind Quest," *Michigan Law Review First Impressions* 105 (2006): 63; Bickerstaff, *Lines in the Sand,* at 386–87.

22. *Houston Chronicle,* June 29, 2006.

23. *Washington Post,* April 5, 2006.

CONCLUSION

1. 5 U. S. (1 Cranch) 137 (1803).

2. 521 U. S. 507 (1997).

3. Id. at 529 quoting Marbury, 5 U. S. (1 Cranch) at 177.

4. Shreveport Rate Cases, 234 U. S. 342 (1914).

5. 426 U. S. 833 (1976).

6. Garcia v. San Antonio Municipal Transit Authority, 469 U. S. 528 (1985). After the decision Rehnquist, writing to his son who was on the *Boston*

University Law Review, asserted, "stare decisis in constitutional law is pretty much a sham." John A. Jenkins, *The Partisan: The Life of William Rehnquist* (New York: PublicAffairs, 2012), 250.

7. 514 U.S. 509 (1995).

8. Lopez v. United States, 2 F.3d 1343 (5th Cir. 1993).

9. Sandra Day O'Connor and H. Alan Day, *Lazy B: Growing Up on a Cattle Ranch in the American Southwest* (New York: Random House, 2002), 257–65.

10. New York v. United States, 505 U.S. 144, 181 (1992).

11. 411 U.S. 1 (1973).

12. 557 U.S. 193 (2009).

13. 133 S. Ct. 2612, 2622 (2013).

14. 74 U.S. (7 Wall.) 700 (1869).

15. 293 U.S. 388 (1935).

16. 491 U.S. 397 (1989).

17. 323 U.S. 516 (1945).

18. 379 U.S. 476 (1965).

19. 430 U.S. 962 (1977).

20. 482 U.S. 451 (1987).

21. I had recommended a denial of certiorari. Douglas buzzed me into his office and said, "Powe, rich people have constitutional rights, too." The Court did as I had recommended to Douglas, and he had me write the dissent to that denial. 2606.84 Acres of Land in Tarrant County v. United States, 402 U.S. 916 (1971).

22. Estes v. Texas, 381 U.S. 532 (1965).

23. Walker v. Sons of Confederate Veterans, 135 S. Ct. 2239 (2015).

24. Allee v. Medrano, 416 U.S. 802 (1974).

25. 530 U.S. 290 (2003).

26. Van Orden v. Perry, 545 U.S. 677 (2005).

27. 489 U.S. 1 (1989).

28. District of Columbia v. Heller, 554 U.S. 570, 626 (2008).

29. 154 U.S. 362 (1894).

30. 410 U.S. 113 (1973).

31. 505 U.S. 833 (1992).

32. 136 S. Ct. 2292 (2016).

33. 539 U.S. 558 (2003).

34. 388 U.S. 1 (1967).

35. 136 S. Ct. 2198 (2016).

36. 457 U.S. 202 (1982).

37. 321 U.S. 649 (1944).

38. Railroad Commission v. Pullman Co., 312 U.S. 496 (1941).

39. Mark V. Tushnet, ed., *Thurgood Marshall: His Speeches, Writings, Arguments, Opinions, and Reminiscences* (Chicago: Chicago Review Press, 2001), 512.

40. 339 U.S. 626 (1950).

41. United States v. Texas, 339 U.S. 707 (1950); Alabama v. Texas, 347 U.S. 272 (1954); United States v. Louisiana, 363 U.S. 1 (1960).

42. Jurek v. Texas decided as Gregg v. Georgia, 428 U.S. 153 (1976).

43. Penry v. Lynaugh, 492 U.S. 302 (1989).

44. Medellin v. Texas, 552 U.S. 491 (2008).

45. LULAC v. Perry, 548 U.S. 399 (2006).

46. On the news I heard claims to the effect that gay marriage cheapens or undermines (the meaning of) heterosexual marriage, but I have never heard the claim that gay sex weakens or undermines (the meaning of) heterosexual sex.

47. Hernandez v. Texas, 347 U.S. 475 (1954).

48. Alabama v. United States, 347 U.S. 272 (1954); United States v. Louisiana, 363 U.S. 1 (1960).

49. 378 U.S. 108 (1964).

50. Illinois v. Gates, 462 U.S. 213 (1983).

51. 380 U.S. 400 (1965).

52. 392 U.S. 514 (1968).

53. 370 U.S. 660 (1962).

54. Allee v. Medrano, 416 U.S. 802 (1974).

55. Medellin; Leal Garcia v. Texas, 564 U.S. 940 (2011).

INDEX OF SUPREME COURT CASES

GENERAL INDEX

Abbott, Greg, as attorney general, 9, 40, 124, 159, 170, 246, 247, 252; as governor, 192

Abilene, 69, 247

Abortion, back-alley, 174; doctors, 174, 175, 183; feminists, 175–76; nineteenth century laws, 173; partial birth, 186; therapeutic, 174; trimesters, 182–83; twenty-first century laws, 186–88; undue burden, 254

Abstention, 79–80

Acker, Louis C., 142

Ad valorem tax, 99

Adams, John Quincy, 2, 3, 4, 5

Adverse possession, 172, 283

Affirmative action: adoption at UT School of Law 55–56; diversity, 55; Fifth Circuit invalidation, 56–57; readoption at UT School of Law, 60; Scalia and 61–62; sustained 2016, 63–64, 257

Alabama, 32, 37

Alamo, 67, 197

Alamo Heights, 101, 108

Alaska, 176

Albuquerque, 242

Alito, Samuel, 35, 61, 62; abortion, 189, 191–92; capital punishment, 235; license plates, 150–53; voting record, 261

Allison, William, 143, 279

Allred, James, 90

All-white primary: at Supreme Court, 19–21, 22, 25; Texas legislation, 21–22

Allwright, S.E., 25

Amarillo, 69

American Bar Association, 206

American Bar Association Journal, 174

American Center for Law and Justice, 165

American Civil Liberties Union, 25, 140, 156, 162, 169

American College of Obstetricians and Gynecologists, 175

American Law Institute, 102, 113, 174, 175

American Medical Association, 173

Amsterdam, Anthony, 216, 219, 221

Anderson, John, 202, 203, 214

Anderson, Ken, 279

Annexation, 6, 256

Anthony, Susan B., 147